JOE KELLY has written a number of books on management
and is professor of management
at Concordia University, Montreal, Canada

Joe
Kelly

HOW
MANAGERS
MANAGE

A SPECTRUM BOOK

PRENTICE-HALL, INC., Englewood Cliffs, New Jersey 07632

Library of Congress Cataloging in Publication Data

Kelly, Joe.
  How managers manage.

  (A Spectrum Book)
  Includes bibliographical references and index.
  1. Management.   I. Title.
HD31.K446   658.4   79–25170
ISBN   0–13–423756–0
ISBN   0–13–423749–8 pbk.

Editorial production/supervision
  and interior design by Heath Silberfeld
Cover design by Vincent Ceci
Manufacturing buyers: Cathie Lenard and Barbara Frick

PRENTICE-HALL INTERNATIONAL, INC., *London*
PRENTICE-HALL OF AUSTRALIA PTY. LIMITED, *Sydney*
PRENTICE-HALL OF CANADA, LTD., *Toronto*
PRENTICE-HALL OF INDIA PRIVATE LIMITED, *New Delhi*
PRENTICE-HALL OF JAPAN, INC., *Tokyo*
PRENTICE-HALL OF SOUTHEAST ASIA PTE. LTD., *Singapore*
WHITEHALL BOOKS LIMITED, *Wellington, New Zealand*

Contents

Preface xv

1
What Is Management?
1

Objectives You Should Meet 2

Elements of Management: Structure, Process, Values 4

The Structure of Management 5

The Executive's Behavior Behaviorally Viewed 7

Middle-Level Management 9

Supervisory Management 10

The Process of Managing 11

Managerial Values 15

A Framework for the Study of Management 17

A Simple Model 18
Review and Research 21
Incident: Ameng, Inc. 22

2
Schools of Management
25

Objectives You Should Meet 26
The Classical School 28
Human Relations 32
Systems Management 38
The Contingency Approach 41
Review and Research 43
Incident: The Top Executive of the Seventies and Eighties 44

I
STRUCTURAL VARIABLES
47

3
Structure of Management
49

Objectives You Should Meet 50
Classical Structure 51
Human Relations Organizing 61
The Systems Approach to Structure 64
Choosing the Structure: A Contingency Approach 66

Review and Research   68
Incident: The Changing Work Force
and Changing Attitudes Towards Authority   68

4
Organizational Politics
71

Objectives You Should Meet   72
The Individual: The Manager as a Political Animal   73
The Group: Cliques and Cabals in Organizations   76
The Structural Bases of Power   83
The Process   85
Politicking: Exercising Influence   88
The Organization: The Conspiracy Theory Versus Pluralism   89
A Contingency Approach to Managing Political Behavior   90
Review and Research   91
Incident: "I Stood Up and Blew My Stack"   91

II
PROCESS VARIABLES
95

5
Objective Setting
97

Objectives You Should Meet   98
The Importance of Objective Setting   99

A Variety of Objectives 103
Composite Objectives 104
Goals 106
Operationalizing Objectives 108
Management by Objectives 110
Review and Research 114
Incident: Organizational Growth Changes Objectives:
What Went Wrong at Chrysler? 114

6
Moving from Strategic Objectives to Operational Goals
119

Objectives You Should Meet 120
A Definition of Planning 121
Strategic Planning 121
Strategic Versus Tactical Planning 123
Developing a Strategy by Exploiting a Weakness of a Competitor 125
Forecasting 126
Forecasting Problems 132
From Strategy to Operational Goals 135
Integrating Strategic and Operating Plans 136
"Group Think" at the Top of the Modern Organization 138
Review and Research 141
Incident: Paul Scott 141

7
Selecting a Management Design
143

Objectives You Should Meet 144
The Principles of Classical Organizing 145

Concept of Role 145
Jobs 148
The Principles of Human Relations Organizing 153
Systems Design 155
Principles of System Organizing 158
Matrix Management: A New Adhocracy Approach 160
Contingency Overview to Organizational Structure 165
Review and Research 166
Incident: Codetermination at Volkswagen 167

8
Staffing: Hiring, Firing, and Evaluating Executives
169

Objectives You Should Meet 170
Hiring 171
Group Selection: The Assessment Center 180
Firing 181
Evaluating 187
Review and Research 193
Incident: George Is Doing Too Much 194

9
Executive Leadership
197

Objectives You Should Meet 198
Trait Approach to Leadership 200
The Human Relations Approach 201
The Systems or Contingency Theory of Leadership 205
Path-Goal Theory of Leadership 209

Leading Existentially: A Modern Executive Style 211
Review and Research 213
Incident: Tim Babcock as Manager 213

10
Managing Information
for Control and Evaluation
215

Objectives You Should Meet 216
Control and Cybernetics 217
Four Steps of Control 218
Information Flow and Control 219
Integration of Information: Decisions and Control 221
International Supplies, Inc. (ISI) 224
Operational Budgeting 225
Operationalizing Control 232
Review and Research 233
Incident: "Small Is Beautiful" 234

11
Decision Making
235

Objectives You Should Meet 236
Information Deciding Action 236
How Firms Make Decisions 239
The Problem-Solving Process 239
Making Creative Decisions 247
The Numbers Game: Models 250
Quantitative Techniques 252
Review and Research 262
Incident: On Working Hours 264

III
VALUE VARIABLES
267

12
The Changing Value Set
269

Objectives You Should Meet   270
The Classical Value: Rationality   271
Systems Values: Black Boxes Within Black Boxes   275
Towards Existential Values: The Mystique of the Black Box   276
Executive Ethics   277
Existentialism and the Systems Approach   280
Review and Research   281
Incident: Problems of Adjusting to Freedom   282

IV
MANAGING PEOPLE
AND BEHAVIOR
285

13
Human Motivation
287

Objectives You Should Meet   288
S-R (Stimulus-Response) Man of Classical Theory   289

S-O-R (Stimulus-Organism-Response) Man:
The Human Relations Model   291
Basic Needs   293
P-G (Path-Goal) Man: The Systems Model   300
E (Existential) Man: The Existential Personality   304
Review and Research   304
Incident: "Old Jim Is Out Again Doing the Housework"   305

14

Managing Groups

307

Objectives You Should Meet   308
Managing Group Meetings   309
The Process of Discussion Leading   313
Group Decision Making   315
Organizational Development   316
Review and Research   323
Incident: Calvin C. Knox   323

15

Managing the Organization

325

Objectives You Should Meet   326
Technology and Organizational Structure   333
The Organization and Its Environment   335
Organization Theory   337
Managing Organizational Change for Performance   337
Review and Research   340
Incident: Selling Management   341

16
Diagnosing and Managing Conflict
343

Objectives You Should Meet 344
What Is Conflict? 345
The Classical View of Conflict 346
The Human Relations View of Conflict 350
The Systems View of Conflict 352
Existential Conflict Management:
Reconciling Conflicting Conceptions of a Job Role 354
Review and Research 356
Incident: Executive Conflict: Shootout at the Johns-Manville Corral 357

17
Executive Behavior, Personality, and Communications
361

Objectives You Should Meet 362
Executive Behavior 363
Three Basic Executive Needs 368
The Executive Career Plan 369
Managerial Communication 370
The Woman Executive 371
The New Manager 374
Review and Research 375
Incident: John Carr, W. C. Penjack Company, Ltd. 376

V
MANAGING THE FUTURE
379

18
The Liberated Manager
381

Objectives You Should Meet 382
The Picture of the Modern "Mobile" Manager 383
The Gamesman 388
Towards an Existential Model of Management 390
Review and Research 392
Incident: Executive Obsolescence 393

Index
395

Preface

This book has two audiences in mind: business executives who wonder what is going on around them and students who are puzzled by management text that assumes what is happening "up front" is the whole story. For example, an easy way of confounding adherents of traditional management is to ask them to define management. The answers tend to be somewhat cliché. "Management is getting results through people;" "management is the coordination of such functions as planning and organizing to reach a measured objective;" "management is . . . "—you can fill in the blanks.

If you are really shrewd, you may well counter with "But what do managers do?" More often than not, you'll get a long pause and a very vague reply.

To overcome this problem, this book develops an existential systems approach to management and attempts to put drama, information, and existentialism together in a way that makes things happen efficaciously. Efficacious in this context implies not only "good things happening" but also "things happening in a way that is meaningful."

To make things not merely good but best, one must manage with certain excellence. To furnish the reader with a model of management that encourages executive excellence, this book utilizes a model that integrates the structure (the cast of executive actors), the process (the sequencing of events through objective setting to control), and values (a judicious mixture of existential and traditional). These factors influence how executives manage organizations, whether they be in the private or the public sector.

A major facet to introduce management is to provide some insight into what managers do. Students need some feel for both the rough edges of corporate life and the effort it takes to fine tune the system to the realities of the marketplace. To meet this problem head-on, I have provided a book that is descriptive rather than prescriptive in nature. As our point of departure we take the empirical facts of executive life— what executives actually do. Only then do we turn to the prescriptive part, which is concerned mainly with the management process.

This book assumes that the management process requires that the functions of objective setting, planning, organizing, staffing, leading, and evaluating be integrated. It attempts to marry structure and process by including a detailed discussion of managerial values.

I have tried to strike a balance between theory and data and between principle and practice. A historical review of management theory shows how management models have progressed from classical theory to a systems approach. This capsule view is a necessary preamble to the contingency theory of management, which gives the student dynamic and adequate framework for both analyzing problems and taking action. We pay attention to the subject of organizational politics, the ideological framework determining the distribution, allocation, and maintenance of power needed to get things done in an institution; this means we discuss not only authority but also power. When there is no consensus of authority, power relations emerge. But an executive can exercise only as much power as is allowed him or her by the other members of an institution. Thus, the exercise of power involves both leaders and followers, and the power play can work only if certain dramas are acted out. Management, like drama, involves subtle and elusive forces that defy logical explanation. This text helps readers figure out the management scenario, recognize the script, work out the roles, follow the action, and keep their places.

I would like to take this opportunity to thank the MBA students at Concordia University, too numerous to mention individually, who helped me with the research and writing.

J. K.
Montreal

1

What
Is
Management?

OBJECTIVES YOU SHOULD MEET

List some of the
rules of effective management.

Diagram the structure in terms of rules, roles,
and relations.

Identify the three levels of management.

Develop a behavioral portrait of the American
chief executive.

Define the basic functions of the management
process.

State the most important managerial values.

Identify two kinds of managers.

Construct a model for the study of management.

Before formally defining management, I would like to take the readers aside and tell them some things they ought to know, even if it means breaking the rules to do so.

First, management has a "something for nothing" aspect; you get more out than you put in. In business we call this profit, and you can feel the dollars in your hand when the selling price exceeds the cost price. Managers are preoccupied with the idea of performance—of producing a better, safer, more elegant, or cheaper item.

The second thing you ought to know is that management requires the exercise of influence, and this can develop into manipulation. A good way of grasping this point is to think of the manager as a person who gets results through people. How does he or she get results? Mainly by influencing people, which means working on their expectations, changing their perceptions, and, on a good day, making them an extension of his or her will—at least as long as they don't find out.

For example, suppose you have to submit a report to your boss by Friday at 5:00 p.m. That is exactly one week away, and you know two things about the secretaries in your office: one, they are overworked; and two, they don't deliver work on schedule. Let's assume it is 9:00 a.m. What steps would you take? If your immediate answer is, "I'd type the report myself," you should probably abandon the idea of becoming a manager. If you are going to manage, you will arrange to get a secretary started on Monday so that you will have the report by Wednesday afternoon for proofreading and correcting.

Which brings us to our third point. It is not sufficient (nor morally correct) to define management as the art of manipulating a person so that he or she will behave in a way that will further your interest. This may be hard to swallow unless perhaps you can think back to some time when you were manipulated. Manipulation is not management.

While the new approach to management recognizes the importance of power (and this can mean manipulation) in getting things done, the manager preoccupied with power can end up falling victim to Lord Acton's dictum, "Power corrupts; absolute power corrupts absolutely." The person who has been manipulated can come away from the experience feeling he has been humiliated. Next time, you may not get the help you need. Yet frequently management has to exercise power to cut through red tape, to get to the core of the matter, to get things moving. Modern research on the executive personality suggests that managers with a strong need for power are likely to get to the top of the organizational tree, but only if they can mobilize the energies of their work teams for good and responsible ends. They succeed because they channel a need to control and dominate others into a socially useful, tempered instrument that turns followers into leaders. They tell their people what is expected of them, give them the resources to do the job, and let them get on with it. They do *not* tell them, "The name of the game around here is power. I can pull a little string and get you fired, and if you don't like it you can quit." The good manager displays a certain grace even under pressure.

Our fourth bit of advice is this: business is complicated, and you have got to be even more complicated if you want to control it. How would you manage a systems analyst group consisting of an economist, a mathematician, a behavioral scientist, an OR man, and a business graduate? Not by learning mathematics, then econometrics, then OR, then behavioral science, and so on. Even if you could, there is not enough time. You would have to stop thinking in linear terms (*B* follows *A*, and *C* follows *B*) and move over to a more sophisticated view of the world. This is what management aims to do: help you to think in a way that makes work *productive* (makes good things happen); *creative* (suggests answers that "going by the book" would have missed); *fun* (transforms work into a game, a sport, an entertainment); and *rewarding* (ensures that you get paid for what you do—usually in cash or capital but sometimes in psychic income).

Now we can turn to more formal matters of defining precisely what management is. We deal here with four basic ideas: management (the managerial structure), managing (the process), the managerial ethos (the values or style), and perhaps most important of all, the person himself, the manager.

ELEMENTS OF MANAGEMENT: STRUCTURE, PROCESS, VALUES

This book is based on certain clearly identifiable assumptions.

Structural Optic

We presume that structural considerations are still very important. Managers need skills in preparing policies and plans, designing organizational charts, writing role descriptions, and producing new rule books. But the new approach to management also emphasizes the sociological aspect. What this means can be illustrated, for example, in the development of role descriptions. Roles cannot be defined in isolation. Just as it is impossible to define the role of the physician without defining the roles of the patient and nurse, it is also necessary to recognize that executive roles have to be defined in sets.

To get into a structure of an organization, one must know something about the politics of organizational behavior. Managers must gain an insight into the operation of cliques, cabals, and coalitions who manage the hidden agenda and determine who gets what, where, when, and why.

Process Considerations

Managers cannot manage the political side of the business without good intelligence about both internal processes and external exchanges. Thus, the new executive is highly involved in the management of the information system. To be effective he or she must be able to set objectives, establish plans, design organizations, people these organizations, and evaluate performance. To do all these things he or she must be involved in communication and decision making.

Values

To manage both the political structures and the information processes, the manager needs a new value system that is appropriate to the turbulent environment of modern times.

THE STRUCTURE OF MANAGEMENT

A useful starting point is to think of management as the rapidly expanding class of persons who manage the organization. But how do you recognize a manager? You can always pick out a doctor in a hospital or an officer in the army. You can usually pick out the managers in a factory by their clothes. They wear suits; the foremen wear white coats with red collars; inspectors wear white coats with blue collars; shop floor people wear jeans or trousers and, traditionally, blue shirts—hence the expression "blue collar."

Quite rightly you may argue that this is all old hat—this management-labor split, this fuzzy white/blue collar demarcation. What with plumbers making what they make and managers wanting to form unions, distinctions based on the color of a collar can be distinctly misleading. A more useful line of approach is to look at managers by level. (See Table 1.1.)

Levels of Management

Sitting on top of the management hierarchy is the board of directors. The board's principal tasks are periodically to force discussions about where the company is going and how effectively it has achieved its objectives. The chairman of the board of directors is known as the chief executive officer (CEO). Members of the board bring acquired knowledge and experience; and they not only appoint but also define the terms of reference of the president and senior vice presidents.

Reporting directly to the board of directors is top management, which is responsible for developing and reviewing the firm's strategic plan. As well as formulating corporate plans, the president, as chief operating officer (COO), evaluates overall performance of key personnel and major departments. To achieve these strategic and critical tasks, top management must establish policy. They maintain a system of communications with the senior managers of the firm, who have the authority and responsibility to implement policy. The senior executives of the firm set objectives, develop organizations, negotiate lines of capital, and participate in decisions on output, price, wages, and personnel matters. They also consider major changes, such as mergers and acquisitions.

Middle management is essentially concerned with implementing policy by developing intermediate plans. Although the exact task varies according to the company's size and technology, most middle-level managers are responsible for establishing departmental policies and reviewing daily production and sales figures. They must also try to get product managers and staff specialists to work together.

The supervisors' main tasks are developing and implementing

Table 1.1 Levels of Management

Level	Titles	Function
Top management	Chief executive President Vice president	Policy
Middle management	General managers Department managers Superintendent	Execution
First-level management	Section managers Foreman Supervisor	Supervision

more detailed short-range operating plans. They supervise the day-to-day operations. They initiate, develop, support, inspect (and sometimes do) shop floor task assignments, sometimes on an hourly basis. Supervisors have an in-between status, being neither completely management nor shop floor people.

THE EXECUTIVE'S BEHAVIOR BEHAVIORALLY VIEWED

What do we know about the behavior of American chief executives? We know a great deal from newspaper gossip columns about such giants as Harold Geneen, who ran ITT, and Henry Ford. But what do we know about chief executives through observational studies?

A Behavioral Portrait

One of the first studies of American chief executives was made by W.H. Whyte, who reported a study of fifty-two company presidents, twenty-three vice presidents, and fifty-three middle managers identified as "comers."[1] Whyte found that they worked excessive hours, included evenings in their work time, and spent most of their time interacting with or influencing people. The question was not how much executives work; it is how they find time to work.

The findings of a more recent study, reported in 1960 by Dale and Urwick, largely confirmed Whyte's data.[2] Dale and Urwick studied ten executives and analyzed in detail the working week of a bank president. More than half of his time was taken up with outside contacts, and a lot of time was spent on public relations.

The whole idea of making executive behavior studies by observation was invented by Sune Carlson, a professor of business studies in Sweden. Carlson was preoccupied with the idea that management studies were largely theological, sterile, and based to a large extent on anecdotes. Carlson was fighting the idea, then and still widely current, that what a manager did could be summed up in the acronym POLE—planning, organizing, leading, evaluating. Carlson's questions were,

[1] W.H. Whyte, Jr., "How Hard Do Executives Work?" *Fortune,* (January 1954).

[2] Ernest Dale and L.F. Urwick, *Staff in Management* (New York: McGraw-Hill Book Company, 1960).

"How do you recognize a manager when he is POLEing? What are his behavioral characteristics? Does he have an identifiable profile?" When nobody could answer him, he set out to find out for himself. Carlson collected his data under five headings: place, person, technique of communication, question handled, and action taken.

What Carlson found confirmed the cliché. He discovered that top executives worked long hours, rarely visited their factories, spent long hours traveling, were slaves to their diaries, and had little time for leisure and contemplation.[3]

Henry Mintzberg, a professor of management at McGill University, set out in 1968 to study the work of the chief executives of five large U.S. corporations.[4] Using a technique called structured observation, he observed each CEO for a period of one week. Mintzberg showed that the American chief executive was on the surface a very superficial person who worked long hours, largely because he was a node in a complex information system. Virtually everything in the business, usually in a digested form, had to pass across his desk.

What Mintzberg is telling us is that grand theories of management are irrelevant: managers don't act; they react. The stuff of managerial life seems to be made up of "brief encounters" and "brief activities" (49 percent of executives' activities in Mintzberg's study lasted less than nine minutes). To get his business done, the manager concentrates on issues that are current, well-defined and nonroutine; he works mainly through the spoken word—few letters, apparently.

The Top Executive Profile

While we don't have much to go on from observational studies, we do know a great deal about the top executive's personality from case histories, personality tests, and interviews. Generally, he or she is bright, well informed, and healthy. He or she is serious and conscientious, forceful and intense, frank and straightforward. They are *not* up to date on technical matters. They are interested in persuasion, manipulation, and Machiavellianism, and they like short, brief books on how to persuade and manipulate others.

One "perceptanalytic" study found that successful top executives exhibited free movements and confident postures and were unimpeded by doubts or hesitations.[5] They experienced basic self-trust and were

[3] S. Carlson, *Executive Behaviour* (Stockholm: Strombergs, 1951).

[4] Henry Mintzberg, *The Nature of Managerial Work* (New York: Harper and Row, 1973).

[5] Zygmunt A. Piotrowski and Milton R. Rock, *The Perceptanalytical Executive Scale: A Tool for the Selection of Top Managers* (New York: Grune and Stratton, 1963).

genuinely confident about their own feelings, decisions, and actions, indicating spontaneity and enterprise. Successful top executives, in other words, are winners; and they know it. The winners were remarkably free from obsessiveness. To be successful, the authors argue, a winner must be a man (the study was reported in 1963), have an IQ of at least 120, be at least 40, and have lots of stamina, initiative, and self-trust.

MIDDLE-LEVEL MANAGEMENT

The function of middle-level management is to translate the policies of top management into operational plans that can be put into effect by lower-level or supervisory management. What do middle-level managers do, how do they do it, and with whom? How and with whom do they communicate? Middle-level managers often have a terrible time trying to answer these questions. To try and throw some light on their activities and communications, we must quickly review an observational study made by Tom Burns, a sociologist at Edinburgh University.[6] Burns' study, which is something of a classic, was an attempt to study the behaviors and interactions of a department manager. The subjects of Burns' study were the department manager, two production engineers, and a design manager.

His results show that his executives spent 80 percent of their time interacting, some on the telephone, a lot of it in meetings. Before he began his study, Burns asked his subjects to estimate how they spent their time. Most managers overestimated time spent on production and underestimated the time spent on personnel.

Another important finding was that most of the interaction took place within the department. A good deal of this interaction was horizontal, between peers.

Reviewing the observational studies of middle managers, we can reach certain general conclusions.

1. The idea that an executive should have only one boss has to be discarded.
2. Middle managers spend a great deal of their time in the horizontal rather than the vertical line of communications.
3. Frequently, when a manager thinks he is issuing instructions, subordinates report receiving advice.

[6] Tom Burns, "The Directions of Activity and Communications in a Departmental Executive Group," *Human Relations*, Vol. 7 (1954), pp. 73–97.

4. The manager does a great deal of the work himself instead of delegating it to subordinates.
5. Authority and responsibility are rarely balanced.
6. The manager is highly involved in personnel work, assessing and training first-level managers.
7. The notion that a middle manager's job is clearly defined and clearly demarcated from other members of the work group has to be abandoned.
8. The kind of work that middle managers do is a function of technology. For example, in highly automated production line work a great deal of time is spent trouble shooting and organizing repairs. In batch production (with a great number of units on the floor at any time) middle managers are highly involved in programming.
9. A significant part of the manager's time is spent bypassing the status circuits of the organization chart to reach the people who can really see that things are done.
10. One cannot describe a middle manager's behavior in systematic terms because he or she spends so much time putting out fires and responding to crises. But middle-management jobs vary primarily according to whether the manager's contacts are mainly within his department or without.

SUPERVISORY MANAGEMENT

The supervisor is part of first-line management and is directly responsible for supervising shop floor operatives. The supervisor's job is to ensure that work of the requisite quality "gets out of the gate" on schedule. Because the supervisor is at the boundary between the middle-management system and the workers' shop floor, he or she is ambivalent to a certain degree. The literature of supervision is replete with terms indicative of this ambivalence. The supervisor is sometimes described as the "man in the middle," "marginal man," and the "manager in no-man's land." Frequently, the supervisor finds himself or herself caught in a bind between the middle managers' formal system and workers' informal system. Because of this bind the supervisor is frequently forced into a variety of conflicting behaviors. (See Figure 1.1.)

The supervisor is the most maligned and least understood of all management personnel. His or her job is usually defined as to oversee, superintend, inspect, lead, motivate, direct, and control.

The production supervisor has three functions:

1. *Programming function.* Find out what work is coming to the section and determine which work has priority.

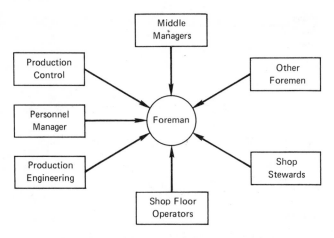

Figure 1.1   The Position of the First Line Manager or Foreman

2. *Technical function.* Organize running repairs to the machines, trouble-shoot, ensure that the work is of the requisite quality and is finished, ensure that the machines required for the next job are properly set up.
3. *Personnel function.* Allocate the work and ensure that it gets done; hire, train, and assess the operatives for the section.

Structure of: Rules, Roles, and Relations

In brief, the manager is the actor who in particular roles, guided by rules (for example, the rights to hire, fire, reward, punish, inform, etc.) and tied to certain relations (other organizational members' expectations) makes things happen in business. (See Figure 1.2.)

THE PROCESS OF MANAGING

Managing is the business of sequencing events so that things come out the way you want them to. To do this, you must know what the management process is: objective setting, planning, organizing, leading, evaluating, and deciding.

The idea of analyzing management into a set of basic functions was first developed by a French industrialist, Henri Fayol, whose ideas reached a wide audience in the 1920s. Not only did Fayol specify how to break the process into its component parts by analyzing the functions,

11

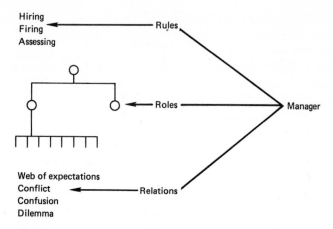

Hiring
Firing
Assessing

Rules

Roles — Manager

Web of expectations
Conflict
Confusion
Dilemma

Relations

Figure 1.2   The Three *R's* Governing Management

but through his ideas of unity of command (one employee—one boss), unity of direction (one group in charge of one function) and chain of command (one line from the president to the shop floor operative), he was able to pull the functions together. Let's take a look at these functions.

Objective Setting

The managerial process naturally begins by formulating the objectives or goals that the firm is trying to achieve. Only when the objectives have been clearly formulated can plans be developed and ultimately performance measured in accordance with these objectives. To a large extent, problems develop and hasty decisions are made because the process of objective setting has not been properly gone through. The absence of objectives leaves the employees without a sense of direction and fails to provide them with a structure within which they can properly exercise their discretion. The absence of objectives impedes planning, organizing, and the other process functions.

Planning

Once the objectives have been defined, planning can be initiated. Planning is concerned with the formation of goals required to achieve a course of action. Plans spell out not only what to do but the "who," the "when," the "how," and the "how much." Planning is essentially concerned with the future, because it anticipates and precedes action.

By providing a factual basis for future action, the act of planning helps managers clarify their thinking and take the necessary steps to meet future needs.

Despite the uncertainties of the environment, an increasing number of firms is engaging in systematic planning. But predicting the future is a hazardous operation. To minimize these hazards, management employs forecasting to establish a pool of reliable information about future business and environmental conditions. For example, the American auto industry is currently trying to make an accurate prediction of future demand for subcompacts. It is trying to reduce the uncertainty of the future.

Although forecasting can consist of a variety of complex and complicated techniques, in its simplest form it is built on rough estimates by salespeople concerning future business. But these sales predictions have to be qualified. One way of qualifying forecasts is to make three different kinds: optimistic, middle of the road, and pessimistic. Since each of these forecasts is tied to a different prediction about how the economy as a whole will behave, forecasting and budgeting are interlocked. When large firms prepare budgets, they usually do so on a contingency basis. U.S. automobile manufacturers consider such contingencies as the rate of growth of GNP, the rate of inflation, the sale of foreign imports, changes in government regulations, and expected changes in consumer preferences.

Organizing

Once objectives, goals, and budgets have been set up, the next step is to get an organization. In broad economic terms, organizing includes the acquisition of physical plant, capital, and personnel. In management, where it has a much narrower meaning, organizing is preparing organization tables, which set out the relationships among functions, jobs, and personnel. Action has to be structured to be effective in achieving organizational objectives. Organizing specifies the structure of the firm; it sets out the lines of authority and communication among managers and determines what information must flow along these lines.

Staffing

Organizing has provided a set of roles. Now it needs people to fill them. The firm needs to be able to recruit, select, train, develop, and direct people in a way that will help the firm both achieve its objectives and give its employees a sense of growth and development.

Leading

Having got the right people in the right place, the next issue is to get the interaction and motivation they need to complete their work. Modern behavioral science has supplied managers with a *contingency theory of leadership,* which guides them toward providing the type of leadership appropriate to the circumstances. The modern approach to leadership helps a manager decide when he should be democratic and employee-centered and when he should be autocratic and directive. Contrary to popular wisdom, it is neither effective nor desirable to be democratic in all circumstances. Modern leadership is more likely to take the view that subordinates are looking for a structure within which they can contribute initiatives and suggestions for consideration by their managers.

Evaluating and Controlling

When the firm has gone through these processes, the question arises as to whether it has achieved its objectives. Control is essentially concerned with measuring the degree of success. This is done by checking performance against standards and then taking necessary corrective action. Control steers and brakes the organization to ensure that it is on the right track and going at the right speed.

It will come as no surprise that not all employees act in a way that is compatible with the firm's goals. Although positive motivation is the most important control, employees require and often welcome sensible and productive constraints on their behavior. But control should be not only coercive but also normative—it must appear to be legitimate to people who have to operate within the system.

Decision Making

Decision making is an integrating function; it permeates the other functions and ties them together. Decision making and doing go together. Recently, decision making has become both systematic and participative. It has become systematic from the application of scientific methods and the use of mathematical techniques to make problem solving more precise. It has become more participative because progressive managers realize that when individuals participate in decisions relevant to their work, they develop a high sense of morale and implement the decisions more effectively. (See Figure 1.3.)

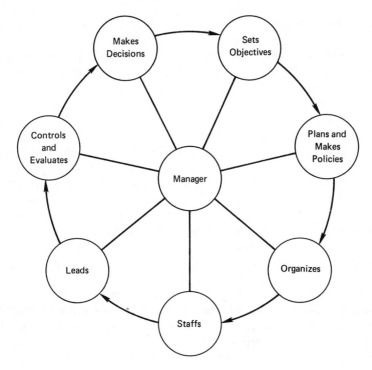

Figure 1.3   The Manager's Functions

MANAGERIAL VALUES

Even after the structure and process in the management system have been defined, it may still not be clear to the individual manager what he or she ought to do. To fill in some of the holes in the system, organizations typically develop an ideology—a set of values that hold the structure and process in position. Values, as broad statements of preferences, help the manager make decisions.

Three values dominate the manager's behavior. First, the manager is basically preoccupied with economic or practical ends. Second, managers see themselves primarily as instruments, as the means of achieving objectives and policies set by shareholders. Third, managers are concerned with achievement. They want to get things done by planning, organizing, and controlling the behavior of individuals, groups, and organizations. American managers, in particular, view the goals of profit, efficiency, and productivity as being of prime importance.

The Changing Success Ethic

Recently, the American Management Association (AMA) issued a report entitled *The Changing Success Ethic.*[7] It cites evidence that executives are developing existential aspirations. They define success as the chance "to be who I am." Apparently, a new concept of success is emerging in the minds of executives, who are beginning to value self-actualization ("What I can be, I must be").

Traditional North American and Western European value systems are changing. Many people are challenging male chauvinism, the worship of science and technology, and the adoration of affluence, achievement, and aggression—the hallmark of the traditional value system. Such competitiveness, many feel, does not further good human relations among superiors, peers, and subordinates.

Traditionally, middle management preferred good human resource planning, in which the important thing was getting highly paid for challenging, innovative work, even if a little angst was introduced in the process. Human relations was left to shop floor operatives and supervisors, and even there it was often a cover for incompetence and lack of effort or planning. Human relations never really caught on with top management, who preferred the strategy of "suboptimizing" the factors of production, technology, and personnel. Top people didn't allow personality to upset their equations.

While executives in the human relations era were busy learning about participation, creativity, and commitment, along came the systems approach, whose central problem of organization was the management of information. The new values were openness and controlling the level of surprise. Now the road was open for the development of the new existential value system. Executives moved from achievement, aggression, affluence, and alienation to the new existential values—self-actualization, self-expression, interdependence, and joy. See Boxes 1.1 and 1.2 for examples of these values.

But in some curious way, American executives want a world that is both traditional and existential. The same is true of college students, who will be tomorrow's executives. Along with the spread of such personal existential values as self-fulfillment and self-expression and such public existential concerns as a just and harmonious society, there has also been a steady increase in such traditional career values as the desire to get ahead and to find economic security. So what we have, in effect, is a fusion of existential and traditional values. This fusion

---

[7] Dale Tarnowieski, *The Changing Success Ethic* (New York: American Management Association, 1973).

The classical theory of management assumes that the executive will always act in the best interest of the firm and behave rationally. Guided by the Calvinist ethic of "work hard, play hard" and with his performance measured by his ability to acquire wealth but not spend it, the classical executive found himself caught up in a value system of the four A's—aggression, achievement, affluence, and alienation. His ability to postpone consumption and endure pain and distress helped to make "the rise of capitalism and the spirit of Protestantism" a beautiful subject for students who wanted to bridge the fields of economics and religion.

The old mythology pictured the manager with a high need for achievement, a strong need to be socially mobile, respectful of superiors, bright in terms of his ability to organize unstructured situations, and keen to make decisions. He knew who he was and he did not fear failure.

Joe Kelly, "Reflections on the State of the Art," *The Conference Board Record XII* (1975), No. 11, p. 33.

should provide some interesting problems, for executive and professional career growth requires conformity and willingness to "go along" with the system. The essence of the matter is that young people want an existential life style but one with career growth and economic security. The critical problem for top management is to provide a work environment that can achieve this integration of existential and economic expectations.

A FRAMEWORK FOR THE STUDY OF MANAGEMENT

It is now possible to set up a contingency framework for the study of management. In its simplist form, the framework is made up of the elements in Figure 1.4.

The critical dimensions can be specified in terms of *structure* (defining direction of information flow), *process* (specifying what is done to information), and *values* (setting out beliefs, ethics, and manners). We can apply these critical dimensions to any system that refers to personality, the group or the organization. If a system is goal-oriented, we should be able to measure its effectiveness by measuring the end products. The only remaining question is, how does one establish the relations between the critical dimensions and the end products of a system? The answer is research.

Two things are important about this framework. First, it has

Box 1.2: The Existentialist

His iconoclasm hits you. He's on something—not necessarily mescaline, LSD, or any consciousness-expanding drugs; little things like small talk matter to him.

He's into body geometry, pizzas, Gallo wine, MacDonald's. He is for Jacques-Yves Cousteau and his exotic shipmates, sea lions, elephant seals, and walruses. He likes to look his age, even a little older, to feel fitter—all through a diet of existential games—mainly tennis, touch football, and biking. He reads (but is against) Ann Landers, Amy Vanderbilt, Evelyn Waugh, Ernest Hemingway, Erica Jong. He likes looking over people's shoulders at *Playboy* centerfolds.

He's for Sir Edmund Hillary and his devil and his explanation of why he climbed Everest. "Science has nothing to do with it; neither does money. . . . I think you sometimes just want to, well, give it a real go." He is for Malcolm Forbes and his balloon flight across the Atlantic. "Why?" as Forbes asked rhetorically. "For a very simple reason: it's the ultimate balloon trip."

Joe Kelly, "Reflections on the State of the Art," *The Conference Board Record XII* (1975), No. 11, p. 33.

generality; that is, it can be applied to the study of personality or the group or the organization. Secondly, the framework suggests different levels of research and different routes across the framework.

A SIMPLE MODEL

A useful and simplified model for studying management is shown in Figure 1.5.

This model has three input variables: structure, process, and values. Although these variables can be much more elaborate and complex, it is perhaps useful to think of them as *who* (structure of actors) did *what, where, and when* (process of events) *why* (values and beliefs).

· Figure 1.4   Step One: Developing the Model

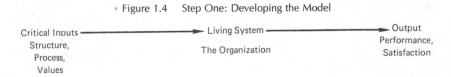

Critical Inputs ——————————————→ Living System ——————————————→ Output
Structure,   Performance,
Process,   The Organization   Satisfaction
Values

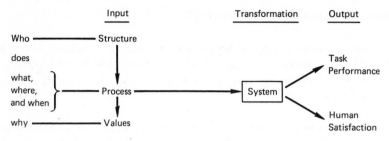

Figure 1.5 Step Two: A Simple Model for the Study of Organization

Structure: The Political Framework
(The Three R's)

Structure describes the political shape of the system, the framework that holds the system together. Think of structure as the three R's: rules, roles, and relations. (See Figure 1.6.)

The *rules* tell you, for example, who can initiate contacts, who can talk to whom, and who can sign expense accounts. The rules are usually based on equity and reciprocity; they bind the group together in an interlocking web of rights, obligations, and gratifications. As long as everyone understands them, rules reduce the need for supervision.

The *roles* describe people's expectations, which makes them respond on cue to what another person does. The role is the behaviors and attitudes appropriate to a particular position regardless of who occupies it. Role always implies duty and obligation.

But how can people be made to assume their proper roles? Once you have the rules in position, most people take up their assigned roles. What about those who don't? Trying to get them in position reveals the importance of relations. Relations essentially describe how one role fits into another, the web of complementarity and reciprocity that is signaled backwards and forwards between role players. Relations are largely a matter of signaling.

Figure 1.6 Structure

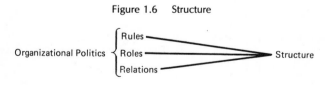

Process: Information Management (OPOSLED)

Structure is essentially theological (it is full of "oughts"), rigid, and fixed. Not so process. Process describes action. Who did what? Where and when? What happened next? But process also includes degree: how and how much.

Process is essentially dynamic, and in management it is usually concerned with information exchanges. Figure 1.7 shows how process fits into our framework.

Values

Values are usually vague verbal statements of imperatives, often in the form of slogans, that mobilize energy and give direction to a group. Values help people make choices among competing behaviors. Every group has values.

Output Variables

There are two kinds of output variables. The first, task output variables, include production and profitability. Task output is measured through productivity. However, there is no method of measuring productivity that is not an exercise in *suboptimization*. The optimum is not necessarily the best; it is more like "the most for the least." Suboptimization means that if you concentrate too hard on winning on one variable, you may well have to pay an inordinate price on another variable. For example, if you run a taxi business and you insist on maximum vehicle utilization, you will have a minimum of vehicle maintenance. In measuring productivity, you must try to get as much as you can from all the variables, recognizing that none will be perfect.

Figure 1.7   Process

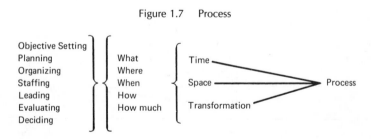

The second output variable is the human variable, which is easy—if fatal—to ignore. This measures the joy you get out of doing something. It is frequently measured by job satisfaction scales. Today, most people take the view that "satisfaction is guaranteed"; they are looking for something better: meaningful work. The challenge for management is to get corporate excellence and still allow people to find their jobs meaningful and satisfying. Figure 1.8 shows how all the management variables fit together in a model of management.

REVIEW AND RESEARCH

1. Draw up a list of what you expect to get out of the study of management. (Suggested headings: technical knowledge, problem solving skills, language, style, interpersonal insights.)

2. Describe the three levels of management.

3. What do managers do? Does their behavior fit your previous ideas about what they do?

4. Describe management in terms of its structure, process, and values.

5. Using the process OPOSLED, set up one of the following: (a) a

Figure 1.8   Step Three: Simplified Model of Management

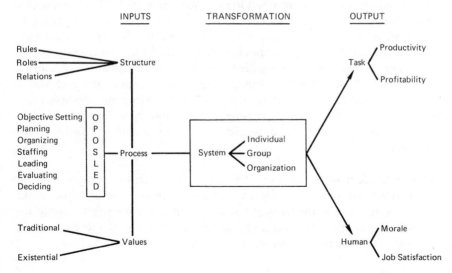

wedding or a funeral; (b) an after football party; (c) the initiation of
new members into a fraternity or a sorority.

6. Compare and contrast the old (traditional) manager and the new
   (existential) executive.

7. Describe the best boss you ever had. Why was he or she the best?

8. Compare and contrast the traditional and the new value systems.

9. Describe how you plan to learn to be a manager.

10. What is the most important point you have learned so far? Why is it
    so important?

AMENG, INC.

Michael Wilson, who is twenty-seven and has recently earned an MBA,
wants to work with his uncle, Don Wilson, who is the president and a
major shareholder of Ameng, Inc. Don joined the company in 1946,
when it was a relatively small manufacturer of accessories for the
automobile industry. He built the business from a $2 million a year
company to a $40 million a year growth stock. Don achieved this
dramatic feat by a combination of precision engeering and aggressive
marketing; he also expanded production from only electrical gas
pumps, the original product, to plain bearings for high-speed engines
and a battery with a guaranteed life of four years. In 1948, Don married
the chairman's daughter, and in the same year he became vice president
of engineering and production. Don is meeting his nephew, Michael
Wilson, to discuss where Michael should begin in the business.

Don is fully conversant with Michael's background and experience.
Besides an MBA, Michael has a degree in physics. Michael was a
helicopter pilot for a short time in Vietnam, before he was wounded
and sent home. He is vocally opposed to the military-industrial complex;
in fact, he took part in a number of demonstrations while at the
university.

Don: I think it would be best if you started off in the company either
   in design or in one of the production sections. See how you make
   out, and when better things come up, they're advertised—apply for
   them. Start at the bottom and come up the hard way, like your uncle.
Michael: You mean actually start near the bottom of the ladder?
Don: Yes.

Michael: What about my MBA?

Don: What about it? Not too many people are going to hold it against you.

Michael: I was thinking of something different, Uncle Don. I was kind of hoping to join one of the project teams—especially the one working on the new computer acquisition.

Don: Let's talk more about this over lunch.

1. What are the advantages and disadvantages of the start that Don Wilson is offering to his nephew Michael?
2. What are the advantages and disadvantages of Michael's idea—to work on a project team?
3. What do you think Michael should do? How should he analyze his choices?

2

Schools
of
Management

OBJECTIVES YOU SHOULD MEET

Identify the three
traditional schools of management.

Outline the assumptions of classical management
theory.

Construct an organizational chart illustrating line,
staff, and functional relations.

Set out the basic characteristics of Weber's
theory of bureaucracy.

Explain how the Hawthorne experiment prepared
the way for human relations.

Diagram Theory X and Theory Y.

Describe how systems management integrates
behavioral science and computer science.

Define the contingency approach to
management.

Defining any academic field is difficult, but defining management theory may be more difficult than most. As a new field, it has yet to stake out its jurisdictions definitively; as an applied field, it draws heavily on such other social science and scientific disciplines as economics, psychology, sociology, and engineering.

In the development of management theory there are three significant themes. The first, classical theory, includes scientific management, administrative management, and bureaucracy theories. Frederick Winslow Taylor, who invented scientific management, made work measurement possible by using the stop watch to measure production. Taylor also orchestrated manufacturing with production planning and budgetary control. Administrative management theory was conceived in the thirties and forties as an attempt to develop rational principles that could be used to design organizations and to help managers make the most effective use of resources. While Taylor was inventing line and functional management, Max Weber, the other great classicist, was developing his notion of bureaucracy. Ideally, he felt, work should be broken down into areas of functional specialization, each commanded by a professional bureaucrat.

But it soon became clear that the classical approach was one-sided. It paid relatively little attention to questions of human needs or motivation. To remedy this situation, managers in the late thirties and early forties began to study human relations. The theoretical infrastructure for human relations was provided by Elton Mayo, who found that employees are guided by a social logic quite different from the economic logic that classical theorists had presumed. Soon industrial psychologists were developing a whole series of principles that helped to humanize the workplace. Human relations made work more tolerable and thus reduced employee dissatisfaction. But by the late fifties, the term *human relations* had fallen into some disrepute. Many managers had come to realize that the human relations approach was not valid in all circumstances. Human relations was replaced by the systems approach.

The systems approach attempts to integrate the best features of both earlier schools. It is a much more subtle approach than either. A major factor facilitating the emergence of this new approach was the development and widespread use of the computer, since information concepts play a large part in the systems approach. Soon organization theorists were working with inputs, transformations, outputs, and feedback.

To understand the systems approach, one must have some familiarity with both computer science and behavioral science. Both of these sciences employ models. In the systems approach, the basic model treats the organization as an organism that interacts with its environment.

THE CLASSICAL SCHOOL

The classical school of management is business's time-honored way of organizing. Its two basic assumptions are (1) that people are rational, analytical, and motivated primarily by economic considerations and (2) that people work best when the job they have to do is broken down into its smallest parts. Starting with Adam Smith's idea of the division of labor, the classical theorist believes in functional specialization: each worker should do one and only one job. (Box 2.1 contains Adam Smith's explanation of the division of labor in a pin factory.) With specialization, individual workers pay attention only to their own small part of the overall task; thus, business needs management to coordinate the different specialists—and, of course, a top manager to keep an eye on the first level of managers.

The value of the classical mode of thought lies in recognizing the necessity of breaking jobs down (functional specialization) and putting them together again (coordination). To understand this business of analysis of functions and their subsequent coordination, we must look at the classical theory in its proper historical perspective.

Scientific Management

Frederick Winslow Taylor, the father of scientific management, was interested in defining the best way to do a job; specifying a "standard time" for each separate motion necessary to perform a task by timing tasks with a stopwatch; selecting the right person for the job; carefully planning the balance of machines, men, speed of working, and payment (usually on a piece basis); and developing line and staff management. Taylor invented a piecework system, which typically led to a threefold increase in productivity for a 50 percent increase in wages. For his system to work, Taylor proposed, first, to make scientific measurements of actual job operations. Secondly, he argued that method and time study should be carried out not by the production foreman but by a foreman specially trained for the task. This was the beginning of functional management, as opposed to the line management then being used.

One man draws out the wire, another straightens it, a third cuts it, a fourth points it, a fifth grinds it at the top for receiving the head; to make the head requires two or three distinct operations; to put it on is a peculiar business; to whiten the pins is another; it is even a trade by itself to put them into the paper. . . . I have seen a small manufactory of this kind where ten men only were employed, and where some of them consequently performed two or three distinct operations. But though they were very poor, and therefore but indifferently accommodated with the necessary machinery, they could, when they exerted themselves, make among them about twelve pounds of pins in a day. There are in a pound upwards of four thousand pins of a middling size. Those ten persons, therefore, could make among them upwards of forty-eight thousand pins in a day. . . . But if they had all wrought separately and independently, . . . they certainly could not each of them have made twenty, perhaps not one pin in a day. . . .

From Adam Smith, *The Wealth of Nations, Representative Selections,* Bruce Mazlish, ed. (New York: The Bobbs-Merrill Co., 1961), p. 5.

This fundamental distinction warrants careful definition. Line managers are people who have a direct responsibility for achieving the objectives of the company. The line managers manage the actual production and "get the stuff out of the gate." The only thing functional managers produce is their function. Functional managers are specialists in the human, economic, technological, or informational aspects of the work. In theory, they serve as advisors or consultants to line managers, who can accept or reject their advice. Taylor started this idea of functional management by separating "planning" from "doing." Figure 2.1 shows which personnel are functional managers and which are line managers.

Administrative Management

Administrative management is the core of classical theory. It is concerned with spelling out the sequence; stating the objectives; and defining who does what, who is in charge of whom, who handles the cash, and so on. What scientific management did for the shop floor, administrative management did for the front office. The author who did most to popularize this new classical style was Lyndall F. Urwick, who read Taylor's theories while serving in the British army during the First World War. Urwick set out to codify Taylor's theories. He argued that if you are going to set up an organization, there are certain steps you must go through:

1. Define the objective (for example, to make automobiles).

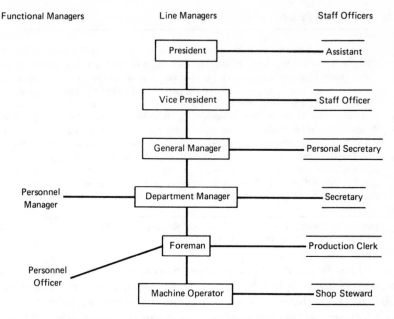

Functional Managers   Line Managers   Staff Officers

Figure 2.1   Line, Function, and Staff Management

2. Divide the task into functions (make engines, transmissions, bodies; assemble them).
3. Draw up an organization chart. (See Figure 2.2.)
4. Prepare proper job descriptions.
   a. Authority and responsibility must be coterminous, coequal, and defined.
   b. Managers should be held personally accountable for all actions taken by subordinates.

Drawing on Taylor's seminal ideas on functional relations, Urwick

Figure 2.2   Part of an Organization Chart

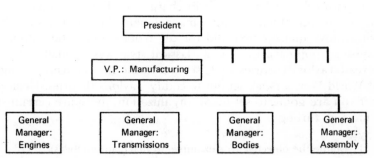

introduced the union of three kinds of formal relations—line, function-al, and staff. The line of command describes the channel of delegated responsibility along which instructions flow and accountability is re-ported. There are several kinds of functional managers at the corporate level. They usually include finance, administration and personnel, marketing, engineering, and research and development managers. At a factory level, functional managers can best be shown with an organi-zation chart of the personnel department. (See Figure 2.3.)

A staff officer who is meant to be a personal assistant to a manager has no authority or responsibility in his own right at all. He is meant to be an extension of the manager he serves. In fact, staff officers can wield tremendous power. The staff officer you are most likely to encounter is the general manager's secretary.

Bureaucracy

The most elegant form of the classical theory is embodied in the idea of the bureaucracy developed by Max Weber (1864–1920). For him, bureaucracy was not a pejorative term but rather a type of organization that was modern and technically efficient.

As Max Weber grew up he was greatly impressed by the manner in which Bismarck had unified Germany. He was struck by how Bismarck ran his government by making all his ministerial colleagues dependent on a bureaucracy. When Bismarck retired, Weber was surprised to note that the ministers continued to manage their offices, unconcerned and undismayed. What Bismarck had done was weld his government into a smoothly operating bureaucratic machine. Thus, to Weber, a bureaucracy meant precision, speed, unambiguity, continuity, discretion, and reduction of friction in the organizational machine.

Figure 2.3   Interlock between Line and Personnel Managers

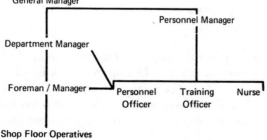

According to Weber, an efficient organization has the following characteristics:

1. *Specialization of function.* The task is broken down into its constituent parts, and each part is assigned to a worker. That becomes his official job.
2. *Hierarchy.* Each manager has the authority to give the commands required for the discharge of his duties. Each lower office falls under the command of a higher one.
3. *A meritocracy.* Individuals are appointed to posts in the bureaucracy by examination and are promoted on the basis of competence.
4. *A written record.* The management of the business is based on written documents.
5. *Specification of relations among specialists.* The relationships among different managers and departments are clearly set out. This description specifies who can consult whom, who can authorize expenditures, and who resolves disputes.

HUMAN RELATIONS

The human relations approach emerged in the thirties as a reaction to the excessive rigidities of the classical school of management. What was ultimately wrong with classical theory was that people don't think rationally; they are limited in their capacity for logical thinking and their ability to assimilate empirical data.

Human relations supplied a new dimension. It emphasized people's capacity for creative activity and self-affirmation and recognized people's need for support from their peers. In brief, we need human relations because we are all sensitive and vulnerable to the impersonal forces of organizational structure.

The Primary Working Group
and the Need for Peer Support

The most important single feature of human relations is the ideology that everybody needs to belong to some kind of primary group and that somehow within this group, he will establish an identity and feel important. If an employee is not satisfied with his formal working group, he will invent or join some sort of informal group. Informal groups not only have their own values, norms, reinforcements, and sanctions, but they also have their own special languages.

The Hawthorne Experiment

The human relations approach was first outlined by an Australian anthropologist and medical doctor named Elton Mayo, In the 1920s, Mayo studied the Hawthorne Works of the Western Electric Corporation in Cicero, Illinois.[1] The Hawthorne experiment, as this famous million-dollar research project came to be known, was based on the work of some British industrial psychologists during World War I. They had discovered that people who work long hours (fifty or sixty hours per week) produce less than people who work a standard eight-hour day and that compulsory rest periods increase performance. They also discovered a correlation between temperature and productivity: workers produce more and have fewer accidents in moderate temperatures than they do when their environment is too hot or too cold. The reseachers at Hawthorne, using the British methods, set out to discover the relationship between illumination and productivity.

Electing elites

The result was that there is no relation between productivity and illumination. Even working under moonlight conditions, workers could maintain their norm. To clinch this point scientifically, the researchers set up two groups, a control group working under constant illumination and an experimental one working under decreasing illumination. The result? Both increased output. Creating a control group and an experimental group created two elites who behaved like superior people and did superior things.

RATR

Mayo set up a Relay Assembly Test Room (RATR), where a small self-selected group of young women were separated by a thin partition from the big relay department, where 100 employees worked. Their job was to assemble small relays (gadgets). Each relay had thirty-five parts and could be assembled in five or six minutes. There was another

[1] F.J. Roethlisberger and W.J. Dickson, *Management and the Worker* (Cambridge, Mass.: Harvard University Press, 1939), pp. 3–18.

person in that room, an observer who suggested various activities. They tried all sorts of things: coffee breaks, light lunches, two rest pauses of five minutes, six five-minute rests, stopping work at 4:30 P.M., stopping at 4:00 P.M., a five-day week, a normal forty-eight-hour week. The odd thing was that no matter what they did in these twenty-three test periods (which ended in July 1932) production went up and up and up—even when working conditions were made worse. What a victory for human relations! All you needed was the right attitude. Create an elite. Don't give people orders; let them determine their responsibilities themselves. Out of these famous experiments came the new participative human relations: supportive, employee-centered supervision.

Revision

Some twenty years after Mayo's death in 1949 along came another Australian, Alex Carey of the University of New South Wales. He came up with a radical and penetrating criticism of Hawthorne. Carey showed that in the RATR two operators who were doing too much talking and not enough working were replaced by two other operators who had the right attitudes and who could and did work. Once the output increased, the supervision eased up. In essence, what the experiment proved, if it proved anything, was that good productivity leads to friendly supervision, not the other way around.

Cliques and cabals on the shop floor

The other great discovery of the Hawthorne studies was in the Bank Wiring Rooms Experiment, where the relays were assembled by a group of wiremen, assembly men, solderers, and inspectors. Here the group produced two units a day, and this figure never varied. To keep production fixed, the men disciplined each other. If one stepped out of line, he was "binged": each of his colleagues struck him a sharp blow in the upper arm with their knuckles. He could return the blow. Perfectly democratic, except that the poor worker got ten bings and they each got one. Supervision by one's peers, even if punishment is token, is extremely effective. (Figure 2.4 shows the findings at Hawthorne.)

Principles of human relations discovered at Hawthorne

Taylor and Urwick "invented" the formal organization; Mayo discovered the informal organization, which inevitably emerged as its counterpart. The informal organization is a network of rules, roles, and

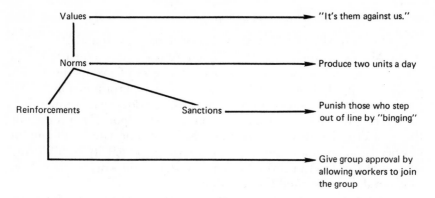

Figure 2.4   Values, Reinforcements, Norms, and Sanctions at Hawthorne

relations that fixes values, norms, reinforcements, and sanctions for a work group.

The principles of human relations include:

1. People do not work for bread alone; they have psychological needs: self-esteem, self-direction, and self-actualization.
2. People like, at least sometimes, to participate in decisions affecting them.
3. People frequently find talking about problems almost as therapeutic as solving them.
4. The informal group can be mobilized to get things done.

A useful caution to keep in mind, however, is the fact that the human relations movement can be used in a manipulative way. People can be lulled, loved, and seduced into doing things.

The Flowering of Human Relations: Theory X and Theory Y

The concepts of the Hawthorne experiments flowed into management's philosophical stream in the thirties. To Mayo, management's task was to mold group opinion in directions favorable to increased production. Although the emphasis on financial incentive was absent and the techniques of implementation were different, on the whole it was not difficult for the earlier classical framework to incorporate these newer elements.

35

Need for supportive supervision

Mayo's work was followed by that of Rensis Likert and Daniel Katz in the Michigan studies in 1947.[2] Their research was aimed at discovering what conditions encourage a higher level of group functioning and a high level of individual satisfaction for the group members. The first of a series of studies came out with strong evidence that supervisory style affected group motivation. From the standpoint of production, the most effective style was one that was more concerned with employees' needs for attention and respect than with productivity itself. Further studies of this kind in several other industries and work settings have, in general, corroborated these findings.

Likert and Katz's work was followed by Frederick Herzberg's Pittsburgh studies.[3] This research came out with the distinction between "hygiene factors" and "motivators." A motivator (for example, recognition for work well done) usually has an uplifting effect on attitudes or performance. Hygiene factors (for example, an improvement in parking facilities) produce no improvements but rather serve to prevent losses of morale or efficiency; they are prerequisites for effective motivation but are powerless to motivate by themselves.

In another study, Chris Argyris found that the restrictions imposed on individuals by industrial organizations for the sake of order and efficiency create resistances that eventually hamstring the organization.[4] He found that by its very nature the organization damages the individual and that too few managers recognized the social effects of their policies. If this was true, organizational policies were bound to collide head-on with the natural growth processes of the individual. Since this collision was and still is a very one-sided affair, the result is wholesale frustration for the worker. Therefore, he suggested that management must look for creativity and sophistication on which to base economic growth.

Theory X and Theory Y

Douglas MacGregor also contributed to changing management philosophies with his Theory X and Theory Y.[5] Theory X holds that

[2] From *New Patterns of Management* by Rensis Likert, pp. 6–7. Copyright © 1961 by McGraw-Hill Book Company. Used with permission of McGraw-Hill Book Company; and R.L. Kahn and D. Katz, "Leadership Practices in Relation to Productivity and Morale," in D. Cartwright and A. Zander, eds., *Group Dynamics* (New York: Harper and Row, 1953), pp. 612–28.

[3] F. Herzberg, B. Mausner, and B. Snyderman, *The Motivation to Work* (New York: John Wiley & Sons, 1959), pp. 113–19.

[4] Chris Argyris, *Personality and Organization* (New York: Harper, 1957), pp. 233–37.

[5] D.M. McGregor, *The Human Side of Enterprise* (New York: McGraw-Hill Book Company, 1960), pp. 15–57.

most people do not like to work, that some kind of club must be held over their heads to make sure they do their work, and that ordinary mortals would rather be told what to do than have to think for themselves. However, Theory Y holds that people do not like or dislike work inherently but rather develop an attitude toward it based on experience. Second, although authoritarian methods can get things done, they are not the only method for doing so; they are not inevitable, and their undesirable side effects do not have to be tolerated. Third, people will select goals for themselves if they think they have a reasonable chance to get some kind of reward, either material or psychic. Once people select a goal, they will pursue it at least as vigorously on their own as they would if their supervisors were trying to pressure them into doing the same thing. Fourth, under the right circumstances, people do not shun responsibility but seek it. According to MacGregor, Theory X is obsolete, and management should operate under the assumptions of Theory Y.

Evaluation of the Human Relations Approach

Human relations provided a necessary corrective for the classical theory of management's excessive zeal for standardization and impersonalization. The classical theory treated people as economic animals who are presumed to be rational in all circumstances. Human relations introduced the idea that people can behave irrationally and have needs for approval, belonging, and group membership. The beauty of human relations was that it introduced management policies that treated the workers with respect and dignity. The problem was that while the classical theory could be summed up as "organizations without people," human relations was "people without organizations." Human relations assumed that good personnel policies would lead to happy and contented workers and that happy and contented workers would be more productive. Unfortunately, research conducted by psychologists in the fifties revealed that there was little direct relationship between morale and productivity or between employee-centered organization and performance measures.

In the sixties, the human relations approach gave way to the organizational behavior approach. Organizational behavior differed from human relations in several important respects. It was concerned not only with the attitudes of individual employees but also with sociological considerations. Social scientists who studied organizational behavior developed the systems approach as a means of understanding what actually happens in the organization.

SYSTEMS MANAGEMENT

Systems management joins the best features of the classical and human relations schools. It uses knowledge and techniques from two fields: management science and behavioral science.

Operations research (OR) began in World War II, when planners began to apply statistics to solve operational problems for the military. They achieved dramatic results in aircraft manufacture, selection of bomber targets, scheduling of repairs, and so on. Box 2.2 gives some uses of models derived from OR.

The object of OR is to find the optimum: the most for the least. But finding the optimum is none too easy. The usual way to get started is to use a model.

Characteristics of Models

Probably the most important change in organizational decision making since 1940 has been the development and use of models. Business schools have been teaching students the skill of model building, which requires a marriage of behavioral and management science concepts and ideas. The basic notion behind modeling is that if a problem is too difficult to solve as it stands, a model can simplify the situation and therefore solve the problem. To invent this simpler problem, model builders use a process of abstraction, which identifies and relates the critical dimensions of the original complex situation.

To abstract,

1. the assumptions must be clearly stated,
2. the critical decision variables must be identified, and
3. the model must allow experimentation with variables, so that "what if" questions can be answered and the answers tested against reality.

Figure 2.5 shows the steps in the modeling process.

Cybernetics

Systems theory draws heavily on the field of cybernetics. Invented by Norbert Wiener, cybernetics is the study of communication of information in mechanical and organic systems. It has largely emerged from the study of feedback systems, or servomechanisms. A thermostat, for example, regulates the temperature in a house because it acts on information it feeds from the environment into the heating system. Organization theorists have developed formulations that can be applied to business firms. As a set of goal-directed behaviors, an organization can be seen as a system of feedback controls that monitor the various processes of the organization. Thus, when social scientists look at organizations, they search for a hierarchy of feedback control systems.

Figure 2.5   The Modeling Process

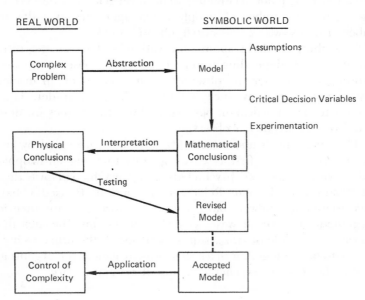

39

Behavioral Science

Management has always drawn on the human sciences, particularly psychology. Classical management depended on industrial psychology to supply technologies for the selection, training, assessment, and safety of personnel. In the 1920s, for example, a group of psychologists who had developed IQ tests to assign enlisted men to trades in the army formed the Psychological Corporation. They developed selection tests to help managers pick the best applicants for a job. Looking back to that period, two things are worth noting. The first is that paper-and-pencil tests were very successful in putting many people in the right jobs. Secondly, managers and psychologists were slow in recognizing that such paper-and-pencil tests favored people with a lot of schooling (middle-class white Americans) and held back the progress of groups with poor educational backgrounds. Nevertheless, psychology supplied classical theory with a whole raft of reliable and valid techniques.

Psychology also contributed to human relations by helping to define the 3 R's (rules, roles, relations) of group dynamics. Soon a great number of studies showed the elaborate ploys workers often used to restrict production. Out of these intriguing shop floor studies, many of which were carried out by sociologists, came techniques for forming working groups based on buddy selection and participation. This brought management into behavioral science. Since behavioral science is about what people do and since what people do can be observed, observation is a major technique. Behavioral scientists observe everything from the number of people a manager sees in a day to the number of times two people switch jobs in a week.

Now the odd thing about observation is that you get different kinds of answers depending upon who does the observing, especially depending on whether the observer is an outsider or an insider. Of course, we are not always lucky enough to have an insider. The next best reporter is a participant-observer, who actually goes in, does the job, and reports his or her observations.

The best reports about work life have been provided by anthropologists. One of the first research groups to bring anthropologists together with sociologists, psychologists, and psychiatrists was the Tavistock Institute of Human Relations in London. It used behavioral science to develop newer, more complex, more relevant theories of management. The result was sociotechnical systems: the idea that an organization is made of two systems—one social, the other technical—that have to be put together in a special way to achieve the organization's task. Box 2.3 sets out ten characteristics of systems theory.

Box 2.3: Characteristics of Systems Theory

1. Treats an organization as a complex, interacting whole—not a set of independent parts.
2. Views an organization as
   a. an energy exchange system with the environment and
   b. an information processing system connected by feedback loops.
3. Comes to terms with the fact that variety can be controlled only by greater variety (for example, a less intelligent person has difficulty in following a much more intelligent person).
4. Remembers that manipulation is preferred to understanding—not everything is knowable anyway.
5. Searches for structure, process, and values.
6. Develops scenarios, models, metaphors, and concepts.
7. Keeps an open mind.
8. Tries to understand nonlinear logic.
9. Tries to find the boundary of the system and identify roles. Looks for territories, technologies, and tasks.
10. Tries to keep conflict optimal.

THE CONTINGENCY APPROACH

The contingency approach is an attempt to resolve some confusions that had arisen in organization theory. To decide which management theory is best, organization theorists would answer, the one that "works." As early as the mid-fifties, laboratory research with simulated organizations revealed

> ... quite dramatically what type of organization is best suited for which kinds of environment. Specifically, for simple tasks under static conditions, an autocratic, centralized structure, such as has characterized most industrial organizations in the past, is quicker, neater and more efficient. But for adaptability to changing conditions, for rapid acceptance of new ideas, for flexibility in dealing with novel problems, generally high morale and loyalty, the more equalitarian and decentralized type seems to work better.[6]

What organization theorists were arguing was that the proper organizational design is dependent both upon the nature of the environment and the technology employed. As a result of their research in

---

[6] Warren G. Bennis and Philip E. Slater, *The Temporary Society* (New York: Harper and Row, 1968), p. 5.

the relationship between the organization and the environment, Lawrence and Lorsch proposed that:

> These findings suggest a contingency theory of organization. . . . The basic assumption underlying such a theory . . . is that organizational variables are in a complex interrelationship with one another and with conditions in the environment.
>
> This contingency theory of organizations suggests the major relationships that managers should think about as they plan organizations to deal with specific environmental conditions. It clearly indicates that managers can no longer be concerned about the one best way to organize. Rather . . . this contingency theory . . . provides at least the beginning of a conceptual framework with which to design organizations according to the tasks they are trying to perform.[7]

The Value of the Contingency Approach

The contingency approach represents a major breakthrough in management theory. It sees the organization as an organism whose response is contingent upon the forces in the environment. Thus, the shape of an organizational system is not simply a matter of executive choice but also a function of external forces.

The contingency approach is directed towards developing structures, processes, and values appropriate to specific situations. The researchers working in this area have shown a surprising amount of consensus on the development of organizational ideas. First, they are unanimous in their rejection of universal principles of management that are presumed to be valid in all circumstances. Contingency theorists take the view that there is no one best way to manage. If management practice is entirely situational, managers have to develop diagnostic skills, which means they have to acquire a repertoire of concepts and techniques that will help them identify different problems. The critical value of the contingency approach is that it focuses the manager's attention on three things: the systems interchange with its environment, the internal dynamics of the system, and the relationship between the two.

---

[7] Paul R. Lawrence and J.W. Lorsch, *Organization and Environment: Managing Differentiation and Integration* (Boston: Division of Research, Graduate School of Business Administration, Harvard University, 1967), pp. 157–58.

REVIEW AND RESEARCH

1. Explain the basic tenets of classical theory, human relations, and systems theory. Connect each theory to its historical antecedents.

2. Can you identify the classical features of your university faculty? Is the faculty bureaucracy efficient? Is it effective in achieving the objectives of the university?

3. If you were appointed as a consultant to a local industrial firm (select one of the plants in your area), what questions would you ask of the management if you used a

   a. classical approach?

   b. human relations point of view?

   c. systems view?

4. Why is the military organized on classical lines? Why does it still need an existential corona?

5. Describe the role of the secretary as a personal assistant to the executive. Why is he or she not paid as a staff officer?

6. Why did human relations catch on in the thirties and forties? Why do you think it worked so well in North America but not so well in Europe? What caused its demise? Its resurrection?

7. Are you a Theory X or Theory Y person? Why? Do you ever change your style? Why?

8. What is a model? List ten different models. Categorize each model according to the following:

   a. static versus dynamic

   b. basic assumptions

   c. critical decision variables

9. Explain the sequence of

   a. industrial psychology

   b. human relations

   c. behavioral science.
      Include some examples of experiments (with their main findings and research methods specified) for each.

10. What is the concept behind sociotechnical systems? Discuss the several subsystems of a jumbo jet. How can these subsystems be synchronized and integrated?

11. Apply the structure, process, and values model to an organization with which you are familiar, for example, your university business school; a firm where you have worked; a military unit; a fraternity, sorority, or club.

12. Find out what a T-group is. Why is attending a T-group such a dramatic experience?

13. Why is it necessary for executives to "act" (that is, to be dramatic) to get things done? Consider in your answer the successes and behavior of such people as General George Patton, General Douglas Mac-Arthur, Presidents Nixon, Johnson, Truman, Roosevelt.

14. How can you liberate your mind to become a more effective open manager? Develop a regime to get there.

15. What are the 3 R's of structure? Define the structure of professor-student, doctor-patient, executive-secretary relationships.

16. What is suboptimization? How does it work? Illustrate your answer with an example from business or education, or discuss the problem of suboptimization of a fighter-bomber's performance.

17. List the assumptions of the new management. Which ones are going to give you the most difficulty? Do you have a plan to meet this situation?

18. Develop a career plan for yourself. What are the main difficulties that have to be overcome to put the plan into action?

19. Why is contingency management popular?

THE TOP EXECUTIVE OF THE SEVENTIES AND EIGHTIES

In spite of the widely-held belief that a new kind of manager had replaced the "organization man" of the fifties, evidence from executive surveys reveals that the traditional executive in the gray flannel suit was very much with us in the seventies and eighties. It has been widely argued that the top managers of U.S. businesses are too inbred to generate the creative insights that are needed to change the quality of our corporate environment. This lack of executive diversity is supported by a survey by Frederick D. Sturdivant and Roy D. Adler. They studied the backgrounds of 444 executives from 247 companies. Of these executives, 400 were among the top office holders, usually the chairmen and presidents, of the largest industrial companies in the U.S. Adler and Sturdivant conclude that

> the executives of 1975 form a *more* homogeneous group than those from earlier time periods. Indeed, a more uniform profile is reflected than the one of the supposedly "conforming 1950s." In addition to being exclusively male and Caucasian, predominantly Protestant, Republican, and of eastern U.S. origin, from relatively affluent families, and educated at one of a handful of select universities, as had been the case in the past, the executives in our sample share some new characteristics. Most significantly, the executives are closer together in age, and more of them have little or no work experience outside their companies.*

Nearly all had been to college, and nearly half of the executives had done some graduate work. Eleven percent had MBAs and nearly 7 percent had a Ph.D. The executives seemed to have attended many of the same schools, most frequently Harvard, Yale, M.I.T., and Columbia. The authors suggest that concentrating decision making in a small, unrepresentative group of executives with common backgrounds, values, and experience may be dysfunctional in terms of meeting the broad social expectations of a democratic society.

Do you agree with the authors' conclusions? If not, why not? If so, what do you think can be done to broaden executive ranks?

* "Executive Origins: Still a Gray Flannel World?" by Frederick D. Sturdivant and Roy D. Adler, *Harvard Business Review* (November-December 1976). Copyright © 1976 by the President and Fellows of Harvard College; all rights reserved.

I

STRUCTURAL
VARIABLES

3

Structure
of
Management

OBJECTIVES YOU SHOULD MEET

Draw an organization chart showing the relationship between line and staff functions.

Diagram authority in terms of the rule of legitimacy, the role of the office, and relation of credibility.

Explain consensus formation.

Develop a check list to facilitate delegation.

Set out the principles of classical structure.

State the advantages of the new, more human assembly line developed by Volvo.

Itemize American reactions to the new kind of assembly line.

Explain "why waitresses cannot give orders to a cook," or how the system structures information flow.

Develop a contingency framework to help in selecting appropriate structures.

The structure of an organization describes its framework, or network of rules, roles, and relations. But what flows along the network? To the classical manager, authority flows through the circuit. To the human relations-oriented manager, "executive electricity"—affiliation, warmth, or support—flows through the network. To the systems analyst, it is information that flows through the structure circuit. What flows through the network, therefore, depends on the structure an organization uses. The contingency approach helps management decide which structure is appropriate.

CLASSICAL STRUCTURE

In the days when almost every organization was based on classical theory, things seemed much simpler than they are today.

The organization chart (see Figure 3.1) spelled out who was responsible to whom; every employee had one boss; role descriptions described in detail what one had to do; if you were in doubt, you could always consult the policy document or the rule book; and if worse came to worst, you did your duty and complained afterwards.

Organizational structure, at least in formal terms, was usually fairly easy to define and could often be presented on an organization chart. The structure, in essence, described the authority and communication network. Line and staff relations loomed large in all discussion of structure. Relations between line and staff were drawn in dotted lines.

No more. Now many firms do not have organization charts, or at least they do not display them publicly. The reason for this rejection of organization charts is not that companies are more democratic; they are not. Rather, flexibility is necessary because of new technology.

Organizational structure refers to the

1. authority/communication network,
2. number of levels of management, and
3. span of control.

Authority Model: Structure

The authority structure is basically an exercise in moral geometry. The authority triangle has three sides, the rule of legitimacy, the role of the "office," and the relation of credibility (see Figure 3.2).

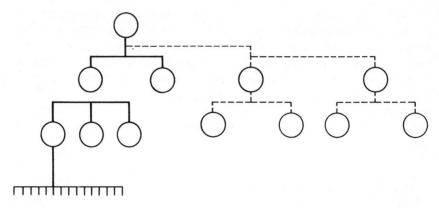

Figure 3.1   Organization Chart Showing Line System with Unbroken Lines and Functional System with Broken Lines

The rule for authority is legitimacy, the presumption of a shared moral frame of reference in which *A* instructs *B* to do certain things. When authority is legitimate, *B*'s critical faculties are suspended. Chester Barnard has described the four requirements for authority to be accepted:

1. *B* must be able to understand the instruction.
2. *B* must believe that communication is not inconsistent with the purposes of the organization.
3. *B* must believe that the instruction is not incompatible with his or her personal interests.
4. The instruction must lie within *B*'s competence.[1]

Typically, instructions are given impersonally. *A* does not exercise

Figure 3.2   Rule, Role, and Relation of Authority

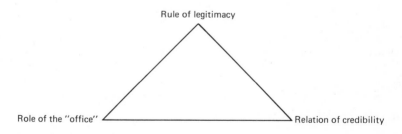

[1] Chester Barnard, *The Function of the Executive* (Cambridge, Mass.: Harvard University Press, 1938), p. 165.

52

authority personally but under the aegis of the "office." If the "office" is abused, a credibility gap emerges. Thus, the third phase of the authority triangle is credibility. Credibility is based on a critical knowledge or competence. In technical terms, sociologists describe this expert aspect of authority as *sapiential* (based on wisdom) authority.

Sapiential authority is the ability to get things done based on expertise. Managers who have a critical know-how are high in sapiential authority. When authority is exercised properly and "the office" is used legitimately, a certain charisma is attached to the manager. This charismatic authority may cause the title holder to experience a certain hubris and overstep the mark. Box 3.1 describes Max Weber's three kinds of authority.

The Authority Process

The authority process is described in Jean Jacques Rousseau's social contract theory. People are born free and enter into contracts that abridge their freedom. These contracts generate obligations and confer rights on both parties. This social contract, which is integral to the employment relation, is achieved through four processes: consensus formation; risk syndication; working within the zone of indifference; and subordination, or delegation.

Consensus formation and risk syndication

Consensus formation is difficult both to define and to achieve. Putting it cynically, the consensus emerges in a meeting when the manager in charge says, "Senior management has made a proposal that the majority are not only going to have to live with but to try to make workable." Consensus management is not majority rule. Minorities have a veto—provided they do not use it too frequently. What keeps consensus management working is risk syndication, which ensures that if you share in the risk taking, you should share in the rewards. In brief, risk syndication makes sure not only that "everybody gets something" but also that rewards are proportionate to risks.

Operating within the zone of indifference

In a challenge to the traditional view of authority, Chester Barnard argued that it was possible for a subordinate to reject the direction of

Box 3.1: Three Types of Authority

> Max Weber, in developing his theory of bureaucracy, identified three types of legitimate authority: rational or legal, traditional, and charismatic.
>
> Rational, legal authority is legally vested power to define roles, to establish norms, to make decisions, and to enforce them through the use of sanctions. In an organization that is governed by rational, legal authority, members are linked by a bond of legitimacy. This legitimacy helps to maintain the stability of an authority relationship. Ideally, rationality implies a style of behavior that is appropriate to the achievement of the organization's goals within the limits imposed by the situation. An action is said to be rational to the extent that it is correctly designed to maximize goal achievement, given the resources available and the competence of the individuals involved. Although in modern times rationality is seen as much more finite (because of people's limited capacity for information processing), managers are still expected to act rationally, that is, to the best of their abilities.
>
> Traditional authority requires that a person be obeyed because he belongs to a certain class or occupies a recognized position. Charismatic authority bases obedience on the subordinate's belief that the superior has some special power. For Weber, a charismatic leader induces an element of emotion, awe, and magic to the conduct of business.
>
> All leadership involves not only rational authority somehow made legitimate but also some charismatic quality, however limited it may be.

a higher authority, especially if he believed that the order was not legitimate. In fact, Barnard believed that the disobedience of subordinates was a fairly common phenomenon. As Barnard pointed out, if a directive is accepted by a subordinate, its authority or legitimacy is established: "Disobedience of such a communication is a denial of its authority."

What Barnard is arguing is that subordinates do not automatically resent and resist all authority; many directions are accepted without question. Orders that are accepted without question fall within what Barnard calls the "zone of indifference."

> The phrase "zone of indifference" may be explained as follows: If all the orders for actions reasonably practicable be arranged in the order of their acceptability to the person affected, it may be conceived that there are a number which are clearly unacceptable, that is, which certainly will not be obeyed; there is another group somewhat more or less on the neutral line, that is, either barely acceptable or barely unacceptable; and a third group unquestionably acceptable. This last group lies within the "zone of indifference." The person affected will accept orders lying within this zone and is relatively indifferent as to what the order is so far as the question of authority is concerned.[2]

[2] *Ibid.*, pp. 168–69.

The whole process of exercising authority involves a litany of ritual, rubric, and routine that turns the business of managing into a sacrament, which ordinary mortals treat with great respect. But when the manager abuses the sacrament by operating outside the zone of indifference, subordinates can "blow the whistle." See Box 3.2.

Delegation

Because executives work through others, they must delegate authority to subordinates. Delegation may be defined as the assignment of authority and responsibility by a manager to subordinates. Through delegation, a subordinate manager is given sufficient autonomy to plan and direct the activities of his unit. Delegation, which has sometimes been described as the secret of executive sanity, arises when an executive has more work to do than he can do himself. When a manager reaches this point of overload, he or she must reorganize the job, divide it into tasks, select a particular person for each task, and make the appropriate task assignments.

But delegating authority does not involve a blank check. When a manager is delegating an assignment to a subordinate he may give him any one of the following instructions:

1. Look into this problem. Give me all the facts. I will decide what to do.
2. Let me know the alternatives available with the pros and cons of each. I will decide which to select.
3. Recommend a course of action for my approval.
4. Let me know what you intend to do. Delay action until I approve.
5. Let me know what you intend to do. Do it unless I say not to.
6. Take action. Let me know what you did. Let me know how it turns out.
7. Take action. Communicate with me only if your action is unsuccessful.
8. Take action. No further communication with me is necessary.[3]

When a manager is delegating, he should have a clear understanding as to which of these patterns he is using.

How much responsibility is delegated?

When a manager delegates authority, he or she places an obligation on the subordinate. If a foreman is given authority in the area of

[3] Ross Webber, *Management* (Homewood, Ill.: Richard D. Irwin, Inc., 1975), p. 392.

Box 3.2: Blowing the Whistle on Your Boss

An organization has been defined as an amoeba originally created for a purpose, molded from the individuals who make up the organization, which takes on a personality all its own. Kenneth D. Walters illustrates the conflict that arises when an employee's conscience does not agree with the organization's policies and practices and declares so by publicly "blowing the whistle."

A whistle blower has been defined as a "muckraker from within, who exposes what he considers the unconscionable practices of his own organization." Several books have been written recently emphasizing the importance of and frequency of whistle blowing. Ralph Nader, who insists "loyalties do not end at the boundaries of an organization," has edited a report titled "Whistle Blowing," which describes the consequences faced by employees who have "gone public on" their companies' defective products, pollution, corruption, or law breaking.

Whistle blowing is viewed as a "notable new development in the history of American reform movements," as an ethical responsibility.

This view differs from the traditional "your organization, love it or leave it." Whistle blowing has also been labeled as "industrial espionage." These views show how the organization forces its morals on individuals.

What factors determine whether a whistle blowing employee should be subjected to an organization's sanctions? Not all organizational loyalty is bad, and whistle

Based on "Your Employees' Right to Blow the Whistle" by Kenneth D. Walters, *Harvard Business Review* (July-August 1975). Copyright © 1975 by the President and Fellows of Harvard College; all rights reserved.

quality control, he has an obligation to ensure that the products are not passed unless they meet the quality control standards. If the foreman is successful in implementing quality control for the products in his section, he will be rewarded; on the other hand, if he fails, he can expect to be penalized in some way. When a manager delegates responsibility, he must still exercise control of the task to achieve coordination.

It is impossible for the manager to delegate his own responsibility; even after the manager has delegated various tasks to his subordinates, the responsibility for coordination and control still remains with him. Here are some guidelines for delegating authority:

1. Break the job into separate tasks.
2. Select individuals with skills and aptitudes to match the tasks.
3. Make the assignment.
4. Define the standards of responsibility for each task.
5. Establish control standards that are clear and that are communicated to subordinates.
6. Retain the power of reward and discipline.
7. Examine the results of delegation at appropriate intervals. Make sure no one thinks he has a blank check.
8. Make sure the subordinate has sufficient authority to achieve his obligations.

blowing isn't necessarily good. The following factors have to be examined: Motive, internal channels, organizational friction, discretion, collective action, rights of employment, and regulatory provisions. Cases in which the employee was reinstated show a similarity in the factors considered.

The motive of one informer was to "publicly expose misconduct, illegality, or inefficiency in an organization." The motive of one teacher was to "protect the health and safety of herself and her pupils." Failure in being able to make oneself heard due to the "bureaucratic runarounds, deaf ears, or hostility coming from the internal channels was generally the cause of employees 'going public' in their whistle blowing."

The time factor can dictate whether to go through the "time consuming bureaucratic maze" of internal channels or to go outside to warn of a fast approaching danger.

Personal relationships within an organization may be disrupted by whistle blowing, causing organizational friction. Court rulings in favor of reinstatement were for the cases where the friction would not prevent the reinstated employee from functioning properly.

The discretion used in the cases was related to whether accusation was true or false.

Collective action like unions backing up the whistle blower greatly influenced his reinstatement.

Continued on next page

9. Make sure the subordinate clearly understands what has been delegated to him, what authority he has, how his work is going to be reviewed, and how he will be rewarded.
10. A manager should keep in mind that he can delegate authority but not responsibility.

Number of Levels of Management

Structure is also a function of the number of levels of management and is, in turn, a function of technology. For example, a chemical plant has a larger number of levels of management than an automobile plant. The most important point to keep in mind is that there is no ideal height of a hierarchy. It all depends on the particulars of the situation.

Span of Control

The span of control refers to the number of subordinates reporting to one superior. The span of control depends on how many people a manager can oversee. This number can vary widely depending upon technology, hierarchical level, and productivity demands.

Rights of employment can be best illustrated with the example of a married woman who the court ruled must be reinstated after being fired for not agreeing to go out on a date with her foreman.

A regulatory provision "prohibits employers from discharging or disciplining an employee who discloses conduct that the statute forbids."

An organization may be able to reduce whistle blowing by following these five procedures, which have been established from a study of whistle blowing cases.

1. It should be made clear to the employees that the organization will not interfere with their political freedoms. Employees should be encouraged to express controversial views.
2. Streamline the grievance procedures.
3. The organization should take a close look at its social responsibility.
4. Organizations should recognize individual consciences.
5. The organization should realize that dealing harshly with a whistle blower may damage its reputation.

These procedures do not eliminate whistle blowing but perhaps would reduce the need to "go public": the individual would be encouraged to use constructive criticism within the organization's boundaries. The amoeba may now develop from within and not suffer damage from public pressure.

Early organization theorists took the view that no superior could supervise directly more than five or six subordinates whose work interlocked. Actual practice, in fact, contradicts this prediction. For example, early studies at Sears and Roebuck showed that some managers supervised up to thirty subordinates. The optimal span of control depends on the managerial expertise of the superior, his mode of supervision, the type of technology, and productivity demands. One company that has made a major effort to determine the optimal span of control is Lockheed Missile and Space Company. After careful research, Lockheed management developed a model that used the following factors:

1. similarity of functions;
2. geographic closeness of subordinates;
3. complexity of functions;
4. direction and control required by subordinates;
5. coordination required;
6. planning importance, complexity, and time required; and
7. organizational assistance received by superior.

Each of these variables was assigned weights. Research at Lockheed indicated that when the span of control was increased, the number of supervisory levels was decreased.

The Principles of Classical Structure

The classical approach requires the development of a structure that arranges divisions and groups of work into functions, subfunctions, and jobs. The principal model is the organization chart with an appropriate set of role descriptions setting out who does what. But behind the classical organization are certain assumptions on which the model is based.

Chain of command

In an organization, decisions flow down, and reports flow up. The chain of command principle assumes that all employees from the bottom of the pyramid to the top should have a superior to whom they are accountable. For example, the chain of command in a business firm would go down from the president to the vice president to the general manager in charge of production. He has under his command departmental managers, each of whom supervises a number of foremen. The foremen oversee the operatives, who do the actual work. The beauty of the chain of command principle is that most people like the clarity of knowing their exact position in the organization chart.

Unity of command

The basic principle is "one employee, one boss."

Functional organization

The principle of functional management presumes that a firm is made up of an essentially hierarchical and differential structure consisting of line and staff functions. Each manager has a certain functional responsibility, which is based either on actual administrative work or expert knowledge.

Span of control

The span of control refers to the number of subordinates reporting directly to a common superior. Experience suggests that the span of control can vary quite widely. The key question for the manager in the classical approach is to decide whether the span of control is appropriate for the organization and the tasks he is supervising.

Clarity of delegation

Delegation arises when the manager has more work than he can do himself. Then the manager must delegate responsibility and authority in selected fields to his subordinates. Many inexperienced managers find it very difficult to engage in delegation because they feel they can do the job faster themselves.

Authority should match responsiblity

When a subordinate is given a job to do, he or she must be given sufficient power and authority to undertake and discharge his duties and responsibilities and make the appropriate decisions. Unfortunately, many managers are incapable of delegating enough of their work to free them for the real work they are being paid to do. For other criticisms of classical organization, see Box 3.3.

The Lordstown Syndrome

One of the most dramatic illustrations of the failure of classical organization took place in 1972 in the Lordstown, Ohio, plant of General Motors. General Motors' automobile assembly plant was planned as one of the fastest production lines in the world. The wage rates were very high but not high enough to stop horrendous levels of absenteeism, especially on Fridays and Mondays. General Motors estimated that production of 12,000 Vegas and 4,000 Chevrolet trucks worth about $45 million was lost due to stoppages and absenteeism. Repeatedly, the management had to close down the assembly line because the workers were slowing down and allowing cars to move along the line without being finished. The management also accused the workers of sabotage. Young assembly-line workers were no longer prepared to accept the boredom of routine, repetitive work, management said.

Yet curiously enough, the Lordstown line was one of the most sophisticated assembly plants in the world. The workers had at their disposal a wide variety of new power tools and other automatic devices. General Motors production engineers had designed the assembly line so that the amount of necessary bending and crawling had been considerably reduced.

Chris Argyris argues that routine, highly structured, machine-paced jobs needle mature individuals:

> ... there are some basic incongruencies between the growth trends of a healthy personality and the requirements of the formal organization. If the principles of formal organization are used as ideally defined, then the employee will tend to work in an environment where (1) they are provided little control over their workday world; (2) they are expected to be passive, dependent, subordinate; (3) they are expected to have a short time perspective; (4) they are induced to perfect and value the frequent use of a few skin-surface, shallow abilities; and (5) they are expected to produce under conditions leading to psychological failure. All of these characteristics are incongruent to the ones healthy human beings are postulated to desire. They are much more congruent with the needs of infants in our culture.

From Chris Argyris, "Personal Versus Organizational Goals," *Yale Scientific*, 1960.

To make this plant efficient, General Motors' assembly division, a management team with an outstanding reputation for toughness and cutting costs, took over the operation. A major reorganization of work began. Unfortunately, this speed-up resulted in a substantial increase of grievances. When the new management team arrived there were about 100 grievances in the plant. Shortly after they came, the grievances increased to 5,000—1,000 of which were protests that too much work had been added to particular jobs.

The union proposed that team assembly be used. This was rejected by the management. Unfortunately, management's effort to increase productivity through classical means mobilized the young assembly-line workers to a full-scale confrontation with management.

Ultimately, the economic recession of the mid-seventies and its attendant unemployment caused the young automobile workers at Lordstown to change their attitudes towards work. Like their fathers, the young assembly-line workers began to place a higher value on job security and the number of grievances began to diminish.

HUMAN RELATIONS ORGANIZING

The New Line

Instead of the clanking high-speed conveyor line invented by Henry Ford, the Volvo Plant in Kalmar, Sweden uses 250 "carriers"

(18-foot-long, computer-guided platforms) that move silently along the concrete floor. Each carrier delivers the frame for a single Volvo 264 to one of the plant's 25 work teams of 15 to 20 workers. Each team is responsible for one aspect of assembly. One team, for example, puts in the Volvo's electrical system; another completes the interior finish.

The man who brought us this existential type of organization is Pehr Gyllenhammar, managing director of Volvo. Under his leadership, Volvo increased its sales by 70 percent (to more than $2 billion in 1973). Soon after taking over, he replaced a centralized management structure with four semiautonomous divisions, each a profit center. He also expanded production of trucks, marine, and industrial engines.

In 1971, two union men were appointed as voting members of Volvo's board, a common practice in Europe but at that time still rare in Sweden. He also automated the heaviest jobs and established an internal placement agency to help people find more satisfying jobs. Convinced that workers were bored by their monotonous assembly-line jobs, Gyllenhammar assigned a task force of young managers to design a new plant, where the machines would be a product of the people and not vice versa. After two months of study, Kalmar, which had a population of 53,000 and a high level of unemployment, was selected.

In the fall of 1974, the *Washington Post* asked, "Are Swedes more open to democratizing work and redesigning jobs than are Americans? Is there some essential difference between Swedish managers and American managers?"

> "I don't think so," says Pehr Gyllenhammar. "It's largely that our young people coming into the labor market will not take jobs which don't provide them with a sense of achievement and personal satisfaction. They are seeking some purpose to their labor beyond mere economic survival. We have an unemployment rate at the moment of only 1.5 percent. In the United States it's a bit different. But eventually American managers will have to face the same situation—that of a highly educated young labor force earnestly seeking job satisfaction."
>
> "Here at Volvo, in fact all over Sweden," Gyllenhammar points out, "we are trying to create small groups of workers who develop into skilled and proud craftsmen, small groups under one large umbrella— craftsmen who set their own work pace, their own coffee breaks. It costs more, but there is evidence that it decreases the rate of absenteeism."[4]

[4] Derk Norcross, "Sweden's Newest Export—Industrial Democracy," *Parade Magazine,* 15 December 1974.

These work groups at Kalmar organized themselves according to their own preferences. While the worker in a traditional assembly line might spend a whole eight-hour shift putting on head lamps, members of a Kalmar work team rotate from tail lights to head lights, from fuse boxes to signal lights, from the fuel injection system to the dynamo or the starter motor.

The new plant, which cost $23 million to build, includes the most modern devices to control production and maintain quality control. At each work station, a television screen displays figures comparing the team's production goal with its "actual." On the screen a yellow light comes on if the team is behind schedule, a green light when it is ahead.

American Realism

Oddly enough, American auto workers are not impressed by such plants as Volvo's. In the early seventies, six auto workers, all employees of G.M., Ford, or Chrysler, spent four weeks at a Saab engine plant in Sweden. The Americans liked the physical working conditions—more space per person, better safety measures, better lighting, and more cool air. They welcomed the change from assembly-line routine. Several of the Americans found the pace of work unexpectedly fast.

On the other hand, the Americans thought the lunch break was too short (24 minutes for the 5 a.m. to 2 p.m. shift and just 18 minutes for the 2 p.m. to 11 p.m. shift). They felt that after a while even team assembly could become tedious. And they doubted whether the techniques used in assembling small engines at a small plant were applicable to the manufacture of V-8 engines at million-unit-a-year U.S. plants. Working with a team also requires "group dynamics" accommodation to others; the American workers preferred to be responsible only to themselves. They found the entire Swedish work system far too regimented and paternalistic. The unions seemed distant and too close to management. Despite the much acclaimed Swedish system of worker participation, the Americans preferred the more informal grass-roots unionism of the U.S.

In the United States, the UAW is participating with management in workplace experiments in several plants. To the UAW's proposal that teams of workers be allowed to assemble one complete car or a large unit, however, management has objected that the cost would be prohibitive. Nevertheless, American plants are trying to make the auto assembly line more human and more democratic by giving shop floor people a say in controlling the flow of materials on the line.

THE SYSTEMS APPROACH TO STRUCTURE

According to the systems approach, organizations are information processing systems that exist in uncertain environments. They may be thought of as formal structures of rules; decisions are achieved because well-defined information channels are followed. These narrow the range of alternatives management must consider.

Thus managers become skilled in editing and classifying information according to its relevance and costs. Inevitably in such a process, damage is done to the raw data as it is pushed and squeezed to fill the taxonomies managers have developed. An example will clarify the systems concept.

A Waitress Can't Give Orders to a Cook

In a brilliant piece of research, William Foote Whyte studied the social system of a restaurant, in particular, the small short-order business.[5] He considered the structure of role specialization, the process of how the flow of information (the order) meets the flow of material and energy (the thing ordered), and the values of the employer-employee hierarchy. After describing the horizontal flow of information and material, Whyte explained how such flows cut across status lines and can give real trouble ("Whoever heard of a waitress giving orders to a cook?").

Systems theory can help explain the restaurant's social and organizational environment. Elias H. Porter has related an administrative parable about restaurants.[6] In this parable, a president of a large corporation of short-order restaurants invites a team of consultants (a sociologist, a psychologist, and an anthropologist) to give him some advice about how to run his business. Each comes up with a different problem, but all recommend the same solution. The sociologist says that the restaurant's problem is one of role and status—how can a person, such as a waitress, who is low on the totem pole, give orders to a high person like a cook? The psychologist says the problem is the Oedipus complex—how can a "daughter" give orders to her "father"? For the anthropologist, it's a matter of culture and values—how can a noncentral value system (a waitress) give orders to a central value system (an

---

[5] W.F. Whyte, "The Social Structure of the Restaurant," *The American Journal of Sociology,* Vol. 54 (1949), pp. 302–310.

[6] "The Parable of the Spindle" by E.H. Porter, *Harvard Business Review,* Vol. 40 (1962). Copyright © 1962 by the President and Fellows of Harvard College; all rights reserved.

owner-cook)? But although they differ in their diagnosis, the consultants all recommend the same thing: a spindle on the order counter. The waitresses simply put their orders on the spindle rather than giving orders to the cook.

Now, what's so revolutionary about a spindle? The spindle acts as a sensor (a radar that picks up data), a data processor (a means of organizing choices into fixed items on the menu), a decision maker (a way for the cook to group orders and maintain a fixed sequence), a controller (a record of who ordered what from whom), and a memory (a daily, weekly, or monthly schedule). This flow of information keeps the informant out of the central food-making process but makes certain that the information gets in. In the technical language of systems, this ability is known as decoupling. What is "decoupled" from what is the essence of systems theory. It explains air traffic control centers, production control departments, credit rating sections, military office selection units, and similar operations. They are all spindles. Of course, the spindle par excellence of modern times is the computer, which we will return to in a moment.

Functions of the Information System

In an organization, the *sensor subsystem* carries out the data collection function. It captures data about events impinging on the organization.

The *data processing subsystem* encodes incoming data. When an event is recorded, it must be defined so that the desired information can be retrieved when it is needed. This is best achieved by data compression. Since the vast bulk of data introduced into the system has little significance, the data processing subsystem should filter out insignificant data and highlight vital intelligence that might be useful for changes in actual plans.

Much of the data collected by the system deals with probabilistic variables, for example, probable sales forecasts, which may include both a pessimistic and an optimistic forecast. This helps reduce uncertainty.

Managing the Information System

Information flows cut across status lines. For managers to be effective, it is necessary for them to develop skill in connecting and disconnecting subunits of the organization. They must be able to break an information processing system into its six subsystems: sensor, data processing, decision making, processing, controlling, and memory.

CHOOSING THE STRUCTURE:
A CONTINGENCY APPROACH

How does a manager choose among different organizational structures? How precisely should he or she define roles and functions? What choices does he or she have as to how these functions can be grouped? Should the organization be centralized or decentralized? To try and answer these questions, managers have to select organizational structures that fit the firm's mission, the type of people employed, and the firm's technology.

Structure, in the most general sense, refers to the variables that define the shape of the organization and the relationship among its subunits. In broad terms, structure describes the degree and extent of differentiation and integration. *Differentiation* includes such considerations as the number of levels of hierarchy and the degree of decision making autonomy among departments. *Integration* refers to the modes of liaison that are employed to ensure that the departments and other subunits cooperate. Inevitably, there has to be a tradeoff between differentiation and integration. Organizations function by either engaging in the division of labor or increasing specialization; the more specialization there is, the more need there is for control and coordination.

Mechanistic and Organic Organizations

Tom Burns and G. M. Stalker, through their study of electronic firms, introduced a useful organizational dichotomy: mechanistic and organic organizations.[7]

Mechanistic organizations, which employ the traditional pyramidal organization, are made up of units and roles that are tightly defined. When people in mechanistic organizations communicate, they do so through the proper channels. Mechanistically organized firms, as the name suggests, employ the machine theory of organization. Each task is broken into parts that are joined together at the end of the work process. Decision making is centralized at the top of the hierarchy. Decisions flow down the hierarchy, and reports flow up. People who work in such organizations are cogs in a large machine. No one is indispensable; everyone can be replaced.

[7] Tom Burns and G.M. Stalker, *The Management of Innovation* (London: Tavistock Publications Ltd., 1961).

This type of organization is appropriate to a task that is stable, well-defined, and programmable. For tasks of this type, the structure is efficient and predictable.

Organic Organizations

Whereas a mechanistic organization employs the metaphor of machine theory, an organic organization uses a biological metaphor. The object of organic organizing is to leave the system open to the environment so that it can make the most of innovative opportunities. The presumption is that the environment is ambiguously defined, complex, and changing. The individuals within the organization have to be able to change their roles and the way they are grouped to cope with opportunities that may arise. The boundaries between the system and environment are deliberately permeable to facilitate this exchange. Thus the organic organization is flexible, and it can rapidly respond to new opportunities. Figure 3.3 shows the difference between mechanistic and organic forms of organization.

Michael B. McCaskey lists key concepts and questions managers should keep in mind when they are choosing between organizational design alternatives.[8]

Figure 3.3   Mechanistic and Organic Firms: Two Ways of Organizing

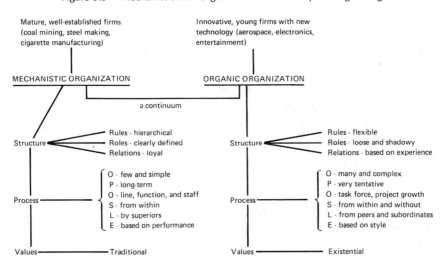

[8] From "An Introduction to Organization Design" by Michael McCaskey. © 1974 by the Regents of the University of California. Reprinted from *California Management Review,* Vol. 17, no. 2, p. 17.

In approaching an organization design problem, some of the important questions to be answered are:

1. How uncertain is the task environment in which the organization operates?

2. In what ways should the organization be mechanistic and in what ways organic?

3. How should the subtasks be divided and how should the organization be differentiated? Should subsystems be organized by the *functions* people perform, by the *products* or services the company provides, or should some other form such as a matrix organization be used?

4. What kind of people are (or can be recruited to become) members of the organization? Under what conditions do they work and learn best?

5. How are activities to be coordinated and integrated? What mechanisms will be used, involving what costs?

REVIEW AND RESEARCH

1. Structure deals with three commodities. What are they?

2. What are the elements of classical structure?

3. What were the three types of authority according to Max Weber?

4. Describe the structure, process, and values of authority.

5. How can delegation be made more effective?

6. What are the dysfunctions of classical structure?

7. How did Volvo develop a human relations structure? Would this work in a U.S. auto plant? Why or why not?

8. "The system concept of structure always involves information flows and spindles." Explain this sentence.

9. Compare and contrast mechanistic and organic organizations.

10. What are the contingency aspects of structure?

THE CHANGING WORK FORCE AND CHANGING ATTITUDES TOWARDS AUTHORITY

The American work force is in the process of changing. White-collar workers now make up one-half of all working people, and this percentage has been increasing steadily. The number of managers and administrators in our society continues to grow. The fastest growing segment in the white-collar group is made up of professional and technical employees, who currently make up one-seventh of the work force. The percentage is expected to increase to one-sixth within ten years. Dennis Chamot, assistant to the executive secretary of the Council of AFL-CIO Unions for Professional Employees, reports that an up-surge in white-collar union membership has increased in the last decade and a half by over one million (to 3.8 million) people.* Several white collar unions—particularly the American Federation of Teachers; the American Federation of State, County, and Municipal Employees; and the American Federation of Government Employees—have experienced spectacular growth in the past few years. At the same time blue-collar unions have not done so well.

Representatives of white-collar professional unions claim that their members are dissatisfied with policies related to authority and decision making. Professional people seek a greater impact on institutional decision making. For example,

> In 1973, NASA engineers at Huntsville, Alabama joined the International Federation of Professional and Technical Engineers (AFL-CIO). A key issue in the campaign was employee disgruntlement over an extremely complex and rigid organizational structure, which they felt would be changed by a union. One might note that, even before they organized, these engineers were earning an average salary of about $20,000 a year. Engineers in federal, state, and municipal agencies have turned to unions in large part because of a strong desire to have greater impact on managerial decisions.†

Chamot concludes:

> 1. The fraction of professionals who are employed by others will continue to grow.
>
> 2. In spite of similarities in educational backgrounds and mores, professional employees and those who employ them have inherently different viewpoints about many aspects of the job situation.
>
> 3. White-collar and professional employees will continue to be attracted to unions in ever-growing numbers.
>
> There should be little disagreement with the first two points. As to the third, all trends point to the increasing organization of professionals.

* "Professional Employees Turn to Unions" by Dennis Chamot, *Harvard Business Review* (May-June 1976). Copyright © 1976 by the President and Fellows of Harvard College; all rights reserved.

† *Ibid.*, p. 123.

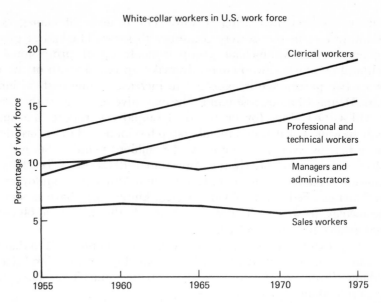

White-collar workers in U.S. work force

Clerical workers

Professional and technical workers

Managers and administrators

Sales workers

Percentage of work force

From U.S. Department of Labor, *Handbook of Labor Statistics, 1974,* Bureau of Labor Statistics.

The most important factor is the growing size and impersonality of employing organizations. This will make the professional ever more remote from the center of decision making and will inevitably increase his frustrations. It is this professional malaise, rather than strictly monetary considerations, that in the long run will result in a union.

A progressive management will recognize that a unionization attempt at the very least indicates widespread employee discontent with existing conditions and that professional employees in particular desire a stronger voice in solving their problems. The union provides the employees with such a voice.

Should management be less than enlightened, then the union will at least fight to obtain for its members a greater measure of dignity and a larger share of the economic rewards.

Do you think professionals and managers will want to form unions?

4

Organizational
Politics

Determine what
it takes to succeed
in management as an individual.

Explain the significance of cliques
and cabals in organizations.

State some useful guides that help
in developing power tactics.

Develop a contingency approach
to managing political behavior.

Organizational politics is essentially concerned with the exercise of authority and power in organizations: who gets what, where, and when. We will analyze the study of organizational politics at three different levels: the individual, the group, and the organization. The first level is essentially concerned with the manager as a political animal who is committed to success and who links success to the ability to influence and change other people's perceptions, emotions, and behavior. The effective manager can create high morale and has high power motivation; he or she is organization-minded, likes to work, is willing to sacrifice his or her own self-interest for the organization, and has a keen sense of justice. Emphasis will be placed on how this new managerial style can be developed.

The second level of analysis deals with the development of cliques and cabals and with the power struggles that arise among departments and functions in business organizations. In organizations, a powerful group that carefully guards and monitors access to the chief executive is sometimes described as the palace guard.

The dominant metaphor of the political theory of the firm sees the organization as a great bureaucratic arena in which the Machiavellians do battle with the humanists. To pursue this organizational firefight, it is necessary to know something about Machiavellian power tactics. The Machiavellian loves means, not ends; he is cool, hyperrational, and a virtuoso actor.

In this chapter, the main issue is the conspiracy versus the pluralistic theory of organizations. While an increasing number of executives in our society believe that the conspiracy theory explains all, the more moderate and liberal argue for pluralism which, briefly, takes the view that no single organization should impose its goals on all other organizations.

The purpose of this analysis is to enable the manager to use a contingency approach to manage the political forces in his own organization.

THE INDIVIDUAL: THE MANAGER
AS A POLITICAL ANIMAL

What Makes a Good Manager?

What makes or motivates a good manager? Some people say that a good manager is one who is successful. They argue that successful management style and a commitment to success are two sides of the same coin. As John H. Johnson (editor and publisher of *Ebony, Jet,* and *Black World;* chief executive officer of Supreme Life Insurance Company; and president of Fashion Fair Cosmetics) puts its,

> Success in business is a time-honored process involving hard work, risk-taking, money, a good product, maybe a little bit of luck, and most of all a burning commitment to succeed. I don't see, never did see, failure as an option. When *Life* went out of business, the guys who made the decision to discontinue it knew that it was not going to disturb their lives. As a matter of fact, Time, Inc.'s stock went up that day. But if *Ebony* didn't succeed, it was going to destroy my life. So I had total commitment; my whole life depended on *Ebony.* I had no options. So I had to learn the rules of the game to win.[1]

When Johnson was asked, "What kind of rules do you mean?" he replied,

> If you're drowning, and two guys are standing above you, one with a long stick and one with a short stick, and the one with the short stick tosses it to you, you can say, "Oh, no, I want the longer stick." But if there's only one stick there, you're going to take it, whatever it is.
>
> For instance, once I was trying to get a second-class permit for *Tan,* which some suggestive stories in it. When I went to the post office, the man said he didn't like *Tan,* he couldn't approve it. I tried all kinds of ways to get him to approve it, including saying, "Well, gee, you must be prejudiced because I'm black, and you've okayed similar magazines, like *True Story, True Confessions,* and so on. Why do you want to do this to me?" But the man just kept rejecting my application. So finally I went down to see him again, and I said, "Mr. So-and-So, I've got to have this second-class permit. I can't survive without it. You're in charge, and I've concluded that the only thing I can do is to do what you want. Will you please tell me what you want me to do?" He said, "Now you're talking, Johnson." And then, really, he told me to do what I was doing right then, namely, being persistent but not hostile. I learned the rules of the game. It wasn't always easy, but I learned them.[2]

David C. McClelland, a professor of psychology, has argued that entrepreneurs have a high need for achievement. But managers *need* a high need for power, because management seems to call for individuals

---

[1] " 'Failure Is a Word I Don't Accept' " by John H. Johnson, *Harvard Business Review* (March-April 1976). Copyright © 1976 by the President and Fellows of Harvard College; all rights reserved.

[2] *Ibid.,* pp. 79–80.

who can influence people. McClelland argues that power must be disciplined, controlled, and directed toward the benefit of the organization as a whole. Thus, power, which can easily lead to authoritarianism, must be tempered by maturity and a high degree of self-control.

McClelland and David H. Burnham discuss the case of Ken Briggs, a sales manager in a large U.S. corporation. Briggs participated in one of McClelland and Burnham's managerial workshops. Ken's profile revealed that his need for achievement was high (over the 90th percentile), and his need for power was low (below the 15th percentile). Ken was perceived by subordinates as a poor manager, because he delegated little responsibility and never rewarded but always criticized. His office was confused and chaotic as well. On scales of effectiveness, his office rated in the 10th to 15th percentile relative to national norms. Ken responded to this failure by setting very high standards, which brought his office to the 97th percentile on the scale of effectiveness. But he achieved this excellence by doing things himself.

According to McClelland and Burnham,

> In the company Ken Briggs works for, we have direct evidence of a connection between morale and performance in the one area where performance measures are easy to come by—namely, sales. In April 1973, at least three employees from this company's 16 sales districts filled out questionnaires that rated their office for organizational clarity and team spirit. . . . Their scores were averaged and totaled to give an overall morale score for each office. The percentage gains or losses in sales for each district in 1973 were compared with those for 1972. The difference in sales figures by district ranged from a gain of nearly 30% to a loss of 8%, with a median gain of around 14%.
>
> . . . the relationship between sales and morale is surprisingly close. The six districts with the lowest morale early in the year showed an average sales gain of only around 7% by years' end (although there was wide variation within this group), whereas the two districts with the highest morale showed an average gain of 28%. When morale scores rise above the 50th percentile in terms of national norms, they seem to lead to better sales performance. In Ken Brigg's company, at least, high morale at the beginning is a good index of how well the sales division actually performed in the coming year.
>
> And it seems very likely that the manager who can create high morale among salesmen can also do the same for employees in other areas (production, design, and so on), leading to better performance. Given that high morale in an office indicates that there is a good manager present, what general characteristics does he possess?[3]

[3] "Power Is the Great Motivator" by David C. McClelland and David H. Burnham, *Harvard Business Review* (March-April 1976). Copyright © 1976 by the President and Fellows of Harvard College; all rights reserved.

The managers who can create high morale were high in power motivation. In the research, product development, and operations divisions, the better managers' need for power was stronger than their need to be liked. The better managers were high in power, low in affiliation, high in inhibition; they cared about organizational power, and they used it to stimulate subordinates' productivity.

The Effective Organizational Manager

According to McClelland and Burnham, effective managers have four characteristics:

1. They are organization-minded; that is, they like to join organizations and to accept responsibility, and they believe in centralized authority.
2. They like to work. Apparently, McClelland found that managers with high achievement motivation tried to process work by becoming more efficient.
3. They are willing to sacrifice their own self-interest for the welfare of the organization.
4. They have a keen sense of justice, which ensures that subordinates get a fair share of the credit.

McClelland and Burnham describe the case of Charlie Blake, who was able to profit from one of their workshops in Box 4.1.

THE GROUP: CLIQUES AND CABALS
IN ORGANIZATIONS

The Political Science of Organizations

The organization is a political system, within which are parties, policies, problems of succession, resistance, and, occasionally, revolution. Therefore, managers such as Charlie Blake are increasingly concerned with political behavior. Viewed as political systems, organizations are mainly concerned with the dispensation of power.

Power is the ability to produce a certain behavior regardless of the feelings and sentiments of the other person. A person is said to have power over another person when he can influence his conduct. Authority is a special kind of power sometimes described as a recognized right to power.

Box 4.1 Charlie Blake Chooses a New Managerial Style

The case of Charlie Blake is instructive. Charlie was as low in power motivation as Ken Briggs, his need to achieve was about average, and his affiliation motivation was above average. Thus he had the affiliative manager profile, and, as expected, the morale among his subordinates was very low. When Charlie learned that his subordinates' sense of responsibility and perception of a reward system were in the 10th percentile and that team spirit was in the 30th, he was shocked. When shown a film depicting three managerial climates, Charlie said he preferred what turned out to be the authoritarian climate. He became angry when the workshop trainer and other members in the group pointed out the limitations of this managerial style. He became obstructive in the group process and objected strenuously to what was being taught.

In an interview conducted much later, Charlie said, "I blew my cool. When I started yelling at you for being all wrong, I got even madder when you pointed out that, according to my style questionnaire, you bet that that was just what I did to my salesmen. Down underneath I knew something must be wrong. The sales performance for my division wasn't so good. Most of it was due to me anyway and not to my salesmen. Obviously their reports that they felt very little responsibility was delegated to them and that I didn't reward them at all had to mean something. So I finally decided to sit down and try to figure what I could do about it. I knew I had to start being a manager instead of trying to do everything myself and blowing my cool at others because they didn't do what I thought they should. In the end, after I calmed down on

Political behavior in organizations requires the formation of coalitions. Coalitions are temporary combinations of individuals for a specific purpose. There are two types of coalitions: cliques and cabals.

A cabal is made up of a group of upwardly mobile people who try to restructure the political situation with a view to achieving their own interests. Cliques are made up of older employees who have come to believe they can make no further progress in the organization. The main objective of the clique is defensive; the members wish to protect their own interests.

These cliques and cabals are always informal groups within the formal organization. As George C. Homans points out,

> When we speak of a number of men as forming a clique, we only mean that they form a subgroup within a larger unit; that is, their interactions with one another are more frequent than they are with outsiders or members of other subgroups.[4]

In the bank wiring room of the Hawthorne study, two cliques

[4] George C. Homans, *The Human Group* (London: Routledge & Kegan Paul, 1951), p. 133. Reprinted with permission of the publisher, Harcourt Brace Jovanovich, Inc.

the way back from the workshop, I realized that it is not so bad to make a mistake; it's bad not to learn from it."

After the course, Charlie put his plans into effect. Six months later, his subordinates were asked to rate him again. He attended a second workshop to study these results and reported, "On the way home I was very nervous. I knew I had been working with those guys and not selling so much myself, but I was very much afraid of what they were going to say about how things were going in the office. When I found out that the team spirit and some of those other low scores had jumped from around 30th to the 55th percentile, I was so delighted and relieved that I couldn't say anything all day long."

When he was asked how he acted differently from before, he said, "In previous years when the corporate headquarters said we had to make 110 percent of our original goal, I had called the salesmen in and said, in effect, 'This is ridiculous; we are not going to make it, but you know perfectly well what will happen if we don't. So get out there and work your tail off!' The result was that I worked 20 hours a day and they did nothing.

"This time I approached it differently. I told them three things. First, they were going to have to do some sacrificing for the company. Second, working harder is not going to do much good because we are already working about as hard as we can. What will be required are special deals and promotions. You are going to have to figure out some new angles if we are to make it. Third, I'm going to back you up. I'm going to set a realistic goal with each of you. If you make that goal but don't make the

---

emerged, each with its own set of behaviors and values. Roethlisberger and Dickson describe one such clique:

> . . . this group of operators held certain definite ideas as to the way in which an individual should conduct himself . . .
>
> 1. You should not turn out too much work. If you do, you are a "rate-buster."
>
> 2. You should not turn out too little work. If you do, you are a "chisler."
>
> 3. You should not tell a supervisor anything that will react to the detriment of an associate. If you do, you are a "squealer."
>
> 4. You should not attempt to maintain social distance or act officious. If you are an inspector, for example, you should not act like one.[5]

---

[5] Fritz J. Roethlisberger and W.J. Dickson, *Management and the Worker* (Cambridge, Mass.: Harvard University Press, 1939), p. 522.

company goal, I'll see to it that you are not punished. But if you do make the company goal, I'll see to it that you will get some kind of special rewards."

When the salesmen challenged Charlie saying he did not have enough influence to give them rewards, rather than becoming angry Charlie promised rewards that were in his power to give—such as longer vacations.

Note that Charlie has now begun to behave in a number of ways that we found to be characteristic of the good institutional manager. He is, above all, higher in power motivation, the desire to influence his salesmen, and lower in his tendency to try to do everything himself. He asks the men to sacrifice for the company. He does not defensively chew them out when they challenge him but tries to figure out what their needs are so that he can influence them. He realizes that his job is more one of strengthening and supporting his subordinates than of criticizing them. And he is keenly interested in giving them just rewards for their efforts.

The changes in his approach to his job have certainly paid off. The sales figures for his office in 1973 were up more than 16 percent over 1972 and up still further in 1974 over 1973. In 1973 his gain over the previous year ranked seventh in the nation; in 1974 it ranked third. And he wasn't the only one in his company to change managerial styles. Overall sales at his company were up substantially in 1973 as compared with 1972, an increase which played a large part in turning the overall company performance around from a $15 million loss in 1972 to a $3 million profit in 1973. The company continued to improve its performance in 1974 with an 11 percent further gain in sales and 38 percent increase in profits.

The Power of Cliques and Cabals

Melville Dalton, a sociologist at UCLA, studied the Milo firm to find out how the political system works in organizations.[6] Dalton discovered that the key ethnic group in the Milo organization was made up of people with an Anglo Saxon or a German background. Although the company officially specified that promotion was based on ability, competence, achievement, and formal education, the key factors, in fact, were being a Mason, an Anglo Saxon, or a person of German descent. It was also helpful to be a member of the local yacht club and a Republican.

To get a better insight into these power struggles in the line, Dalton identified a whole variety of different coalitions. These included the vertical clique, which is made up of a superior and one or more of his subordinates; the horizontal clique, whose members are made up of

[6] Melville Dalton, *Men Who Manage* (New York: John Wiley & Sons, 1959).

people at the same level; and the random clique, whose membership is based on friendship. Dalton found that the horizontal cliques operated to the disadvantage of the company. In response, the company tried a variety of techniques to break up such cliques. Dalton also found that rate busters came from different socioeconomic backgrounds and had different political and religious views from other shop floor people.

What Dalton's work spelled out was that the organization is a political arena within which there is a considerable degree of conflict not only between cliques and cabals but also among departments. Dalton found that powerful production department managers blackmailed the managers of the maintenance section to force them to step outside the planned maintenance schedule. When staff managers were sent out from the head office to set this right, they were blocked from getting the information necessary to get the situation under control.

Dalton also identified important political conflicts between staff and line managerial officers.

> Even before presenting an idea to the line, staff agents must face the obstacle that many first-line foremen view them as tools brought in primarily for control of the lower line. Foremen are likely to regard most staff projects as manipulative devices. They cooperate with production workers and general foremen to defeat insistent and uncompromising staff people. . . . foremen may cooperate with lower staff personnel in trouble with superiors. But this is also an attack on staff chiefs. The staff function inherently threatens some part of the line because any contribution is likely to mean change in the line.
>
> Staff innovations are opposed for several reasons. In view of their longer experience, intimate knowledge of the work and higher pay, line chiefs feel an obligation to make the contributions themselves, and they fear being "shown up." They know that changes in methods may bring personnel changes, break up informal arrangements, reduce their authority or enlarge that of rivals (including staff people), and bring reorganization with possible change of superiors. To some line chiefs, change based on staff ideas will be disastrous for they represent instability, impracticality, and unpredictability. They are "snoopervisors" who may uncover workable but forbidden practices and label them "inefficient" and "unscientific" in terms of their holy procedures.
>
> Hence middle and lower line will often oppose staff-initiated change openly until top line shows firm support. Then verbal conformity will screen lower level resistance and malpractices to bring a return of the earlier arrangement. Knowing this, staff officers may withhold real improvements when they believe attempts to introduce them will be defeated or that forcing resistance into the open will hurt their future.[7]

[7] *Ibid.*, p. 100.

Machiavellian Power Tactics

In business, government, education, or the church, Machiavellians have power, understand power, and use power. They maneuver and manipulate to get a job done and to strengthen and enhance their own position. They are in fact politicians. Now, people can exercise only the amount of power that other people allow them. The ultimate source of power is the group; and a group, in turn, is made up of people—each with his own consciousness and will, his own emotions and irrationalities, his own intense personal interests and tenaciously held values. The successful functioning and advancement of the executive is dependent on the vast intricacy of human relationships that make up the political universe of the organization.

How can power be used most effectively? What political stratagems must the administrator employ to carry out his responsibilities and further his career? Norman H. Martin and John Howard Sims have not only searched the biographies of well-known leaders of history from Alexander to Roosevelt, but they have also explored the lives of such successful industrialists as Rockefeller and Ford. Their tentative conclusions regarding power tactics are worth paraphrasing.[8]

Taking counsel

The able executive is *cautious* about how he or she seeks and receives advice. He takes counsel only when he himself desires it. His decisions are made in terms of his own grasp of the situation, taking into account the views of others when he thinks it necessary. To act otherwise is to be subjected not to advice but to pressure; to act otherwise too often produces vacillation and inconsistency.

Alliances

In the struggle for power and influence, if he or she is to protect and to enhance his status and sphere of influence every executive needs a devoted following and close alliances with other executives, both at his own level and above him. Alliances also provide ready-made systems of communication.

Maneuverability

The wise executive maintains his or her flexibility and never completely commits himself to any one position or program. An

[8] "Power Tactics" by Norman H. Martin and John Howard Sims, *Harvard Business Review* (November-December 1956). Copyright © 1956 by the President and Fellows of Harvard College; all rights reserved.

executive should preserve maneuverability in career planning as well. He ought never to get in a situation without several escape hatches. He must be careful that his career is not directly dependent on the superior position of a sponsor.

Communicating

It simply is not good strategy to communicate everything one knows. Instead, it may often be advantageous to withhold information or to time its release, especially when information may create a schism or conflict within the organization or when another executive is a threat to one's own position. Thus, information is an important tactical weapon. The executive should be concerned with determining "who gets to know what and when" rather than with simply increasing the flow of information.

Compromising

The executive should appear to accept compromise as a means of settling differences. It is frequently necessary to give ground on small matters, to delay, to move off on tangents, even to suffer reverses in order to retain power for future forward movement. Concessions, then, should be more apparent than real.

Negative timing

The executive is often urged to take action with which he is not in agreement. To give in to such demand would be to deny the executive's prerogative. To refuse might precipitate a dangerous crisis and threaten one's power. In such situations, the executive may find it wise to use what might be called the technique of negative timing. He initiates action, but the process of expedition is retarded. He is always in the process of doing something but never quite does it, or finally he takes action when it is actually too late. In this way the executive escapes the charge of dereliction, and at the same time the inadvisable program "dies on the vine."

Self-dramatization

The skill of the actor, whose communication is "artistic" as opposed to "natural," represents a potential asset to an administrator. Dramatic art is useful for the purpose of arousing the emotions, of convincing, of persuading, of altering the behavior of the audience in a planned direction. The actor's particular gift is in deliberately shaping his own speech and behavior to accomplish his purpose. A good executive considers the "how" of communicating as well as the "what."

Confidence

Related to self-dramatization is the outward appearance of confidence. Once an executive has made a decision, he must look and act decided. If genuine inner conviction is lacking, the executive should postpone any contact with his associates to avoid appearing in an unfavorable light.

Always the boss

An atmosphere of social friendship interferes with the efficiency of an operation and acts to limit the power of the manager. Personal feelings should not be a basis for action, either negative or positive. The executive should never permit himself to be so committed to a subordinate that he is unable to withdraw from this personal involvement and regard the subordinate objectively.

Thus a thin line of separation between executive and subordinate must always be maintained. The executive must sustain a line of privacy that cannot be transgressed; in the final analysis, he must always be the boss. If we assume, then, that the traditional "open-door" policy of the modern executive is good strategy, we must always ask the question, "How far open?"

THE STRUCTURAL BASES OF POWER

Power to influence behavior is derived from a number of sources. Amitai Etzioni has identified three different kinds of power: utilitarian, normative, and coercive.[9] Organizations achieve control over their members partly by coercion (conformity or nonconformity results in rewards or sanctions), partly by utilitarian considerations (employees are paid inducements both to join the organization and to do things that further its objectives), but also by normative considerations (organizations require value assimilation).

A person's power base is a function of four characteristics:

1. organizational factors,
2. information management and control of access,

[9] Amitai Etzioni, *A Comparative Analysis of Complex Organizations* (New York: Free Press, 1961), p. 5.

3. personal expertise, and
4. personal qualities.

Organizational Factors

A manager's role gives him or her power, for each role specification explicitly or implicitly contains a definition of the power adhering to that role. Managers have authority to hire and fire, reward and punish, make expenditures, and authorize expense accounts. Indeed, so attractive are the powers associated with particular offices that frequently executives are actually prepared to forego financial advantages to obtain offices of greater power, which allow them to exercise more control over others. But such organizational-based power resides in the office, not in the person.

Information Management
and Control of Access

An executive's standing in the system can be measured by his ability to have access to and manage the information system. On one level, power is the ability to restructure and mold the perception of others in a way that will enable you to achieve your goals. Closely tied to information management is personal access to key figures.

Members of the lowerarchy also exercise considerable power as either gate keepers or controllers of critical resources.

Personal Expertise

Many executives have power because of some expertise, know-how, specific information, or creative skill. Modern organizations cannot function without professional experts—accountants, lawyers, scientists, mathematicians—to supply critical information and skills. Such professional experts have considerable power although, in fact, it is task specific.

Personal Qualities

Some individuals operate not from structural or information management bases but rather from a personality base. A good example of a politician with a powerful personal appeal, which he used as a power base, was President John F. Kennedy. Kennedy's New Frontier approach derived its strength from what French and Raven call "referent power," which has as its base the "feelings of oneness that a person has for another."

Referent power denotes a manager's ability to generate an ambiance or lifestyle that is seen as attractive by his colleagues and makes them want to identify with him. Such leaders are charismatic because they have the ability to articulate the values and aspirations of the group in a way that makes them sophisticated, relevant, and vivid. Politicians like Roosevelt, Churchill, and Hitler could generate this kind of charisma, which in turn mobilized unbelievable energies and loyalties that could be focused according to the interests of the leader. Many executives, perhaps emulating such historical figures, set out to generate a charismatic image both of their executive style and their personal demeanor and dress.

THE PROCESS

Executive Power in Action

Howard R. Hughes, the charismatic, legendary, and mysterious American executive, operated in a way that made a maximal use of power. *Time* described his executive style:

> "Those who dealt with him were almost always driven to absolute fits of frustration," wrote *Time* Associate Editor David B. Tinnin in his book, *Just About Everybody vs. Howard Hughes* (1973). Continued Tinnin, who interviewed scores of people who had dealt with him: "One banker who did business for many years with him maintains that Hughes operates according to four principles. One: Never make a decision. Let someone else make it and then if it turns out to be the wrong one, you can disclaim it, and if it is the right one, you can abide by it. Two: Always postpone any deadline—for a week, a day, or even half an hour. Who knows, the situation may change in your favor if only you have the patience to wait. Three: Divide and conquer—both your foes and friends. Play off everyone against each other so that you have more avenues of action open to you. Four: Every man has his price. The only problem, therefore, is finding out what the price is."[10]

[10] From "The Hughes Legacy: Scramble for the Billion." Reprinted by permission from *Time*, The Weekly Newsmagazine; Copyright Time Inc. 1976.

Power! How to Get It, How to Use It

An increasing number of books full of practical advice on how to exploit organizational power have been written. A good example of this new genre is Michael Korda's *Power! How To Get It, How To Use It*. Following Korda's advice, executives should practice a "power gaze" in front of a mirror, learn to pick the power seats at meetings, and cultivate an appropriate air of mystery. Here is a sampling of Korda's recommendations.[11]

1. *The strategy of raises.* Get more for those under you and over you, and your raise is almost inevitable.

2. *Shaking things up below.* About one such executive, someone said: "He likes to stir the pot to show he owns the spoon." An effective strategy.

3. *A new and bigger title* can protect you (against being fired, for one thing).

4. *If two people always agree* in business, one of them is not needed.

5. *How to handle gossip.* Listen closely, don't comment. Bide your time.

6. *Creeping helplessness.* That's the first sign of a rise to power. "The less you have to do, the more power you have."

7. *When to offer your opinion.* Be silent, impassive, alert, visible until everyone else has spoken his piece—then fire away, in complete safety.

8. *Clocks and watches.* The ultimate power symbols. The more intricate the watch, the less powerful the executive who wears it.

9. *The art of accepting bad news.* Learn to stay cool, as if you already knew and didn't care.

10. *The miracle word.* "No." Every time you say it, your power increases.

11. What smart executives with power *never give up is control* of other people's expense accounts.

12. *Hysteria as a source of power.* Most people will do anything to avoid a scene.

13. *Don't cross your legs.* Plant your feet firmly on the floor. This projects an aura of solid power.

14. *Speak low,* to make others lean forward to hear what you have to say.

---

[11] Based on Michael Korda, *Power! How to Get It, How to Use It* (New York: Random House, Inc., 1975), pp. 253–61.

A Caution: Executive Life Is Complex

It is a good idea to keep in mind that assertiveness, or the push for power, can become dangerous. Executives who take Korda's advice too seriously may well end up in trouble. To many senior executives, the advice of power-game gurus seems repulsive, unsound, and even ludicrous. For example, Korda lays great stress on immobility, the capacity to sit still while others vibrate in response to a crisis. Korda is also against beards and moustaches on the curious basis that executives who sport them look as if they have something to hide. .

Among academics the criticism is even stronger. It centers on the notion that manipulation advocated by self-help experts requires raising bullying, cheating, and lying to an art form. Their books are described as a sort of moral pornography. The student of management might do well to consider why so many executives uncritically accept power-game writers' advice. There is a vast market of people who would like to become successful executives and who hope by following the simple aphorisms of these self-help books to get there. Unfortunately, executive life is a good deal more complex than these self-help books imply. To be effective in management requires high motivation, good problem-solving skills, a capacity for good human relations, and a feel for organizational politics. Organizational politics presupposes that the executive should know something about power and how to use it, but it also requires an awareness that those who talk about power make their colleagues feel anxious. Power is important, but it is important to keep power in its place. It is a means of influence that should be exercised only in extremes, a last resort to get good things done.

Power Values

The swiftest way to understand the value system underscoring the process of power is to look at the psychosis of power. When a manager is getting things done in a big way, he or she experiences a feeling that he could capture the world. In brief, he suffers from and gives off the illusion of grandeur. Of course, he is usually more familiar with the negative end of paranoia—that he is being got at; that his phone is bugged; that the memo is aimed specifically at him; that "they" are out to get him. The "they" is always there with power. The power ethos is characterized by the Machiavellian manager who is calculating, crafty, and dissembling. The effective manager knows how to use power and does not condemn people for exercising power, provided it is used for good purposes. The effective manager knows that the corporate world is held together by a set of somewhat interlocking conspiracies who understand only power. Having dealt with authority and power, let us turn now to the organizational influence of authority, or politicking.

POLITICKING: EXERCISING INFLUENCE

"Getting in Role"

Getting people to do what you want them to means putting them in role. Getting them into role means you have got to get into role yourself. Existential role playing is a major part of the drama of executive life. Playing a role is like playing a hand in poker. Since roles, rules, and relations are socially ordained, behavior conforms to probabilities and perceptions. "Play it as it lays," "playing it by ear," "play it again, Sam"—all are expressions descriptive of the double dealing of good role playing.

A good example of old-fashioned double dealing is the diabolical role playing of Bobby Fischer at the chess board. Fischer scares his opponents to death, even though his behavior is impeccable. For Fischer, as for many executives at their game, a chess match is psychological warfare waged at nerve-tearing intensity—sometimes for as long as two months. Like a good executive, Fischer is a sportsman while he plays. He never squirms while he is losing, never crows when he is winning. Just as task-oriented, tough-minded executives try to outwit their opponents, so chess players try to get ahead of their challengers.

The Conspiracy Theory

The conspiracy theory is the notion that the world is organized on a monolithic basis with one group deciding everything that happens. Basically the presumption is that a group of people—the mafia, the church, the press, Free Masonry, the Eastern establishment, or whatever powerful interest group you wish—controls your world. A conspiracy theory of organization presupposes

1. a powerful autocratic clique in charge, who wield power with great force,

2. a sense of paranoia or persecution among subordinates,
3. other institutions of society (the government, the press, the universities) that are prepared to acquiesce, and
4. nonexistent unions or unions that have been bought.

THE ORGANIZATION: THE CONSPIRACY
THEORY VERSUS PLURALISM

Since the Watergate disclosures, the conspiracy theory has captured the popular imagination. A number of contemporary movies have dealt explicitly with political and organizational intrigue. Executives find this theory comforting because it provides a rational explanation for many bewildering corporate experiences. Furthermore, executives, like other ordinary mortals, can find meaningful patterns in both drama and life if they approach them with the right point of view.

Pluralism

In opposition to the conspiracy theory of organizations, more moderate social scientists tend to see power structures in pluralistic terms. According to the moderates, no single organization or set of organizations is dominant. Rather, society consists of a set of interest groups with conflicting goals. These groups join and leave coalitions depending upon which issues are current. According to the pluralistic thesis, power can be understood as a balance of prudence, which presumes that our society is a set of countervailing interest groups who cooperate and conflict with each other to maintain some kind of equilibrium.

In macroeconomic terms, there are many examples of pluralism. One is a balance of power between big business and big unions. Historically, trade unions developed as an ideological response to the power of large companies to impose upon workers unacceptable working conditions. But as negotiations became more complex and systematic, trade unions were inevitably forced to create their own bureaucracies with the necessary bargaining expertise to take on large, industrial organizations.

A CONTINGENCY APPROACH TO
MANAGING POLITICAL BEHAVIOR

Stephen P. Robbins has proposed a contingency theory of organizational politics. To understand the political process, Robbins suggests four propositions.[12]

1. The more ambiguous the formal roles and authority of organization members, the more developed will be the internal system of political competition.

2. Positions with high discretionary powers are held by individuals who have developed political skills.

3. Those in discretionary powers will seek to maintain power equal to or greater than their dependence on other organizational members.

4. Where those in discretionary positions have less power than those upon whom they are dependent, they seek a coalition.

For Robbins, political behavior can be classified into three categories: offensive, defensive, and neutral. Often political behavior, which includes power building, developing loyalties, and sabotaging and exploiting others, requires the offensive strategy of developing useful coalitions. Defensive political behavior takes as its point of departure the notion "if you cannot look good, make others look bad." Neutral strategies are mainly concerned with the preservation of the status quo.

Bureaucracies were designed to manage political behaviors; they lay out impersonal and rational ground rules that enable organizations to achieve effectiveness and equity. Therefore, bureaucratic organizations with clearly defined policies, specified job definitions, established career plans, and impersonal rules were developed originally not only to restrain the landed gentry who wanted to purchase commissions in high offices but also to afford an opportunity for the ordinary person who had the necessary talents. Bureaucracies were meant to be meritocracies.

Dealing With Dysfunctional Political Behavior

A major problem in organizations is to keep dysfunctional political behaviors within some kind of limits. Many organizations, such as the military, forbid all forms of political and religious discussion in official

---

[12] Stephen P. Robbins, THE ADMINISTRATIVE PROCESS: Integrating Theory and Practice, © 1976, p. 63. Reprinted by permission of Prentice-Hall, Inc., Englewood Cliffs, New Jersey.

settings. And most business organizations are usually very careful to meet demands of junior and middle management when a failure to do so would provide a rallying point for the formation of bargaining groups.

Generally, in business and government organizations it is regarded as bad form to conspire openly against one's superiors. Until very recently, executives adopted a somewhat dependent and subservient attitude to both the system and their superiors. But our turbulent economic and political environment makes large corporate changes necessary. For example, thousands of professional and managerial people were recruited by NASA to get to the moon. Subsequently many had to be let go. The dramatic cyclical changes in the automobile industry have caused companies like Chrysler to fire a considerable number of executives. With this kind of economic turbulence, executives no longer experience a high degree of job security. In such a changing climate, political action becomes not only more probable but also something of a moral duty.

To meet such a contingency, top management's best strategy is to adopt an open, democratic problem solving style that brings everything into the open and makes managers realize that often they are competing one with another.

REVIEW AND RESEARCH

1. Why is the attitude of Nicolo Machiavelli so relevant to the operation of a modern organization?
2. Why is it necessary for Machiavellians to be such good actors?
3. What can Norman H. Martin and John Howard Sims tell us about power tactics?
4. What power tactics did Sam Ervin use to bring the Watergate conspirators to justice? Were they completely legal?
5. Why is the conspiracy theory of organizations so much in vogue today? Why is it necessary to conspire?

"I STOOD UP AND BLEW MY STACK"

In 1978, I was the sales manager for a division of a large multinational corporation located in a small Ontario town. I had been with the firm for some thirteen years and was reasonably happy with the job situation. For purely personal reasons, I had come to a decision to return to Montreal, where I preferred to live and work. I obtained subscriptions to Montreal newspapers and prepared a resumé. On a business trip to Montreal, I contacted several placement agencies and was interviewed by two of them. Resumés were left with both, but the job market at the time did not look promising.

Several months later, I was contacted by one of the agencies, who had a client who might be interested in me for a senior staff position. The salary range was mentioned, and they wanted to know if they could set up an interview with the client's director of industrial relations, who was going to be in Toronto for a few days the following week. I indicated that the upper end of the salary range was substantially below what I was currently earning and that I was not particularly interested in a staff position. The agency felt that the salary was negotiable and suggested that I take a run at it anyway. I agreed to an interview in Toronto but asked that it be made in the evening, as I preferred not to take time off work for what I felt would turn out to be a wild goose chase. The agency called back a short while later to tell me that the director of industrial relations would not see me in the evening and was prepared to meet me at 10:00 a.m. the following Monday in the agency's Toronto office. I reluctantly agreed to the appointment.

I set out for Toronto early Monday morning and arrived at the agency's office a half an hour early. The receptionist asked me to wait, which I did for about one hour. A good part of that time I spent trying to decide whether my man was late or was still interviewing an earlier arrival. I was waiting for some sign of traffic in or out of the office, but there was none. Finally the receptionist's phone rang. She answered and then announced that my man was ready to see me, pointing to a door directly off the room I had been waiting in.

I knocked and entered, confronting my interviewer, who was tilted back in the chair, both feet on the desk, wearing a blue blazer with brass buttons. I noted that there was no other door to the office and realized that he had been in the office alone while I was cooling my heels for over an hour. Without getting up, he introduced himself, reached out to shake my hand, and waved me to a chair. By this time I was getting pretty upset. I sat down while my friend began to read my resumé, periodically looking up to scowl.

"I see that you've got Commerce and Science degrees. That's all you have, eh? No M.B.A., huh? That's too bad. We wanted an M.B.A. You don't seem to have any accounting experience either. A fair knowledge of accounting is certainly a requirement for this position."

I had no real accounting experience. I did have a major in

accounting in my Bachelor of Commerce degree. I conceded however, that that probably wouldn't do.

"I see also that you're forty years old," he said in a horrified tone. "We wanted someone around thirty or so. Certainly not more than thirty-five."

I stood up and blew my stack. "For Goodness sake—you've had my resumé for two weeks—it's all there! If I'm such a misfit and I'm too bloody old, why the hell are we talking to each other? Why bother dragging me in for this interview? We are obviously both wasting our time," and I turned to leave.

"Whoops, hold it," he said. "Sit down, don't get carried away." Smiling slyly, he confided, "I was just trying to see how you would react. I like to see how far I can push a guy. Now, let's get down to the main issue. Let me tell you about the position we are trying to fill ... "

I excused myself. As I walked to the washroom, I began to formulate a plan of action.

1. What power plays were involved in this situation?
2. Why would the interviewer behave the way he did?
3. How does this person's story relate to Chapter 4?

II

PROCESS
VARIABLES

5

Objective
Setting

OBJECTIVES YOU SHOULD MEET

Diagram the relationship
between objectives and plans.

Develop skill in spelling out objectives.

List a variety of objectives
extending market share,
increasing earnings,
and maintaining social responsibility.

Explain how firms reconcile
multiple objectives.

Distinguish between objectives
and goals of the firm.

Describe how MBO can be used
to get subordinates involved in setting
their own targets and reaching them.

Explain how Chrysler is trying to improve its
position by redefining its objectives.

The process of making the firm's dreams and strategic visions meaningful begins with objective setting. The prudent executive carefully reviews the firm's comparative advantage and its resources to develop a set of possible objectives. Effective executives build on their own and their colleagues' personal strengths; they concentrate on what they can do best. Second, they try to figure out what kinds of results they can produce. This is a tough, searching process to ascertain what results are really worthwhile. Third, they concentrate their resources on a few major areas, with a high probability of producing superior performance.

In this chapter, we emphasize the variety of corporate objectives managers try to achieve, including increasing or maintaining market share, increasing profits, and accepting some social responsibility. But these aims will not be achieved unless they are communicated. A widely used technique for formulating corporate aims is called management by objectives (MBO), in which both the manager and his team establish goals for their unit. The second part of this chapter is devoted to an explanation of MBO. In going through this chapter, the reader should keep in mind that objective setting and planning are fundamental to the enterprise's sense of direction. Since objective setting is frequently couched in terms too general and abstract to guide day-to-day behavior, the manager must make a real effort to translate operating objectives into concrete and specific goals.

THE IMPORTANCE OF OBJECTIVE SETTING

Recent research has highlighted the fact that there is a direct relationship between the clarity of organizational goals and business success. High-growth companies develop clear objectives and undertake to accomplish them. George G. Gordon and Bonnie E. Goldberg found that "organizational clarity—clear goals, formal planning, complete planning, and existence of defined plans" lead to high performance. They continue:

A clear picture of the highly successful company thus emerges. It is characterized by a formal system for planning that provides a large number of managers with a clear picture of where the company is going and how it intends to get there. This is backed up by a good deal of communication of relevant information—that is, information needed in decision making and performance measurement. Furthermore, this philosophy of identifying objectives, planning for their accomplishment, and measuring performance is implemented relatively widely throughout the organization. While the formal processes of management by objectives have rightly come under severe attack, it appears that their action-orientation—perhaps without the encumbrances of an overly detailed procedure—are alive and well in highly successful companies.[1]

In selecting the objective, managers might follow this sequence:

1. Formulate objectives: "Should we do this, or should we do that?"
2. Develop scenarios: "If I do this, he'll do ——." "What if ——-?"
3. Select an objective: "I will do this."
4. List all factors affecting the objective's achievement:
   a. "What have I got going for me?" (Comparative advantage)
   b. "What is it going to take?" (Resources)
   c. "How am I going to keep score?" (Results)
5. Setting priorities: "What comes first?"
6. Make a plan: "First we'll do this, then that."

Figure 5.1 shows this sequence.

Figure 5.1   A "Logical" Sequence For Selecting an Objective

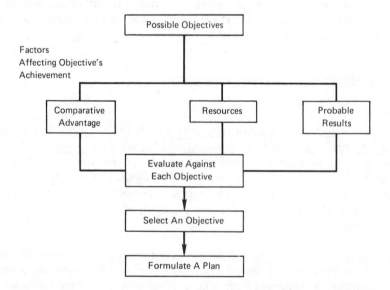

[1] Reprinted by permission of the publisher, from "Is There a Climate for Success?" by George C. Gordon and Bonnie E. Goldberg, *Management Review* (May 1977), p. 41. Copyright © 1977 by AMACOM, a division of the American Management Associations. All rights reserved.

Formulating Objectives

Because human beings are not always logical, the process of formulating objectives seldom follows a set plan. Basically, formulating objectives is a matter of asking yourself the right question, or at least not asking the wrong question (see Box 5.1). The most difficult problems in management arise not from failures of problem analysis but from failures arising from solving the wrong problem (asking the wrong question).

Types of Objectives

Firms usually have a variety of objectives. These include making profits, extending their share of the market, and improving their social standing. Fundamentally, the business of a firm is to make a profit. Everyone agrees that profit is a basic concept of the philosophy of the free enterprise system, and most educated people are coming to realize that profit, in some disguised form, also plays a significant part in nationalized or state-owned industries. Thus, for business the notion of enlightened self-interest is the mainspring of all economic activity.

Profits, the ultimate measure of the firm's success, may be reported as a return on investment, the degree of market penetration, a percentage of sales, or a percentage of net worth. All successful top executives realize that profits and their continuing growth are absolutely essential for continued tenure. Failure to generate satisfactory profits usually portends a change in top management.

Box 5.2 gives a terse but useful statement of objectives. It catches the spirit of both traditional and existential aims. Figure 5.2 classifies the objective of an automobile manufacturer.

Profits, The Lifeblood of the Economic System

Hardly anyone questions the basic right of a firm to make a profit. The question is, how much? Ever since Adam Smith argued that profits are the legitimate return for an entrepreneur's risk and effort, some economists have been arguing the opposite. Nevertheless, it is generally recognized that in a capitalist free enterprise society, profit is the motivator to take a risk, to start a new business, to introduce a new product, or to continue to produce an old one.

In business theory, profit is an important measure of efficiency. Why is there so much suspicion of profits? In one poll conducted by the

Box 5.1: Asking the Wrong Question

Question:
If Jack is worse than Jill and Jill is better than Jean, who is worse?
Answers:
Jack
Jill
Jean
Can't tell
   Although the correct answer is "Can't tell," many will select Jack. If the question is rephrased, "Who is best?" the number of mistakes will be sharply reduced.

Opinion Research Corporation, a majority of those surveyed thought that profits averaged 33 cents, for each dollar of sales. The actual figure is below 5 per cent. According to a *Fortune* survey, the 1975 median profit margin of the nation's 500 largest industrial corporations was 3.9 percent of sales.

Another major problem is how profitability should be measured. As Peter Drucker has pointed out, the three main measures used by corporations today—gross income, net income, and earnings per share—are far too superficial. But as David B. Tinnin points out,

> Equally bad, under the present system, earnings are compared only with the preceding quarter—or year. This leads to wild gyrations in the loss and gain columns. The profit may be up 75% from a year ago, but then, a year ago may have been miserable. These swings are, humanly enough, magnified by corporate officers, who pooh-pooh losses while boasting about profit increases in hyperbolic press releases. The press then magnifies the problem by often reporting profits in language more appropriate to space shots or sporting events: profits leap, soar, skyrocket—or plunge, plummet, nosedive.
>
> It is time for a more sober analysis of profits and their importance as the engine of economic growth. It is a historic irony that in the U.S., the stronghold of world capitalism, so few citizens understand that profits provide the basis for the prosperity on which rests the well-being of both individuals and the nation.[2]

But firms are concerned not only with profits. They also have other objectives, which include technological excellence, long-term economic flexibility, and the capacity to discharge their social responsibilities. For the firm to function properly, the manager must be able to operationalize these objectives.

[2] From "Profits: How Much Is Too Little?" 16 August 1976. Reprinted by permission from *Time*, The Weekly Newsmagazine; Copyright Time, Inc. 1976.

Edwin H. Land, chief executive officer of the Polaroid Corporation, describes the strategies of his company:

"We have two basic aims. One is to make products that are genuinely new and useful to the public, products of the highest quality and at reasonable cost. In this way we assure the financial success of the company and each of us has the satisfaction of helping to make a creative contribution to the society.

"The other is to give everyone working for the company a personal opportunity within the company for full exercise of his talents—to express his opinions, to share in the progress of the company as far as his capacities permit, and to earn enough money so that the need for earning more will not always be the first thing on his mind. The opportunity, in short, to make his work here a fully rewarding and important part of his life."

A VARIETY OF OBJECTIVES

Objective: Market Share

"Our principle," Hoffman-LaRoche president Adolf W. Hann said in 1971, "is that we do not enter a field unless we can play first violin." In the field of tranquilizers, Hoffman-LaRoche plays both first and second violin. This commanding position is due to their exclusive

Figure 5.2   Characteristics of Objectives According to Level, Function, Quantity, and Data

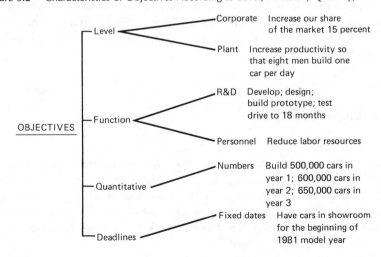

patents on valium and librium. *Fortune* magazine described the company as "one of the most profitable organizations of earth" (one share of Hoffman-LaRoche is currently worth nearly $45,000).

This distinguished pharmaceutical company has achieved leadership in the tranquilizer market not only because of its research and development genius, but because of its ability to plan and carry through market strategies, mainly through medical journals aimed at physicians.

Objective: Increasing Earnings

Under the leadership of chairman Ray W. MacDonald, Burroughs Corporation has reported forty-eight consecutive quarters with profits exceeding those of the same period of the previous year. The company's explicit goals are to double sales every five years and to increase profits even faster. Such growth is possible because the computer market is growing at a rate of 10 to 15 percent a year compounded. The main competition for Burroughs is IBM, which is nine times Burroughs' size and is planning to grow at a rate of 10 percent a year.

Objective: Social Responsibility

Companies have not only economic objectives, such as increasing market share or increasing the return on investment; they also have social responsibilities. For example, Burroughs, which has been very tough minded about costs and personnel, has shown a distinct social conscience in Detroit. In 1968, the year after the Detroit riots, the company announced plans to build a $35 million headquarters complex in the new center area. Top management at Burroughs felt that if they abandoned Detroit in 1968, the social effect would have been devastating.

COMPOSITE OBJECTIVES

Because of the complexity of the external environment, organizational goals cannot be described by one simple objective. For example, General Motors' portfolio in the early seventies was categorized by the company's slogan "Sixty, sixty, sixty". It revealed a variety of objectives: to win 60 percent of the market, to get their stock up to $60 a share, and to achieve these goals in the sixtieth year of the company chairman and president (which was 1976). GM's competitors must also have diversified goals, among them responsiveness to GM's strategies and any of a multitude of unexpected external events—a gas shortage, for example.

What General Motors Did Yesterday

Many organizations derive their objectives not from a basic analysis of their critical resources, special expertise, or the demand of the market, but rather by doing "what General Motors did yesterday." Since General Motors dominates the market, when it starts pushing fuel economy, cutting cars' weight, and designing new models, its competitors are forced to follow suit.

Much the same can be said about university business schools, which frequently pursue a "follow the leader" policy in formulating school objectives. The principle then becomes "what was good for Harvard last year is good for us this year." Many organizations tend to inherit their objectives from the leaders of their particular industries.

Suboptimization of Multiple Objectives

The organization is the meeting ground for a number of inter-locking constituencies. These include the share holders, who want a fair return on their capital investment for the speculative risk involved; the employees, who want to prosper personally in the working community; and the consumers, who want to buy a good product at a reasonable price.

The existence of these multiple objectives inevitably leads to the process of suboptimization: trading off the margins of achievement between different performance variables. Given multiple objectives and the process of suboptimization, managers inevitably have to bring into play their creative intuition, know-how, and experience. They have to formulate strategies, plans, and decisions that will help them achieve complex and complicated objectives.

Formulating Objectives and Goals of the Firm

To a great extent, problems arise in firms because objectives have not been properly specified. Subordinates function best in a structure within which they can exercise discretion. It is necessary to distinguish between objectives and goals. Objectives provide general and strategic targets that implicitly and explicitly suggest guides to action that emerge in the form of plans. Goals emerge from plans, and they provide standards of desired performance by which success or the lack of it in the various divisions of the firm can be measured. Thus, the formulation of objectives is essentially a top management function to which middle management contributes ideas, concepts, and facts. Goals, on the other hand, are more likely to emerge from the upper echelons of middle management and to be reviewed by top management.

GOALS

Objectives tend to be broad, general, philosophical statements of where the company wants to be. Goals must be operative and must provide identifiable and usually quantitative solutions. For example, an objective might be to achieve an economically viable and profitable operation. Such an economic objective could be translated into such operational goals as selling 100,000 cars, or opening 20 new franchises in 10 different states in the next year.

Goals are also important because they provide the operational criteria for measuring effectiveness. As such, they make it possible to identify and develop critical decision variables, which, in turn, become a key part of the control system. To enable all this to happen, the goals must be attainable; they should be set out in writing; they must be communicated to subordinates; they must be related to rewards; and they must be integrated into the control system.

Goal Optimization and Effectiveness

There is a lack of consensus on what organizational effectiveness means. For the investor, it means high profits or a significant return on investment. For the line executive, it means getting the right quality and quantity out of the gate on schedule within a specified cost structure. For the research scientist, it means the number of brilliant ideas developed, or perhaps, papers published.

The problem of defining organizational effectiveness is bedeviled by the fact that too many managers define effectiveness in terms of a single criterion—profitability or productivity or job satisfaction. To try to overcome this difficulty, Richard M. Steers has developed a useful table on criteria used in measuring organization effectiveness (see Table 5.1).

The need for goal optimization

As Table 5.1 reveals, only one criterion, adaptability-flexibility, was mentioned in more than half the models. Steers' general conclusion is that organizational effectiveness is an abstract concept that involves a number of dimensions, and these dimensions may conflict with one another. To solve this problem, managers must engage in the process of goal optimization. It may be possible, for example, to improve job satisfaction and morale but only at the expense of productivity. Further, it may be a mistake to assume that the criteria used in assessing one organization may be applicable to another. Profitability and market shares are fine for organizations but irrelevant for a hospital or university.

Steers gives an example of organizational ineffectiveness.

There are many examples of organizations that correctly identify the nature of the problem and set relevant goals but then select a less than optimal strategy for attaining those goals.

One such example can be seen in the activities of the first Henry Ford as he tried to maintain the profitability of Ford Motor Company during the depression of the 1930s—when, of course, the demand for new

Table 5.1 Frequency of Occurrence of Evaluation Criteria in 17 Models of Organizational Effectiveness

Evaluation Criteria	No. of Times Mentioned (N = 17)	Percent of Total
Adaptability-flexibility	10	59
Productivity	6	35
Job satisfaction	5	29
Profitability	3	18
Acquisition of scarce and valued resources	3	18
Absence of organizational strain	2	12
Control over external environment	2	12
Employee development	2	12
Efficiency	2	12
Employee retention	2	12
Growth	2	12
Integration of individual goals with organizational goals	2	12
Open communication	2	12
Survival	2	12
All other criteria	1	6

Reprinted from "Problems in the Measurement of Organizational Effectiveness" by R. M. Steers, published in *Administrative Science Quarterly*, Vol. 20, 4, by permission of *The Administrative Science Quarterly*. © 1975 by Cornell University.

cars had declined. Alfred Chandler reports in his book *Strategy and Structure* that Ford decided to enter the farm tractor market in order to employ some of his unused plant capacity. Within a relatively short period of time, his engineers had designed and built a versatile yet inexpensive tractor. Unfortunately, however, Ford selected an inappropriate marketing and distribution strategy for the new product. He tried to market the tractors through his existing automobile distribution system, which was largely concentrated in major cities and was not attuned to the needs of farms. Hence his product (however good it may have been) never really reached its intended market. The venture failed commercially until Ford realized his mistake and created a supplementary distribution system that reflected market realities and communicated with the farming audience in its own terms.[3]

A Definition of Organizational Effectiveness

Steers defines organizational effectiveness "in terms of an organization's ability to acquire and efficiently use available resources to achieve their goals."[4] Thus, organizational effectiveness must be measured against the real intended strategies of an organization. It presupposes a degree of goal optimization. In Figure 5.3, Steers identifies the major influences on organizational effectiveness.

The concept of effectiveness has to be developed in relation to the real objectives of the organization. Thus, effectiveness is best understood in terms of a continuous process rather than an end state. Second, since the criteria for effectiveness vary from moment to moment in an organization, contingencies are critical in any discussion of effectiveness. When managers understand these vital aspects of effectiveness, they can respond to the realities of organizational life.

OPERATIONALIZING OBJECTIVES

To operationalize objectives effectively, managers have to establish a climate that will allow things to happen. Management climate is a unique combination of policies, structures, and reward systems. The

[3] Reprinted by permission of the publisher, from "When Is an Organization Effective?—A Process Approach to Understanding Effectiveness" by Richard M. Steers, *Organizational Dynamics* (Autumn 1976). Copyright © 1976 by AMACOM, a division of the American Management Associations. All rights reserved.

[4] *Ibid.*, pp. 55–56.

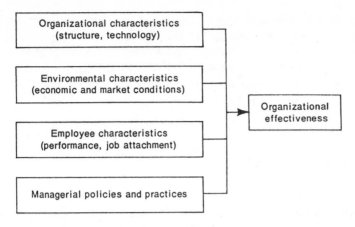

Figure 5.3   Major Influences on Organizational Effectiveness

climate of an organization is based on such factors as goal clarity, autonomy, rewards, supportiveness, tolerance of conflict, and the need for innovation. Basically, climate describes how people perceive their work environment.

Research suggests that managers can change the work climate if they realize that there is a problem and are willing to try to solve it. Gordon and Goldberg discuss the case of International Harvester, which was experiencing severe difficulties in both net income and earning during the years from 1967 to 1971.[5] A new chairman insisted that a climate study be conducted among senior members. The study produced the following perceptions:

1. a lack of a sense of direction;
2. insufficient delegation of authority and discouragement of individual initiative;
3. a short-term emphasis on decision making; and
4. highly strained communications.

The new chairman developed a climate that improved not only planning, delegation, and performance but also profitability. How are these climate changes to be achieved? Most successful managers and experienced behavioral scientists argue that members of organizations must

[5] Gordon and Goldberg, "Is There a Climate for Success?" p. 42.

have a broad understanding of the objectives and some of the plans that guide their firm's managers. Development of managers' objectives can proceed top down or bottom up. Usually effective goal formation starts at the top, but somehow or other it mobilizes the people at the bottom. One way to make the route of objective setting a two-way street is through management by objectives.

MANAGEMENT BY OBJECTIVES

To achieve organizational objectives, the people who do the work, make the decisions, and implement them must get involved. A widely respected method for doing just this is management by objectives, or MBO. MBO has been a major topic of discussion and debate for the last 20 years. Developed by Peter Drucker, the management consultant, MBO is a process that requires a manager to use participation in establishing objectives for his unit. These objectives must be defined in terms of their contribution to the larger organization of which the manager's unit is a part. The whole point of MBO is that subordinates participate in the establishment of viable objectives; thus, their commitment is achieved. Box 5.3 tells a little about Drucker and his philosophy of management.

Making Management by Objectives Effective

Too often, systems of MBO become ends in themselves rather than tools to help managers do their jobs more effectively. Too many organizations have plunged into MBO without considering the complexities of the situation. Figure 5.4 shows how activities interlock in MBO systems. Frequently, MBO is approached in a bureaucratic manner; to get the program operational, someone invents appropriate forms, instructional manuals, review dates, and check points. As a consequence, the system supersedes the people. MBO has typically been used for planning, control, evaluation, and compensation.

To get MBO programs operational, there must be a workshop for the prospective participants. The underlying philosophy, objectives, processes, and limitations of MBO must be explained. The firm needs a consultant who can sit down with individual members of a work group, help them write objectives, and then be a third party in the group's objective-setting sessions. MBO programs cannot change man-

Box 5.3: Peter Drucker

Many of the most interesting developments in modern management have come from Peter Drucker, who invented management by objectives. Drucker, a Viennese-born lawyer, had to flee Europe when Hitler came to power. When Drucker came to the United States, he acted as a management consultant to a large number of important U.S. firms, including General Motors. For Drucker, the first responsibility of management is human relations.

Some quotes from Peter Drucker:

Management

Management says the first job of the supervisor is human relations. But when promotion time comes they promote the fellow who puts in his paperwork.

Management by objectives works if you know the objectives. Ninety percent of the time you don't.

The main impact of the computer has been the provision of unlimited jobs for clerks.

Specialists and Experts

Many believe that if people are sufficiently poor and live in sufficiently

From John J. Tarrant, *Drucker, The Man Who Invented the Corporate Society* (Boston: CBI Publishing Co., Inc., 1976).

agerial behavior and attitudes en masse; to be successful, they must catch on at the bottom.

Objectives should be few in number, and statements of objectives should concentrate on "what" and "when" and not on "why" and "how." There are four categories of objectives:

1. innovative,
2. problem solving,
3. administrative-ongoing, and
4. personal.

One expert provides a useful set of guidelines for writing objectives:

Start off with an action verb.

Identify a single key result for each of the objectives.

Give the day, month, and year of estimated completion.

Identify costs, i.e., dollars, time, materials, and equipment.

State verifiable criteria which signal when the objective has been reached.

horrible conditions, they become honest. In all recorded history there has not been one economist who had to worry about where the next meal would come from.

Organizations

Growth that adds volume without improving productivity is fat. Growth that diminishes productivity is cancer.

People

Strong people always have strong weaknesses. The question is not, "How will he get along?" but "What will he contribute?"

Himself

Most corporations consider me harshly critical. My clients don't consider me a management consultant but a management *in*sultant. Measurements are cheap, so I use all of them. When you have 186 objectives, nothing gets done. I always ask, "What's the one thing you want to do?"

Be sure the objective is controllable by the person setting the objective and, if not totally controllable, at least isolate the part that is.[6]

In preparing lists of objectives, people should limit themselves to ten key objectives that are clearly set out and represent things that need to be done. One value of having a clear statement of an objective is that it can be easily changed.

MBO cannot operate effectively unless you have committed people working in your organization. The aim of the program is to help people manage by objectives and results rather than crisis and charisma. This aim can only be achieved by getting people committed.

The Widespread Use of MBO

MBO is widely used not only in the U.S. but in Canada, Britain, Europe, and Japan. Its appeal is based largely on its common-sense

---

[6] "Make Your MBO Pragmatic" by John B. Lasagna, *Harvard Business Review* (November-December 1971). Copyright © 1971 by the President and Fellows of Harvard College; all rights reserved.

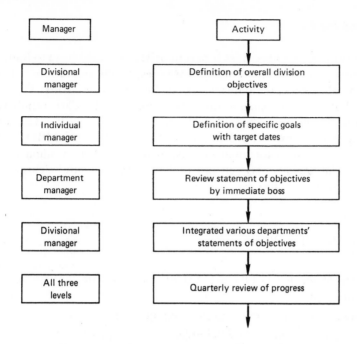

Manager	Activity
Divisional manager	Definition of overall division objectives
Individual manager	Definition of specific goals with target dates
Department manager	Review statement of objectives by immediate boss
Divisional manager	Integrated various departments' statements of objectives
All three levels	Quarterly review of progress

Figure 5.4   MBO: How Activities Go from Level to Level

approach and its simplistic format. It is valuable because it enables planning to take place at a fairly low level in the organization, provides a valid review of progress, improves motivation and commitment, focuses organizations on the achievement of results, increases interaction between managers and their subordinates and, last but not least, creates a pleasant and stimulating climate.

Some research suggests that MBO has not always been an unqualified success. Many MBO programs lack any scientifically organized evaluation. What evaluation is carried through is usually done by the researchers who install the program. Second, there appears to be no one best way of implementing, modifying, and evaluating MBO. The cost of implementing the various phases of diagnoses, preparations for objective setting, intermediate reviews, final examination, and feedback is substantial. Although the costs of consultants' fees and the time the managers spend away from their regular tasks are relatively easy to measure, the benefits from increased profitability and improved motivation are more difficult to tally. Much more evaluation of MBO must be done before hard-pressed managers can become convinced of its payoffs.

MBO and the Future

In spite of the difficulties inherent in MBO, it continues to flourish. According to George S. Odiorne, MBO is especially relevant in fields in which the objectives are financial (profits, ROI, sales, and costs). Odiorne argues that "the charismatic, intuitive manager's days are numbered. The costs of failure are becoming higher, and the necessity of advance planning has become more apparent to most firms."[7] MBO makes management more functional because it leads to better management control: relationships between pay and performance, and clearer definitions of strategic objectives.

REVIEW AND RESEARCH

1. What do the letters OPOSLED stand for? How are the various steps connected?
2. How are planning and controlling connected?
3. How does a scenario link the objective to the plan?
4. Using the concepts of comparative advantage, resources, and probable results, formulate a new plan of action for an organization with which you are familiar.
5. List all the possible objectives you can think of for General Motors. Organize these objectives into a pattern.
6. Compare and contrast the objectives of the major U.S. automobile manufacturing firms.
7. What is lateral thinking?
8. Describe how you would introduce MBO to an organization with which you are familiar.

ORGANIZATIONAL GROWTH CHANGES
OBJECTIVES: *What Went Wrong at Chrysler?*

Like organisms, organizations are conceived and born; they grow, mature, achieve uniqueness, decline, and die. For a long time, we thought large organizations were immortal. Then Penn Central, Rolls

[7] George S. Odiorne, "MBO in the 1980's: Will It Survive?" *Management Review* (July 1977), p. 40.

Royce, and Lockheed all either had close calls or went bankrupt and had to be resuscitated. The latest case is the Chrysler Corporation. Financiers and bankers are periodically forced to debate whether Chrysler is a chronic invalid or a stripped-down corporation with the ability to bounce back after each cyclic downswing of the market.

Chrysler, with sales of $11 billion, is one of the biggest U.S. manufacturers. As such, it is particularly vulnerable to the ups and downs of the market. Although it has 15 to 17 percent of the U.S. car market, Chrysler has only 6 car assembly plants (G.M. has 23 and Ford 15). Therefore, Chrysler cannot fine-tune its production; it takes more risks with market forecasting. Large inventories of cars can be deadly dangerous. In the 1975 recession, Chrysler had to spend $2 million a week to finance the 135-day backlog of unsold cars.

Corporate health is measured by the ability to mobilize, develop, and operationalize the structures, processes, and values that will generate productivity and satisfaction. But production of what, and satisfaction for whom? The answers vary from year to year, even from minute to minute. Effectiveness means innovation and adaptation.

A smaller, leaner Chrysler Corporation has shown the auto world how to adapt by not innovating. General Motors and Ford have had subcompacts since 1970. With the U.S. market for compact and subcompact cars consistently increasing, Chrysler, which has no subcompacts, has been progressively forced into a corner. Chrysler's answer is essentially nontechnological and managerial in character. Its strategy is to import the small Plymouth Arrow made by Mitsubishi, Chrysler's Japanese partner. (This strategy is essentially a repeat of the scenario Chrysler followed in 1970, when it imported two "new" subcompacts: the Plymouth Cricket from England and the Dodge Colt.) And instead of shrinking the size of its big cars, as Ford and G.M. are doing, Chrysler is simply moving the names of its bigger cars to existing smaller models.

Chrysler is bringing in cars, tooling, and components from its English and Japanese "members" instead of designing its own new four-cylinder engine and chassis. By copying tooling, design, and planning, Chrysler has a sure-fire capability. Thus, in spite of a fantastic debt-equity ratio (37 percent, compared with G.M.'s 7 percent, Ford's 24 percent, and American Motors' 20 percent), Chrysler had a blueprint for a trimmed down company that could break even under even the most pessimistic conditions.

Traditionally, innovation means responding to the mandates of technology and the whip of the marketplace. It means living dangerously. Chrysler has shown that to stay healthy, the corporate organism does not in fact need to grow.

Organizations, like human beings, get sick, suffer from growing pains, and sometimes grow obese. They get flabby and have to be trimmed down. Each time Chrysler has a slump, its recovery has less bounce, and its profit margins are smaller.

What went wrong at Chrysler was that Chrysler never had a clear idea of what its purpose was. Top management could never really decide what kinds of cars they ought to build or what kinds of customers they ought to reach. While it is clear that Chrysler had both high costs and financial weaknesses, its real problem was the lack of a clear concept of its product and of the market that it served.

The essence of the matter is that the concept of the product dominates strategy. Henry Ford's idea of an inexpensive car for the masses still dominates the Ford Motor Company. Although Ford makes expensive products such as the Continental, most Fords have been designed as low-price models.

Chrysler's strength lay in engineering; the company has done an outstanding job in developing products with engineering break-throughs. Unfortunately, the company is dominated by engineers' judgments. Most of the time Chrysler has been unable to get a competitive advantage from new engineering features as, for example its introduction of the push-button transmission in the mid-50s. What it amounts to is that Chrysler has responded to engineering inventions rather than to the needs of the market.

Although most teen-agers can rank different G.M. products in some kind of hierarchy (a Buick is better than a Chevy), very few know that a Dodge is supposed to outrank a Plymouth. Chrysler needs to study the demographics and psychographics of its customers. Chrysler buyers are a little older than average; their incomes are a little lower in almost every category of car. They also tend to be significantly more conservative than other car buyers.

Chrysler apparently made a mistake in pushing the racing image tied up, for example, with the Dodge Charger and the Plymouth Road Runner. One of the reasons was that Dodge's traditional owners are not very youthful. But Chrysler has been strong in selling small cars, especially the Plymouth Valiant and the Dodge Dart.

What it amounts to is that Chrysler has pushed too hard for distinguished styling and has not paid enough attention to the strategy of avoiding the loss of established customers, who are interested in economical and reliable cars.

Towards the end of 1975, John Riccardo and Eugene Cafiero took over the reins of the Chrysler Corporation. They rejected the approach that had been Chrysler dogma for ten years: instead of great gambles for great gains, the new goal simply was to make a good, steady profit.

In 1978, Ford's Iacocca assumed the top position. The important thing about the Chrysler case from our point of view is that it illustrates what a complex process objective setting is and how publicly stated goals are frequently at variance with privately held views. Second, business organizations seem to live from crisis to crisis. Each time they are rebuilt, they come out with a different portfolio of objectives. When all is said and done, it is impossible to deny the role that luck plays in determining outcomes. Management is a very difficult business, full of hazard and risk, and objectives frequently have to be trimmed if they are to be in line with means.

Chrysler is going through tremendous adjustment pains, in spite of the success of the Aspen and Volare. Nevertheless, in April 1978 Chrysler sales led both G.M. and Ford. Of course, Chrysler was helped by the decline of the value of the dollar, which has forced many foreign car makers to increase prices. In brief, Chrysler is responding to dramatic changes in environment dictated by new government standards on fuel efficiency and safety and by the competition from G.M., Ford, and imports. Our brief look at the Chrysler Corporation shows that organizations can be adaptable to their environment. They can be ready to respond to changes by repudiating outdated concepts and firing people who have outlived their usefulness. This is a tough proposition for modern managers to accept.

6

Moving
from
Strategic
Objectives
to
Operational
Goals

Define planning.

Explain the differences among strategic, operational, and tactical planning.

Specify the techniques used in forecasting.

Illustrate how forecasting can go wrong.

Describe how corporate planning works.

Illustrate how General Motors put strategy into action to market the Chevette on schedule.

Translating objectives into operational realities takes strategic planning. Planning operationalizes both goals and ways of achieving them. Planning is an interpretation of the past as a means of changing the future. But to change the future, something must be done in the present.

Plans cannot be formulated unless we make some attempt to predict the future. Forecasting involves realistic and knowledgeable estimates of future facts. A whole raft of techniques has been borrowed from futurologists to help managers predict what is going to happen. As you read this chapter, keep in mind that management is essentially a translation process, a process of translating strategy into action.

A DEFINITION OF PLANNING

Planning means working out where you want to go and developing a possible sequence of events that will get you there.

In brief, plans spell out goals and ways of achieving them. Figures 6.1 and 6.2 show simple and more complex plans. Only the simpler plans are free of contingencies, or blockages. Now the odd thing about planning is that business executives have such an ambivalent attitude towards it. American executives, for example, are hostile towards government planning of the economy, yet they try to control their own share of the market very carefully.

Although few firms follow the strategic plans they have prepared, firms that have corporate planning departments are more successful than their nonplanning counterparts. More planning is needed because of:

1. uncertainty about the future,
2. longer lead times, and
3. the necessity of larger investments.

STRATEGIC PLANNING

One of the most intriguing developments in the last decade has been the rapid spread of the strategic planning concept. Strategic planning

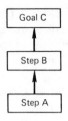

Figure 6.1   Simple Plan

is a systematic means by which a firm can become what it wants to be by:

1. specifying long-term objectives or purposes of the firm.
2. identifying the constraints on resources, and
3. identifying strengths and weaknesses.

The company sets out to identify its present position and where it would like to be. The strategic plan is the bridge between the present and the desired positions. Once again, we must highlight the differences between objectives and goals. They have these dimensions:[1]

1. *Time frame.* An objective is timeless, enduring, and unending; a goal is temporal, time-phased, and intended to be superceded by subsequent goals.
2. *Specifity.* Objectives are stated in broad, general terms, dealing with matters of image, style, and self-perception; goals are much more specific, stated in terms of a particular result that will be accomplished by a specified date.

Figure 6.2   More Complex Plan

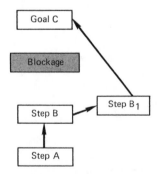

[1] Richard F. Vancil, "Strategy Formulation in Complex Organizations," *Sloan Management Review* (Winter 1976), pp. 1–18. Excerpted by permission.

3. *Focus.* Objectives are usually stated in terms of some relevant environment that is external to the organization; goals are more internally focused and carry important implications about how the resources of the organization shall be utilized in the future.
4. *Measurement.* Quantified objectives are stated in relative terms. A quantified goal is expressed in absolute terms.

Figure 6.3 shows a hierarchy of plans with specific detailed goals.

STRATEGIC VERSUS TACTICAL PLANNING

Reviews of the literature and actual observation of executives at work show that there is considerable confusion about the distinction between strategic and tactical planning. Part of the problem is that the decisions

Figure 6.3   Hierarchy of Plans, Including Production, Marketing, and R&D

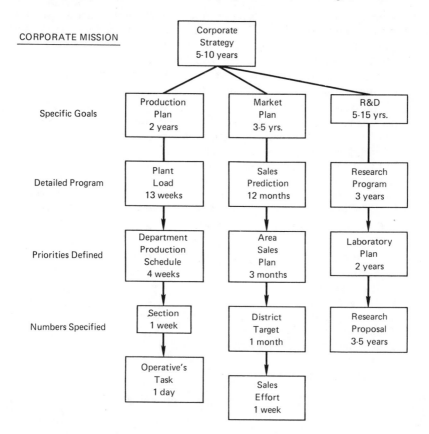

which appear to be strategic to one person may, in fact, be tactical to another. As one expert says:[2]

> 1. The longer the effect of a plan and the more difficult it is to reverse, the more strategic it is. Therefore strategic planning is concerned with decisions that have enduring effects that are difficult to reverse; for example, next week's production planning is more tactical and less strategic than planning a new plant or distribution system. Strategic planning is long-range planning. Tactical planning is of shorter range. But "long" and "short" are relative terms and therefore so are "strategic" and "tactical." In general strategic planning is concerned with the longest period worth considering; tactical planning is concerned with the shortest period worth considering. Both types of planning are necessary. They complement each other. They are like the head and tail of a coin: we can look at them separately, even discuss them separately, but we cannot separate them in fact.
>
> 2. The more functions of an organization's activities are affected by a plan, the more strategic it is. That is, strategic planning is broad in scope. Tactical planning is narrower. "Broad" and "narrow" are also relative concepts thus adding to the relativity of "strategic" and "tactical." A strategic plan for a department may be a tactical plan from the point of view of a division. Other things being equal, planning at the corporate level is generally more strategic than planning at any organizational level below it.
>
> 3. Tactical planning is concerned with selecting means by which to pursue specified goals. The goals are normally supplied by a higher level in the organization. Strategic planning is concerned with both formulation of the goals and selection of the means by which they are to be attained. Thus strategic planning is oriented to ends as well as to means. However, "means" and "ends" are also relative concepts; for example, "advertising a product" is a means to the end of "selling it." "Selling it," however, is a means to the end of "profit," and profit is itself a means to many other ends.

A strategic plan has the following characteristics:

1. It is high-level.
2. It is general.
3. Its time span is long-range (more than 3 years).
4. It affects the whole organization.
5. It is developed from the ground upwards.
6. It plans a wide diversity of activities.
7. It exploits a particular concept.

[2] Russel L. Ackoff, *A Concept of Corporate Planning* (New York: John Wiley & Sons, 1970), pp 4–5.

Determining Feasible Strategies

In developing a feasible strategy, an executive must consider potential market available resources and opportunities and constraints of the environment. Figure 6.4 shows an example of these three factors and a possible strategy. The strategy, which may be useful for an engineering consulting company, takes all three factors into account.

DEVELOPING A STRATEGY BY EXPLOITING A WEAKNESS OF A COMPETITOR

For the engineering consulting company in Figure 6.4, strategic planning is oriented towards the deployment of resources. Developing a strategic plan requires describing your company's past position, its present position, and its future goals.

A good strategic plan takes into consideration not only your own company's strengths and weaknesses but the competition's as well. In assessing the competition, remember that most companies gradually

Figure 6.4   An Engineering Consulting Company's Strategy Formation

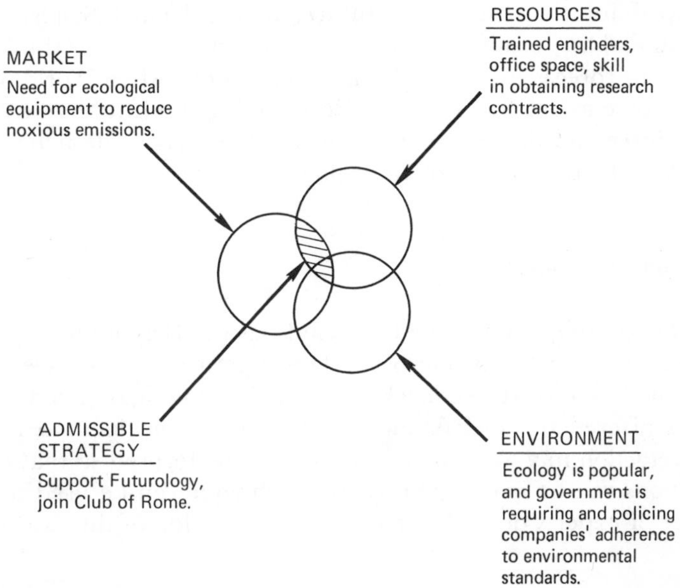

RESOURCES

Trained engineers, office space, skill in obtaining research contracts.

MARKET

Need for ecological equipment to reduce noxious emissions.

ADMISSIBLE STRATEGY

Support Futurology, join Club of Rome.

ENVIRONMENT

Ecology is popular, and government is requiring and policing companies' adherence to environmental standards.

adjust their products and prices over a period of time. As a result of these gradual, small changes, a company may have moved out of one market and into another. Perhaps it has left a hole in the market system that you may be able to fill. A good example of such a marketing opportunity is Holiday Inn. After beginning as a low-budget motel chain, Holiday Inn gradually traded up. After a while, the market was ready for new types of low-budget motels built by other firms. A similar phenomenom compelled Sears Roebuck to cut prices and bring its stores back to Sears' original market. Companies must continually ask themselves not only "what business are we in?" but also "are we acquiring old and tired images?" One technique for answering such questions is forecasting.

FORECASTING

The Basis of Planning: Forecasts

If planning is to be action-oriented and concerned with deciding what is to be done in the future, it must be based on sound information. This information must include realistic and knowledgeable estimates of future facts. Such "guesstimates" are collectively known as forecasts.

Box 6.1 describes some of the research techniques that have been developed for forecasting the future. In the United States, in fact, forecasting has become a major growth industry. One "think tank" devoted to forecasting is the Rand Corporation. After World War II, the air force asked Rand to assist in planning the future role of both the air force and the aerospace industry. Rand has made many contributions to the technology of futurology.

The Delphi Technique

One technique developed by Rand was the Delphi method, which polls experts on various questions. The experts need not meet face to face, but they receive feedback both on the data aggregated and the reasons offered for specific judgments. The Delphi method manages this interaction in a way that allows views to be focused so that realistic predictions can be made. The Delphi technique can be used to poll a number of experts on such topics as the population of the world in the

Box 6.1: Forecasting Methods

Jury of executive opinion. This method consists of combining and averaging top executives' views concerning the item to be forecast. Generally, the company brings together executives from areas such as sales, production, finance, purchasing, and staff operations in order to get the benefit of broad experience and opinion. Often staff groups supply background information to the members of the executive group. This approach has the advantages that forecasts can be provided easily and quickly without elaborate statistics and that a range of management viewpoints can be considered. Also, it requires fewer data than mathematical techniques do.

Time series analysis. Several different methods belong in this category. The most common are exponential smoothing methods and moving average methods. The general approach is to identify a pattern representing a combination of trend, seasonal, and cyclical factors based on historical data for that variable. That pattern is then smoothed to eliminate the effect of random fluctuations and extrapolated into the future to provide a forecast.

Regression analysis. Regression analysis assumes that the variable to be forecast (the dependent variable) can be predicted on the basis of the value of one or more

year 2000, the price of a barrel of oil in 1990, or the passenger-carrying capacity and speed of airliners in 1985.

Scenario Writing

Herman Kahn of the Hudson Institute invented the technique of scenario writing, which involves writing a hypothetical story triggered by a specific event. Box 6.2 describes the scenario for a nuclear disaster. Another scenario might begin, "General Electric has developed a solar cell, which can heat a four-bedroom house." The scenario writer may go on to describe the effect of this development on house building companies, electric heater manufacturers, and family life styles and leisure activities.

One of the major criticisms of Herman Kahn and his associates at the Hudson Institute has been that they have achieved their predictions mainly by extrapolation. Until recently, all of Kahn's predictions have seemed to indicate that such "up-and-coming" countries as Japan and Germany will produce more and more, and such "less effective" countries as Britain will produce less and less.

The unstated assumption of the Kahn argument is that economic

independent variables. For example, if company sales were the variable to be forecast, they might be dependent on time, the economy, or sales of major customer industries. Regression analysis is a statistical technique that fits the specified model to the historical data available. One of its major attractions is that, as independent variables take on new values, the dependent variable will also change. Thus it goes beyond simple time series extrapolations and bases a forecast on a casual relationship.

Sales force composite. The sales force composite approach to forecasting involves obtaining the views of salespersons, sales management, or both, on the outlook for individual products and/or total sales. This is generally a bottom-up approach, since different salespersons can estimate sales for only some subdivision of the company, and these can then be combined to get an aggregate forecast of sales. Like the jury-of-executive opinion, this approach is not statistical but has the advantages of integrating judgmental factors and experience in situations where historical data may not be available or applicable. However, it has the disadvantage of being susceptible to the biases of those who are most influential in the sales group.

Index numbers. Index numbers are most commonly used to provide a basis for anticipating short-term fluctuations caused by seasonal or cyclical patterns. For exam-

---

growth is good and big is best. This assumption has produced a strong reaction from the neo-Malthusians, who regard such social scientists as growth maniacs.

Computer Simulation

The neo-Malthusians have developed another technique for forecasting the future. Their technique uses computer simulation. A mathematical model developed by Jay W. Forester allows them to make predictions about how capital, population, food, fuel, and pollution will grow in the future. The computer simulation developed by Dennis Meadows and his wife reveals what has been called the Doomsday Syndrome—"No matter what the world does before the beginning of the 22nd century, everything is going to end in disaster."[3]

While the Meadows' computer simulation has been challenged both on its conceptual basis and on the accuracy of their computer calculations, their work has been useful. It has forced academics and executives to think that "small is beautiful." This concept has had a tremendous effect on the consumer movement, which in turn has put pressure on the U.S. auto industry, for example, to produce small cars

---

[3] Dennis H. Meadows, D.L. Meadows, J. Ronders, and W. Behrens III, *The Limits to Growth* (New York: Universe Books, 1972), pp. 23–24.

ple, seasonal indices are often projected in order to determine how a company's sales might be distributed by month of the year. Such indices can be determined by simply looking at the ratio of sales for a given month to annual sales for each of the past several years. The most common use of index numbers is that made by the federal government for seasonal adjustments of variables describing unemployment and general economic activity. Another use is for the index of industrial production, which predicts a general trend for the aggregate level of output of the industrial sector. In preparing their own forecasts, many companies use index numbers from a government agency.

Econometric models. This approach to forecasting uses a system of simultaneous regression equations that takes into account the interaction between various segments of the economy and/or areas of corporate activity. Often, companies use the results of national or regional econometric models as a major portion of a corporate econometric model. While such models are useful in forecasting, their major use tends to be in answering "What if?" questions. These models allow management to investigate the impact of various changes in the environment and in major segments of the company's business on the performance and sales of the company.

Customer expectations. Like the method of sales force composite and the jury-of-

Continued on next page

that are safe, do minimal damage to the environment, and get more miles per gallon of gas.

Technological Forecasting

Closely related to computer simulation is technological forecasting (T.F.). Businesses are increasingly using T.F. as a means of assessing the effects of technological changes on their development. For example, T.F. has been used to predict the consequences of having relatively inexpensive television tapes with "playback machines" in middle-class homes in the U.S. Such machines would allow families to purchase current movies, which they could show in their own living rooms.

In deciding which of these techniques to use—T.F., scenario writing, the Delphi method, or computer simulation—corporate planners are guided by the tecnnique's accuracy, its cost, and especially whether it provides information or merely gets management to start thinking.

Estimating Four Economic Climates

Forecasting assesses or predicts future developments that have to be taken into consideration before an organization can formulate a

executive opinion, this technique seeks to combine managerial judgements in arriving at forecasts. However, rather than using judgments from those strictly within the company, this method seeks to use customers' expectations of their needs and requirements as the basis for forecasting. This is often done through selected surveys administered by a corporate staff group, or it may be done by the sales force gathering information from selected customers. While it has the advantage of recognizing changes in customer expectations at a fairly early date, this technique is difficult to use in markets where customers are numerous or not easily identified. Much of the forecasting done by market research groups is based on variations of the customer expectation approach.

Box-Jenkins method. This technique is a highly sophisticated approach to time series forecasting. It seeks to identify patterns in the historical values of a time series and then to extrapolate those patterns into the future. It has the advantage of being able to handle a wide range of time series patterns and to provide statistics indicating the level of accuracy that can be expected in a given situation. However, it is extremely complex and somewhat difficult to understand.

---

plan. In preparing forecasts, business firms must be able to make reasonable predictions about four kinds of economic climates: international (for example, the price of oil), national (rates of inflation), industrial (what will be our market share?), and entrepreneurial (will unions have a strike next year?). Even the largest firms have relatively little control over national and international events, although their impact is greater than we once thought.

Getting the Information Together

Business executives use a wide variety of information sources for forecasting. These sources vary all the way from newspapers, trade magazines, and management journals through computer simulations all the way to industrial espionage.

The American Management Association reports that most companies separate economic forecasting from specialized sales forecasting. In the sixties, corporate planners typically developed a consensus on how the economy was likely to perform over a period of time and developed a sales forecast to match that economic prediction. In the seventies' climate of double digit inflation, firms made more use of "what if" planning. Companies use "what if" planning to deal with high rates of inflation, dramatic interest rates swings, higher fuel costs, and greater government intervention in business.

130

The Great Nuclear Debate
    The trouble is first recorded by sensitive, computerized instruments in the control room of the nuclear power plant. They warn that temperatures inside the reactor are rising fast toward a danger point—so fast that only one explanation is possible: somehow, the main pipes carrying water to the reactor core have broken or clogged. As white-coated technicians look on helplessly, the back-up water system also fails. Deprived of the coolant that controls its temperature, the reactor begins melting in its own heat. Then the machine and its fuel collapse into a molten mass that explosively converts the coolant water into steam. The resulting blasts rip open the power plant's massive concrete dome, releasing a cloud of radioactive gases. Tens of thousands of people living near by are contaminated by radioactivity. Many die within days. Others suffer lingering illnesses and develop cancer years later.

Econometrics

There may have been a time thirty or forty years ago when executives could have done forecasting on the back of an envelope. Now very few can feel comfortable operating without access to an econometric model. Very large companies in the United States make extensive use of econometric models to forecast the national economy and the place of their industry in it.

Econometrics provides a mathematical portrait of economic phenomena. This portrait is drawn up by a computer and typically uses hundreds of interacting equations. These equations are theoretical but may be tested against historical data. Once a model has been developed, its predictive capacity is tested against various policy moods: higher (or lower) rates of inflation, changes in interest rates, higher oil prices, a looser monetary policy.

One firm, Data-Resources, Inc., has been perfecting a national econometric model. Into it are built 1,200 equations, to which 600 client corporations can have access through computer terminals located in their own offices. Using such a time sharing system, corporate planners in their head offices can ask the model certain "what if" questions. They can see how the answers affect the growth of their industry and the growth of their companies.

Computer-Assisted Forecasting

In the early sixties, systems analysts predicted that the computer would take over the business of making corporate decisions, and

131

executives would be relegated to setting out goals and handling human and public relations functions. Since the midseventies, a more realistic relationship has been established between the executive decision maker and the management scientist. Although more than half the companies in the *Fortune 500* have access to computer programs that model national and world economies, managers are still needed. Recent experiences with rigid long-range forecasts have forced managers to adopt a more flexible approach in the use of econometric models. As one expert points out:[4]

> The company maintains an elaborate mathematical model of the U.S. economy. This model consists of some 1,100 equations and other relationships, which are augmented by such exogenous factors as the anchovy catch off the west coast of South America, the Soviet grain harvest, elements of the energy crisis, OPEC decisions, and even the gross national product of Kuwait.
>
> Through multiple regression analysis, the model is manipulated by one of the fastest computers available. One object is to direct attention to relationships of particular concern—for example, the interplay between disposal personal income and automobile buying, both of which are estimated in the model. Another object is to encourage questions that can be answered by special computer runs and that can help to resolve doubts about major risks and uncertainties that might disrupt a company's planning and operation.
>
> Such econometric models also turn out economic forecasts of varying length and detail. On the whole, they are quite reliable for the short term of about 90 days, and those for 10 to 15 years ahead are worthy of confidence, although they are scanty on detail about fluctuations during that period. But econometric forecasting is probably soundest when projected roughly 2 years into the future. Strangely enough, there seems to be a parallel with weather forecasts, which are surprisingly credible about 2 weeks to a month ahead, whereas daily forecasts have improved only slightly over the past 50 years.

FORECASTING PROBLEMS

Especially in an inflation-ridden economy, forecasting can be treacherous. Such relatively simple techniques as moving or weighted averages

[4] "Shaping Decisions with Systems Analysis" by George A.W. Boehm, *Harvard Business Review* (September-October 1976). Copyright © 1976 by the President and Fellows of Harvard College; all rights reserved.

and regression analysis can be counterproductive, because the basic economic factors are changing in unpredictable ways. During the 1973–75 recession, for example, prices moved down far more slowly than they had in previous economic downturns. According to a 1976 study of the White House Council on Wage and Price Stability, this phenomenon was caused by the removal of wage and price controls, the quadrupling of oil prices, massive food exports and poor crops, speculation on raw materials, and worldwide inflationary pressures.

Floating exchange rates may play havoc with the company that is selling abroad. A good example of this problem is provided by a quick look at the British pound. In December 1975, the pound stood at $2.05, having fallen from $2.80 in 1967. In the first five months of 1976 the pound dropped to as low as $1.65. Such large changes in currency make forecasting an extremely difficult affair.

Equations Don't Always Behave as They Should

To make their estimates, forecasters look at such measures as rate of change of GNP, wholesale price indexes, percentage of manufacturing capacity utilization, and the cost of living index. Economists set up equations and attempt to show the relation between different factors. But occasionally these equations do not work effectively. To help executives make forecasts, the *Wall Street Journal*, *The New York Times*, and other newspapers produce frequent summaries of how the economy is doing and how particular industries are faring. In the forties, estimates of GNP growth were linked to such factors as the annual production of sulphuric acid. Now automobile sales, housing starts, and the purchase of other consumer goods are used as guides to the state of the economy. Particular attention is paid to measures of productivity, capital outlays, and short term bank rates. But things can still go awry.

The Difficulties of Forecasting

Economists have great difficulty in making forecasts mainly because they are unable to determine how long present trends are likely to continue. In brief, their difficulties stem from problems of defining the length and gradient of the business cycle. Ever since John Maynard Keynes published his general theory in the 1930's, economists have been committed to the idea that the government should accept responsibility for the management of aggregate demand. Out of this concept emerged the idea that permanent prosperity was only a matter of careful fiscal management. But the 1973-75 inflation turned economic theory upside down, as economists had to grapple with double-digit inflation. In fact, economists did so badly in forecasting in the early seventies that Walter Heller dubbed 1973 "a year of infamy in inflation forecasting." Nearly all economists missed the economic implication of the jump in oil prices, and they failed to forecast the deflationary consequences. Thus, for the last few years, the forecasts of economists have been treated with considerable reserve. To remedy this situation, economists are trying to make shorter forecasts.

Dramatic changes in the environment have compelled companies to invest more efforts in corporate planning and to define the relationship between short-term and long-term planning. Typically, firms plan on a five-year basis; increasingly, however, disturbed by the difficulty of forecasting in the turbulent contemporary environment, many firms are projecting for only three years.

Forecasting activities can be divided roughly into three forms. The first, short-term forecasting, usually has a period of one to two years. This forecast becomes the basis of the second form, a broader, less detailed five-year plan. Third, a long-range plan raises broad questions about broad issues. Make no mistake about it; top executives can make terrible mistakes in planning. Vast sums of money were tied up in the building and operating of huge transatlantic liners which faced more competition from jet planes than company executives counted on. The forecasts were wrong, and some firms faced disaster. Several factors make forecasting very difficult:

1. The contemporary environment is uncertain and turbulent. For example, the disappearance of low-cost energy has had a great unforeseen impact on American life styles.
2. It is no longer possible to rely on economic forecasting alone. Political, social, and technological forecasts are also required.
3. Single-line forecasts are no longer appropriate. Contingency ("what if") planning is needed to meet the multiple possibilities that can affect both short-term and long-term evaluations.
4. To meet the complexity of the situation, firms are increasingly using futurology in middle-term planning. Scenario writing, the Delphi method, and T.F. make the actual act of planning even more complex.
5. Short-term planning is essentially operational in nature and is greatly preoccupied with ensuring cash flows.
6. Corporate planners are finding it very difficult to reconcile short-term planning (month-to-month estimates of cash flows, sales forecasts, and budgets), with middle-term planning (time horizons of three to five years, which are greatly influenced by inflation and interest rates), and long-term planning, which deals with basic issues (are we in the automobile business or the transportation business?).

Corporate Planning In Action

To overcome some of these difficulties, planners in large corporations are recognizing that managing is more of a gamble than it has ever been. They are developing a sceptical attitude towards the basic laws of planning, which experience has shown to be faulty. I.B.M., for example, develops short-term forecasts that fit its two-year operating plan. But the company also has conditional forecasts and slightly longer ones to facilitate the development of new production lines. These forecasts are regularly monitored to take into consideration such economic surprises as the actions of O.P.E.C. Furthermore, I.B.M.'s forecasts are only the top of the planning iceberg, which extends right into the organization. Firms like the General Electric Company, with more than 100 production lines, plan for each product separately. This is because the typical cycle of a new model toaster lasts only about three years, whereas the cycle for a new jet engine may last twenty years.

FROM STRATEGY TO OPERATIONAL GOALS

For I.B.M. and G.E., management is essentially a translation process—a process of translating strategy into action, of translating concepts into working systems. The sequence is something like this. Someone has an idea. This leads to the formulation of strategy. Strategy must be translated into action through the development of operating goals.

For example, in the sixties the Ford Motor Company asked, "What business are we really in?" Instead of taking the view that its business was primarily the production and distribution of cars and trucks, the company argued that its job was "making devices to move people and goods with whatever radical kinds of hardware were most likely to meet the needs of future customers." Ford began to form a "transportation research group" that would plan for the manufacture of auto trains, rapid transit systems, and other means of transportation beyond Ford's traditional product line.

Developing Specific Goals

To be effective, an organization must move from a strategic plan through an overall objective to specific goals. In 1975, for example, Chairman William Seawell of Pan American World Airways, which was in severe financial difficulty, developed and operationalized the following plan:

> *Strategy:* Survival of Pan Am
> *Overall Objective:* Cut Costs
> *Specific goals:* 1. Cut kerosene costs by $30 million.
>   2. Drop unprofitable flights.
>   3. Lay off 10 percent of the labor force.
>   4. Get and hold breakeven point at 49.9 percent of seats filled on an average flight.
>   5. Sell least efficient airliners.
>   6. Prepare to buy Boeing 747 SP that can fly New York-Tokyo nonstop.
>   7. Swap routes with TWA and American Airlines.
>   8. Evaluate possibility of merging TWA and Eastern Air lines to acquire domestic airline.
> *Result:* Third-quarter profit of $42.1 million (versus loss of $520,000 for the same period of 1974)

Meaningful Objectives for Each Executive

To achieve this kind of turnaround management Chief Executive Seawell had to ensure that his senior executives would provide a guide for action for the middle managers of his company. It is not enough to provide "the big picture"; specific objectives must be spelled out. These objectives must have a quantitative measure and a definite date for achievement.

INTEGRATING STRATEGIC AND OPERATING PLANS

For business organizations to be effective, they must interlock strategic and operating plans. Many companies make considerable investments in terms of time and money to develop long strategic plans; few companies make the effort to integrate plans at different levels. The following case illustrates how operating plans can become uncoupled from the very strategy they are supposed to achieve.[5]

[5] "Coupling Strategy to Operating Plans" by John M. Hobbs and Donald F. Heany, *Harvard Business Review* (May-June 1977). Copyright © 1977 by the President and Fellows of Harvard College; all rights reserved.

The manager of a consumer durable goods business concluded that, in a climate characterized by recession and rapid inflation, the fastest way to improve profitability was to fill out his product line. Accordingly, he authorized engineering to design a new appliance and asked manufacturing to tool up for an initial production run of 2,000 units. For his part, this manager included in his strategic plan profit targets that reflected the market's (hypothesized) favorable response to this new offering.

Signs that something was amiss soon reached his desk. Performance data revealed that the field failure rate for the new product was significantly higher than that for older models.

An investigation pinpointed waht had gone wrong. Engineering had prepared an operating plan that recognized the broad intent of the new strategic plan. Unfortunately, the design engineers had not specified a quantitative quality standard for the initial prototypes. It seemed safer for engineering, if not for the business, to await field results on the initial 2,000 appliances. This low-level decision took little heed of the following facts:

1. Manufacturing had invested millions of dollars in a new production line for this prototype. If engineering were to renege on the original product specifications that manufacturing had followed in laying out that line, much of this investment would have to be written off.
2. The financial goals that the profit center manager had set depended on the timely and profitable introduction of the new appliance. If engineering took six months to finalize product specifications, these goals would not be met and the corporate office would be asking why.

When this instance of uncoupling was eventually brought to the attention of the profit center manager, he could not believe his ears. How could such an obvious deficiency in functional planning skills go undetected for so long? He intervened. The linchpin between the strategic plan and engineering's operating plan was reinserted, by edict.

If corporate managers are going to be effective in introducing change and minimizing strategic shock waves, they must give careful attention to integrating plans at various levels. If companies are developing functional plans in the areas of personnel, marketing, and logistics, top management must make sure that they can be interlocked into the company's strategic plan. This adds increasing complexity to planning. Box 6.3 gives a specific illustration of how logistics, marketing, and strategy are interlocked. To achieve this integration, top management is using a form of "group think" in developing corporate strategies.

Logistical considerations play a critical part in the development of a strategic plan. Logistics is the study of supply, the management of inventories, and the location of plants and warehouses. In essence, logistics deals with matters of plant location, sources of raw materials, and standards of customer services. As James L. Heskett of the Harvard Business School has pointed out,

> Logistics can spell the difference between success and failure in business. For example, a few years ago a young engineer-entrepreneur began to build a company from scratch. His first product was liquid bleach. Actually, he didn't know much about the business at the time. He knew that liquid bleach is nearly all water and that the U.S. market is divided among two large manufacturers, Clorox and Purex, and a number of smaller producers that sell branded and private-label bleach on a regional basis. He also knew that the market for private-label bleach in New England, where he wanted to be,

"GROUP THINK" AT THE TOP OF THE MODERN CORPORATION

Because of the increasing complexity of planning at the top in the large corporation, a growing number of companies are creating the "office of a chairman." The object of this exercise is to develop a cabinet of four or five top officers who share the responsibility for decision making and planning.

Two U.S. companies who have recently adopted this "group think at the top" are Trans World Airlines and Sears Roebuck. At T.W.A. this cabinet approach enables the chief executive and his two senior vice presidents, one for corporate affairs and the other for finance, to work as a team. At Sears, the office of the chairman is manned by the chairman, the president, and the senior vice president. In fact, many other companies, large and small, use the cabinet approach. An especially good example is I.T.T., which developed a multiple management plan to prepare for the retirement of its chief, Harold Geneen.

There are great advantages in this "group think" arrangement. For one thing, it is a useful way to achieve continuity. Second, it provides excellent on-the-job training for budding chief executives. Third, it provides companies with the opportunity to give additional attention to such optional extras as corporate planning. But it also has a supreme disadvantage in that it allows ambiguity of command.

138

was dominated by a manufacturer located in New Jersey.

So the entrepreneur decided to found a private-label bleach manufacturing company near Boston. This location provided his company with a distinct transport cost advantage over its chief competitor. But he didn't stop there. He located his plant near a concentration of grocery chain retail outlets. This enabled him to sell his bleach under an arrangement in which retailers' trucks were loaded with his bleach after making their retail deliveries and before returning to their respective distribution centers. Given this double cost advantage, he was able to go one step further. By adding other items to his product line, he was able to obtain efficient truckload orders from his retail chain customers.

Thus logistics have a critical role in formulating strategy, particularly where the goal is increased market shares or increased profits.

Planning and Policy

With cabinet "group think," planning and policy are intimately interlocked. It is often forgotten that major developments in planning come not from econometric analysis but from bold changes in policy. General Motors has always known how to lead the U.S. automobile industry. An example of this leadership was G.M.'s decision to make every year a new model year, as opposed to Ford Motor Company's reliance on one particular model that did not change from year to year.

General Motor's 1977 models were a foot shorter and 700 pounds lighter than their 1976 counterparts. Instead of G.M.'s old policy of "longer, lower, wider" cars, their 1976 cars were shorter, higher, and narrower. According to the Environmental Protection Agency, G.M.'s "fleet wide" gas average rose from 16.7 to 18.4 miles per gallon. In spite of such gas savings, this new G.M. policy was considered risky by its top executives. The big question was, do people really want small cars? Do they want cars like the Chevette?

Getting the Strategy into Action: The Chevette

A good example of getting the strategy into action is provided by General Motors' development of the Chevette. The Chevette, whose name is a hybrid of Chevrolet and Corvette, is a subcompact. G.M.'s strategy was to meet foreign competition, particularly from Toyota, Datsun, and Volkswagen.

General Motors had two basic alternatives: build the car from scratch, or adapt an existing model. Faced with a choice, G.M. executives set up a list of criteria that helped identify the correct option:

1. The subcompact had to be in the sales rooms in the fall of 1975.
2. It had to have an MPG comparable with Volkswagen's and Datsun's.
3. It had to use some of the toolings General Motors had available in U.S.
4. The car had to meet American safety requirements, especially in regard to low-speed collision characteristics and emission standards. In particular, the car had to withstand a five mile-an-hour crash into a barrier without damage to lights, gas tank, tailpipe, radiator or hood, and trunk latches.

G.M. decided to adapt an existing model.

Steps in the development of the Chevette

The twenty one months that it took to put the American Chevette on the market were gruelling ones. Several weeks were spent acquiring the blueprints from Opel in Germany and General Motors in Brazil. G.M. decided to modify the body and develop a hatchback. A number of features of the European underbody had to be modified, including the bumper and the anticorrosion requirements. The body also had to be redesigned to get the fuel tank out of the passenger cabin.

It was decided to offer the Chevette in two versions: a four-seater base model, which cost anywhere from $3,100 to $4,000, and a two-seater scooter model.

Operating objectives

A major objective of the Chevrolet engineers was to adapt the design of the German-Brazilian car to American production lines. This meant, for example, that some of the parts of the body were made from a number of pieces that fitted American dies and presses rather than from a single piece.

Why the Chevette strategy worked

By employing a particular strategy, General Motors was able to beat out the opposition by two years. The Chevette policy was successful because:

1. The G.M. executives knew from the moment they made the decision that there would be twenty-one months to design, test, manufacture, and distribute the car. Normally it takes forty-eight months to accomplish these goals; the best G.M. had ever done was forty-six months.
2. Top management decided that rather than going for an entirely new car, they would capitalize on the design of one of their foreign subsidiaries.
3. G.M. decided to Americanize the German-Brazilian model. This increased the chances of appealing to the American driver.

REVIEW AND RESEARCH

1. Why do firms plan? Why do they not make full use of their plans? Why is planning so difficult?
2. Distinguish between strategic and tactical planning.
3. Develop a plan for your business school to help small businesses in your area.
4. How can planning be made more participative? How can junior management be more involved in planning? Why are American shop floor workers reluctant to be involved in company planning?
5. Use the Delphi technique to poll faculty members on their estimate of the population of the U.S. in the year 2000.
6. Why are corporate executives frightened by econometric models? How can this fear be conquered?
7. What does the planning of the Chevette tell you about the corporate methods of G.M.? Were the G.M. planners right? What was wrong with their assumptions? How could these problems be anticipated?

PAUL SCOTT

In March of 1975, Mr. Dickinson, manager of financial planning for a major manufacturing concern, hired Paul Scott for the position of financial analyst. The financial planning department was a closely-knit group of three, consisting of the manager, a market research specialist, and a specialist in corporate-level financial analysis.

Paul was thirty years old, unmarried, with a bachelor of commerce degree and a work background in accounting and finance, coupled with office management experience. After three weeks on the job, Mr. Dickinson was impressed with the quality of Paul's work papers. The papers were, in fact, an accountant's dream—neat and beautifully cross-referenced, with source data and computation methods well-defined.

Over the next two months, the following events took place:

- ☐ Paul was commended on his work papers and took this opportunity to indicate what a terrible mess the previous incumbent had left behind. Mr. Dickinson, who had worked with Paul's predecessor for three years and frequently referred to the work papers, knew this was not the case.
- ☐ On two consecutive Mondays, Paul telephoned in ill. On both occasions, the air conditioner in his apartment had gone off in the night and his sinuses were bothering him.
- ☐ Paul was sent on a two day course to become conversant with a computerized financial planning model recently designed by Mr. Dickinson in conjunction with a computer service bureau. Paul asked for an extra day's instruction because of "inadequacies on the part of the instructors" and this was arranged.
- ☐ Subsequent to his course, Paul reported to Mr. Dickinson that he had gone to the in-house terminal, "talked to the computer to build his own model, and input data to his model but could not get it to work."
- ☐ Mr. Dickinson received a visit from George, the head office manager responsible for the computer terminal. George said that he had a secretary in tears over Paul. It seemed that Paul had asked her for the key to the terminal room, gone about his business, and, when returning the key, gave the young lady a scathing attack for turning over the key for something as critical and costly as a terminal to someone she did not know. Mr. Dickinson then spoke privately to Paul who repeated essentially the same story, except that his verbal attack was reported as being not harsh but well deserved.

Mr. Dickinson, after reflecting on Paul's performance over three months, called Paul into his office and . . .

1. What should Mr. Dickinson do about Paul Scott?
2. Develop a plan for the interview that will enable Mr. Dickinson to attain his objectives.

7

Selecting a Management Design

Define roles, and show why roles
have to be defined in groups.

State the principles of design
for the classical organization.

Describe Likert's linking-pin
human relations design.

Link systems design to project management,
task forces, and matrix management.

Outline why an organization changes
from a functional structure to a matrix.

Develop a contingency approach for the
selection of organizational designs.

After setting the objectives and developing a plan, the next step in the management process is to select an organizational design. Basically, organizing is made up of two steps: analysis, which breaks the mission into jobs, and synthesis, which puts the jobs together into units.

THE PRINCIPLES OF CLASSICAL ORGANIZING

Before discussing classical organizing, it might be helpful to review structure. As you may remember, structure can be broken into three elements: rules, roles, and relations. There are two basic types of *rules:* break tasks into bits, and arrange the tasks into sets, *Roles* are determined by people's expectations, not by the person occupying the role. A role cannot be defined individually; it must be defined in a set. *Relations* in organizations come in three forms—line, function, and staff. Now, how can we put these three elements of structure together to get the business done?

CONCEPT OF ROLE

Structure, which describes the shape or framework that holds the system together, is essentially static in nature. Expectations, when they are organized around particular functions, are called roles. Like actors in the theatre, executives usually have a script, props, prompters, players, acts, scenes, scenarios, producers, directors, and rehearsals to help them fulfill their roles.

As an aspect of organizational structure, a role may be defined as a social position. It is marked by three characteristics:

1. The person occupying the position is expected to behave in a particular and predictable way that is appropriate to his function, regardless of his personal needs.
2. To perform these functions, the role holder has certain rights and duties.
3. Each role has a particular status which defines its relative standing in the hierarchy. (Box 7.1 humorously shows status symbols associated with roles in one company several years ago.)

When a person takes up a position, he is said to be "playing a

Box 7.1: A System of Status Symbols

Visible Appurtenances	Top Dogs	V.I.P.s	Brass	No. 2s	Eager Beavers	Hoi Polloi
BRIEF CASES	None—they ask the questions	Use backs of envelopes	Someone goes along to carry theirs	Carry their own—empty	Daily carry their own—filled with work	Too poor to own one
DESKS, Office	Custom made (to order)	Executive Style (to order)	Type A "Director"	Type B "Manager"	Cast-offs from No. 2s	Yellow Oak—or cast-offs from Eager Beavers
TABLES, Office	Coffee tables	End or decorative wall tables	Matching tables Type A	Matching tables Type B	Plain work table	None—lucky to have own desk
CARPETING	Nylon—1 inch pile	Nylon—1 inch pile	Wool-Twist (with pad)	Wool-Twist (without pad)	Used wool pieces—sewed	Asphalt tile
PLANT STANDS	Several—kept filled with strange exotic plants		Two—repotted whenever they take a trip	One medium-sized; repotted annually during vacation	Small; repotted when plant dies	May have one in the department or bring their own from home
VACUUM WATER BOTTLES	Silver	Silver	Chromium	Plain painted	Coke machine	Water fountains

	Private Collection	Autographed or complimentary books and reports	Selected references	Impressive titles on covers	Books everywhere	Dictionary
LIBRARY						
SHOE SHINE SERVICE	Every morning at 10:00	Every morning at 10:15	Every day at 9:00 or 11:00	Every other day	Once a week	Shine their own
PARKING SPACE	Private in front of office	In plant garage	In company garage—if enough seniority	In company properties—somewhere	On the parking lot	Anywhere they can find a space—if they can afford a car
LUNCHEON MENU	Cream Cheese on Whole Wheat Buttermilk and Indigestion Tablets	Cream of Celery Soup Chicken Sandwich (White Meat) Milk	Fruit Cup— Spinach Lamb Chop— Peas Ice Cream— Tea	Orange Juice Minute Steak French Fries— Salad Fruit Cup— Coffee	Tomato Juice Chicken Croquettes Mashed Potatoes Peas—Bread Chocolate Cream Pie—Coffee	Clam Chowder Frankfurter and Beans Rolls and Butter Raisin Pie à la Mode—Two Cups of Coffee

Monsanto Company, *Exec-Chart: A Ready Guide for Evaluating Executives*. Reprinted by permission.

role." This refers to how the self is presented, to what people who interact expect of each other. Roles must be learned. Thus, it is useful to think of the role as a patterned sequence of learned actions. When an individual carries out his role, reciprocal expectations are always involved. The instructor cannot instruct unless the members of the class act like students. Likewise, an executive cannot assume the role of the superordinate unless some other person takes up the role of subordinate. Reciprocity always implies the existence of a relation between role holders. A role never exists in a social vacuum; it always exists in relation to other roles—the role set. In management, the position to be defined is the focal role. In defining a particular position, it is necessary to specify not only the focal role but the role senders. For example, if we wish to define the role of foreman, we must also define the superordinate (department manager and personnel officer), collateral (other foremen with whom he interacts, production planner, and work-study officer), and subordinate roles.

Typically, the official role description includes a job title, an introductory paragraph setting out to whom the person is responsible, his colleagues, the numbers and kinds of subordinates, a list of functions and duties, kinds of decisions to be made, the physical and mental requirements for the job, tools and equipment used, lines of promotion, and the terms of employment. Box 7.2 describes a number of roles managers play.

JOBS

A job is something somebody does on a regular basis for something else, usually money. How has it come about that "just doing my job" has become such a chore? To get at the root of this problem, it is necessary to go back to Taylor and his associates, who invented the modern method of defining jobs.

Job Analysis

Job analysis is the purely theoretical study of a job in order to discover its component parts, duties, physical and mental requirements, and necessary tools. Job analysis typically also includes a statement of the minimal IQ, education, age, and aptitude requirements; the conditions of the workplace are also specified. Job analysis is "purely theoretical"

Managerial activities may be divided into three groups—those that are concerned primarily with interpersonal relationships, those that deal primarily with the transfer of information, and those that essentially involve decision making. It is for this reason that the ten roles are divided into three groups—three *interpersonal* roles, three *informational* roles, and four *decisional* roles.

The manager's position provides the starting point for this analysis. Earlier the manager was defined as that person formally in charge of an organizational unit. This formal authority leads to a special position of status in the organization. And from formal authority and status come the three interpersonal roles. First and most simple is the role of *figurehead*. The manager has the duty of representing his organization in all matters of formality. Status enables the manager also to play the *liaison* role, in which he interacts with his peers and other people outside his organization to gain favors and information. The third interpersonal role, that of *leader*, defines the manager's relationships with his subordinates—motivating, staffing, and so on.

The interpersonal roles place the manager in a unique position to get information. His external contacts bring special outside information and his leadership activities

Continued on next page

because so few jobs are scientifically analyzed. What typically happens is a person leaves his job and has to be replaced.

Let us assume you are his boss. You contact personnel. Personnel tells you to complete an "indent for labor replacement form." You get a copy of the form, which asks you to specify job title, to whom responsible, list of duties, decisions to be made, hazards, special clothing, and so on, including "the kind of person to fill the role." You complete the form and send it to personnel. Personnel has a set of job definitions, which they assemble from their records, other companies' records, and the American Management Association's files. Personnel writes up a job description from your invention and his.

Now, you may wonder why jobs are *not* scientifically studied. The first reason is that the process is expensive and time consuming; second, jobs change with new technology and material; third, people do not like being studied, and thus they frequently try to mislead the job analyst. Fourth, we do not have a good theory of work.

We do not know in a complete sense what the elements of work are. Certainly, we know and can classify activities such as "grasping a bolt, placing it in the hole . . . ," but we have no ready means to measure such perceptual elements as "visually check insulin level in ampoule."

Trying to develop scientific job descriptions can be a long, frus-

serve to make him a focal point for organizational information. The result is that the manager emerges as the key nerve center of a special kind of organizational information. Of the three informational roles, the first—*monitor*—identifies the manager as receiver and collector of information, enabling him to develop a thorough understanding of his organization. The second role, termed *disseminator,* involves the transmission by the manager of special information into his organization. The third, the *spokesman* role, involves the dissemination of the organization's information into its enviroment.

The manager's unique access to information and his special status and authority place him at the central point in the system by which significant (strategic) organizational decisions are made. Here four roles may be delineated: In the *entrepreneur* role the manager's function is to initiate change; in the *disturbance handler* role the manager takes charge when his organization is threatened; in the *resource allocator* role the manager decides where his organization will expend its efforts; and in the *negotiator* role he deals with those situations in which he feels compelled to enter negotiations on behalf of his organization.

trating, and soul-destroying task. Employees hate them because they limit variety, reduce autonomy, cut down interactions, abbreviate knowledge and skill, reduce responsibility, and dehumanize the job. (Hence the need for job enrichment, which we shall deal with in Chapter 13.) As a postscript, perhaps it is worth mentioning that managers' jobs are hardly ever studied, scientifically or otherwise.

Departmentalization: Grouping Jobs

The next step is to organize the jobs into groups according to some principle—purpose, process, procedure, person, place, or function. Frequently a manufacturing plant is broken into departments according to such activities as production, marketing, finance, research and development, and engineering. (See Figure 7.1.)

Figure 7.1   Some Companies Are Organized According to Geographical Area (See Figure 7.2)

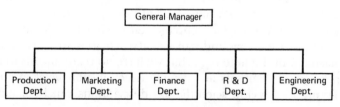

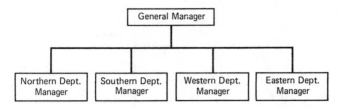

Figure 7.2   Sometimes Companies Organize by Product (See Figure 7.3)

The Managing of Roles

Roles are managed primarily through the exercise of authority and power. The exercise of authority always involves moral considerations. To issue orders a superior has to be seen as legitimate by his subordinates. He has to act "out of the office," and his instructions have to be seen as credible. The authority process presupposes a social contract between the two or more parties concerned. To maintain this particular contract, a social ritual has developed. When authority is properly exercised, certain values—legality, precedent, and legitimacy—are invoked.

Roles can be managed in a number of different ways. Classical managers have developed a whole range of techniques for putting subordinates in roles and making them follow the formal job description. Human relations managers take quite a different view and approach the subject of role management in an indirect way, through establishing a climate of values that allows employees to expand their conception of the role in a way that is appropriate to their personal needs.

The Classical Model of Organizing

What model does the classical manager use as a means of stimulating what happens in a business? Until about twenty years ago, the

Figure 7.3   Often the Process is Broken Down into a Number of Subprocesses, which Are Allocated to Separate Departments; These Departments Are Grouped into Divisions (See Figure 7.4)

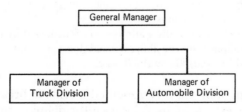

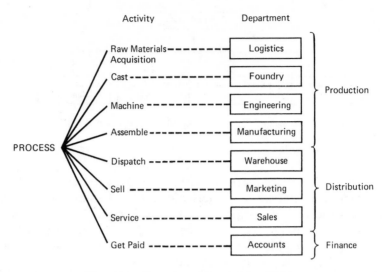

Figure 7.4   Departments Grouped into Divisions

principal model was the organization chart, which had sets of role descriptions defining who was who on the chart. What were the assumptions on which this model was based? Some of the assumptions were:

1. Organizations are like pyramids—decisions flow down, and reports flow up.
2. Unity of command—one employee, one boss.
3. The chief executive is like a conductor of an orchestra. He knows all the players; they can all see him; they know both the score and what he wants; they are all going to play the same tune. They are going to play only well-established works.
4. The chief executive likes an organization chart with "line" and "function" clearly delineated.
5. The ultimate satisfaction for the chief executive is a clearly written role description with an introductory paragraph, a list of functions and duties, a schedule of events and decisions, and a note specifying "the kind of person to fill the role."
6. The chief executive enjoys discussions about the span of control, product organization, process organization, and the various minutiae of managerial functions.
7. The model is essentially static—action is achieved by pulling strings.
8. The metaphor of the map is used for communications, which are achieved by going through channels.

The organization chart represented a brilliant breakthrough in its day and was an extremely useful device for defining roles and formal communication routes. But it is less relevant when you try to describe what is happening in terms of either process or values. To include these two other characteristics, we need a different model.

THE PRINCIPLES OF HUMAN RELATIONS ORGANIZING

The classical form of organizing generates some problems. In organizations that are too rigidly structured, employees feel stifled and alienated; they have a general feeling that the organization is not making the best use of human resources. To overcome these difficulties and make. the best use of the potentials that people bring to work, a more human relations orientation is required.

The basic assumptions of human relations organizing include these assumptions:

1. that people are creative, responsive and responsible;
2. that people function better in an open work environment with superiors who are supportive, employee-centered, and democratically oriented;
3. that people work better in groups where they belong and where they have good standing; and
4. if people participate in the decision making that affects their work lives, they are more likely to feel involved and give of their best.

The Linking-Pin Structure

Rensis Likert developed these principles of human relations in an attempt to integrate the principles of group dynamics and business efficiency studies. Likert starts from the basic proposition that employees have basic needs for recognition, exercising influence, accomplishment, and respect from people they hold important and trust. In brief, a person wants to feel that he is somebody who counts. In his book *Patterns of Management*, Likert takes as his point of departure the principle of supportive relationships. He states that management must in all interactions and relationships be supportive and build and develop a sense of personal worth. To do this, management must make full use of employees' potential.

Based on his research, Likert has argued that managers are effective when they are supportive, friendly, and helpful rather than threatening. To be supportive, a manager must be kind but firm, just if not generous. He must show confidence in the integrity, ability, and motivation of subordinates. To do all this, the manager must be ready to coach and assist subordinates whose performance is below par. This means that the manager has got to spend a lot of time, not only in planning and scheduling the work carefully, but in providing adequate technical competence.

In this approach to organizing, the manager develops high group loyalty by using participation in all aspects of work. Likert also proposes an *integrating premise*, which argues that effective firms are made up of integrated work groups. These work groups are coordinated into an overall organization by people who have a linking-pin function. For example, the foreman links his primary work group of shop floor operatives to the departmental manager's group of which he is a member and such functional specialists as production planners and production engineers. Figure 7.5 shows Likert's principles of organization graphically.

Likert postulates an overlapping group form of structure in which groups are linked by members of more than one group. The emphasis is on effective group functioning.

When the group process of decision making and supervision is used properly, discussion is focused on the decision to be made. There is a minimum of idle talk. Communication is clear and adequately understood. Important issues are recognized and dealt with. The atmosphere is one of "no nonsense" with emphasis on high productivity, high quality, and low cost. Decisions are reached promptly, clear-cut responsibilities are established, and tasks are performed

Figure 7.5   Overlapping Group Form of Organization. From Rensis Likert, *New Patterns of Management*. Copyright © 1961 by McGraw-Hill Book Company. Used with permission.

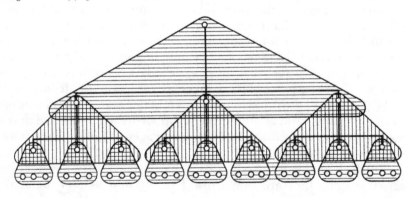

rapidly and productively. Confidence and trust pervade all aspects of the relationship. The group's capacity for effective problem solving is maintained by examining and dealing with group processes when necessary.[1]

Box 7.3 provides a good example of Likert's ideas in action.

SYSTEMS DESIGN

Beyond Human Relations

The human relations approach views the organization as a set of interacting groups and treats the employee as a social animal. In the late thirties and early forties, managers began to realize that work involved not only economic but social activity. In the human relations approach, an employee is seen as having a need to belong as well as having needs for recognition, achievement, and growth. The firm still behaves rationally, but rationality is tempered by human considerations.

But as managers gained more experience in applying the new human relations, they came to realize that it was not valid in all circumstances. They needed a new theory that would integrate the best features of the classical and human relations approaches. To achieve this integration, managers and social scientists invented the systems approach, which treats the organization as an organism that interacts with its environment. Information concepts play a very important part in the systems approach. Indeed, it is possible to liken the organization to a computer. The human model employed in this theory is called "administrative man." An early explanation of the concept stated,

Administrative man recognizes that the world he perceives is a drastically simplified model of the buzzing, blooming confusion that constitutes the real world. He is content with this gross simplification because he believes that the real world is mostly empty—that most of the facts of the real world have no great relevance to any particular situation he is facing, and that most significant chains of causes and consequences are short and simple. Hence, he is content to leave out of account those aspects of reality—and that means most aspects—

[1] Rensis Likert, *The Human Organization* (New York: McGraw-Hill Book Company, 1967), pp. 50–51. Copyright © 1961 by McGraw-Hill Book Company. Used with permission.

An example of participative management in action can be found in Donnelly Mirrors, Inc. Many managers regard D.M.I., which is located in Holland, Michigan, as the company that does the most to make it possible for people to succeed. D.M.I. holds 70 percent of the domestic market in automobile mirrors. From 1965 to 1975, its sales rose from $3 million to $18 million, and the number of its employees rose from fewer than 200 to more than 500.

D.M.I. achieves this kind of effectiveness because it operates on two basic assumptions:

1. Employees work better when problems are presented to them in terms they can understand.
2. The employees share equitably in any improvement made.

Shop floor operators are involved in the selection and design of equipment. At the same time, the workers are protected from the negative effects of improvements in productivity.

For instance, here's the sort of thing that happens: a team of five people was

that are substantially irrelevant at a given time. He makes his choices using a simple picture of the situation that takes into account just a few of the factors that he regards as most relevant and crucial.[2]

The computer has revolutionized not only data processing but how managers think. Thus, the computer has led not only to the development of control systems but has also dramatically changed how managers look at organizations. Increasingly, managers have turned to general systems theory for a better insight into the firm as an information processing system. This means that managers have to understand such abstruse subjects as probability if they are going to be able to bring corporate uncertainties under some measure of control. And of course, decision making is greatly influenced by information management.

As a manager ascends the hierarchy and spends more time making strategic decisions, he or she operates more by feel and intuition than by programmed technical techniques. He or she must become expert in communicating, must decide what he or she is trying to communicate,

[2] H.A. Simon, *Administrative Behavior: A Study of Decision-Making Processes in Administrative Organization*, 3rd ed. (New York: The Free Press, A Division of Macmillan Publishing Co., Inc., 1976), pp. xxix–xxx.

feeding and unloading a multistage injection molding machine. By their own decision, they modified the work so that four could keep the machine loaded. Since there were two machines operating three shifts, six jobs were eliminated. The holders of those jobs, though, were guaranteed a continuation of their wages for six months. All were placed in new jobs before the end of the six-month period.

Great emphasis is placed upon teamwork and communication at D.M.I. The key to communication between work teams is the linking-pin person. Owner and manager John F. Donnelly gives an example of how work teams make decisions.

Yes, we had an interesting thing happen recently. During the course of a decision-making process, one supervisor fell ill and an assistant took over for him. Somehow a rumor got into his department, the night shift, that his was the only group working in that factory that night and that the company had decided on a 2 percent or 3 percent wage boost for the year, which seemed utterly out of line. And so people decided to have a meeting right then and there. They had

Continued on next page

to whom the message is addressed, how his or her audience is likely to react, and how to ensure sufficient feedback.

The Organization as a Computer

The modern approach in our field is to view organizations (or any behavioral system) as information processing systems, which is essentially what the computer is. The computer analogy suggests that a system has subsystems, which are linked by information. (Information is defined as whatever reduces uncertainty. An organization's purpose is to reduce uncertainties as much as possible so it can plan with confidence.) The information network of an organization is equivalent to the nervous system of an animal. Components in the system perform such functions as searching the environment (the sensor subsystem), classification (data processing subsystem), decision making (decision-making subsystem), evaluation (control subsystem), storing and retrieval (the memory subsystem). Without information, there can be no planning or control. Information is the internal currency of a system. It is bought and sold, stored, and retrieved; it travels along the structures of an organization, both formal and informal. Box 7.4 explains how systems dynamics can model an organization.

the meeting, and the assistant foreman got the proper information and got them back to understanding what had really been said—that no decision about raises had been made. And they all went back to work, having decided that no injustice had been done.

D.M.I. has two systems, an executive system and a representative system. The executive system is made up of work teams. The representative system deals with frictions and problems that arise in the course of work. Every thirty-five or so employees elect a representative to sit on the Donnelly Committee, which is the essence of the representative system. Although every member of the committee has a vote, unanimous agreement is required for passing a recommendation. The critical question is, does the Donnelly approach to management work? Bill Melton, material control supervisor, answers.

... it's clearly understood by all of us. When something comes along—something like a schedule increase, a product variation, a method change—we

PRINCIPLES OF SYSTEM ORGANIZING

Open Systems

Systems adherents view organizations as open systems that trade with their environment. They import information, material, and energies and export them in another form to another system. The advantages of the systems approach is that it reveals organizations as social institutions; they achieve effectiveness by reducing disorganization.

Use of New Informational Technologies

In the modern view, organizations are systems of information flows—sets of black boxes connected by a series of inputs, transformations, and outputs. Information is the real organizational currency; it has to be researched, bought, processed, and sold to some other system. As a serial processer of information, the contemporary executive needs to reduce all the sensory data about his environment to a level he can handle. It is possible to develop a theory of organization in which everything—including role, status, and power—can be defined in informational terms.

158

try to decide how we can do that with the least amount of trauma and expense to the individual people. The people who are doing the routine manufacturing every day can be very helpful in developing a common-sense way to do it. In fact, even if they can't, it's worth involving them in it to the point that they understand completely what's going on. We don't get change orders that say, "You used to do that, but now you must do this." We minimize the number of failures on anything new we try by deciding ourselves. You'd be surprised how often people take pride of authorship in what they think up and what kind of effort they put in to make it work. Let me give you a recent example of what I call "participation." The group I supervise was going to have to face the task of taking the annual inventory. The amount of direction that I had to give for that was super nothing. The only thing I did was to get the group together and say, "Hey, you know annual inventory's coming up, and I want to know what-all we have to do yet and how long it's going to take." We had about six people, and in about six hours one evening they had the whole cotton-pickin' warehouse all organized, ready to go.

Creative Uses of Conflict

The modern view of conflict accepts conflict as integral to corporate life and seeks to exploit it.

New View of Authority

In the traditional definition of authority, the subordinate was presumed to suspend his critical faculties while receiving instruction from his superior. Nowadays, subordinates are more likely to think of themselves as responding to the ideas and needs of senior colleagues. Modern authority involves consensus management.

The Mobicentric Manager

The new manager, deriving his authority from and owing allegiance to some kind of professional association, considers himself or herself a consultant. He or she seeks out organizations that offer interesting opportunities. If one's present position loses interest, he or she moves on to the next place. Modern executives seek something challenging that will allow personal growth, recognition, and achievement.

Box 7.4: Systems Dynamics Can Provide a Complete Business Model

Jay Forrester and his colleagues at M.I.T.'s Sloan School of Management have developed a model based on systems dynamics. It uses feedback control in the form of "loops" to develop a complete model of the business. G. A. Boehm explains:

A complete diagram of a business—or even a segment of it—looks forbiddingly complex at first glance; it may contain hundreds of circles and squares connected by a maze of lines. But since each element is labeled and connecting lines explicitly show relationships, a persistent person can read and understand such a diagram. The same is not true for the ranks of equations in econometric models. Both types, of course, require computers for drawing conclusions. The procedure with systems dynamics is "simulation," which, in effect, makes the model act out its function under whatever conditions the analyst might specify.

When carefully constructed, a systems dynamics model often spells out an important lesson: complex systems generally behave counter to intuition. An obvious solution can, in many cases, exacerbate a problem.

For example, the management of a young and expanding company with slumping sales quite understandably thought of doubling its sales force, but computer simulation showed that the company had actually been putting too much emphasis on sales. Consequently, quality control and distribution had been seriously overtaxed so that previously satisfied customers were shopping elsewhere. Analysis suggested firing some salesmen, and taking that step restored the company's equilibrium.

MATRIX MANAGEMENT: A NEW ADHOCRACY APPROACH

"Adhocracy" is a term describing a new type of organization that is challenging the traditional bureaucracy. A short life span—a built-in obsolescence resulting from rapid and unexpected change characteristic of the turbulent environment of the 1970s—is the single most salient characteristic of the adhocracy. This approach requires radically different perspectives and postures: instead of permanence, it demands transience; instead of the organization man, we are confronted with the "mobicentric" (mobile) manager who thrives on high mobility between organizations and constant reorganizations within.

With the development of computer-based management information systems, there arose a need for new approaches to systems development organizations. First came the "functional groups" organization. This was soon replaced by the "project" organization, an adhocracy approach in which project teams were made up of individuals with the various necessary skills to implement the system. The newest concept, which is fast replacing the project organization approach, is the matrix organization. The matrix design attempts to benefit from both technical performance and coordination. Box 7.5 describes how the new matrix organization will be organized. Another organizational form is the project team. Box 7.6 describes this form of organization.

Management of the Matrix

Not all organizations need a pure matrix, and in those that do, it takes a special type of management to make the matrix work effectively. Figure 7.6 shows the matrix structure as a diagram.

Figure 7.6   Diamond Diagram of Communications

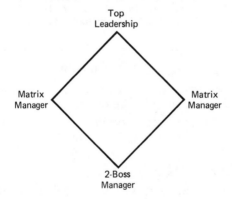

The leader must develop a peculiar blend of democracy and autocracy. This has been described as "I'm okay; you're okay; but I'm still the boss." The diamond diagram of communications, unlike the hierarchical pyramid, is basically unstable.

Given this instability a fair measure of conflict is to be expected. The focal center of this conflict is the two-boss manager, who experiences a great degree of anxiety and stress. Experts give this advice:[3]

---

[3] Reprinted by permission of the publisher, from "The Human Side of the Matrix" by Paul R. Lawrence, Harvey Kolodny, and Stanley M. Davis, *Organizational Dynamics* (Summer 1977). Copyright © 1977 by AMACOM, a division of American Management Associations. All rights reserved. Figure 7.6 is also from this article.

Groups are necessary for executive decision making because computer technology now makes it possible to generate and organize information that is beyond the capacity of one man to understand, much less to evaluate, and because they can generate internal commitment to decisions. Some executives doubt this and still hold the view that, if they had the right information, they could come up with the right decisions individually. This commitment is generated by "strong" and directive executives. However, research has demonstrated that directive, controlling executives become strong at the expense of the subordinates who became weak. Weak subordinates, in turn, protect themselves from the strong superior by carefully censoring the information they send to the superior, or "timing" the moment when he would receive it. These subordinates had learned that the safest tactic was to censor information or delay its transmission until a corrective solution could be shown. After all, they had learned to think positively, which usually meant, as one executive put it, "Do not bring up a problem without a solution." As a result, dry runs became a way of life; timing became even more valued than thinking; fighting and polarizing issues more rewarded than open cooperation and problem solving.

All these consequences tended to make the organizations increasingly rigid and sticky. The presidents soon became upset with these signs of organizational illness and responded by becoming even "stronger."

From Chris Argyris, "How Tomorrow's Executives Will Make Decisions." Reprinted by permission from THINK Magazine, published by IBM copyright 1967 by International Business Machines Corporation.

"Practices for Managing Matrix Relationships":

• Lobby actively with relevant two-boss counterparts and with your matrix boss to win support before the event.

• Understand the other side's position in order to determine where tradeoffs can be negotiated; understand where your objectives overlap.

• Avoid absolutes.

• Negotiate to win support on key issues that are critical to accomplishing your goals; try to yield only to the less critical points.

• Maintain frequent contact with top leadership to avoid surprises.

• Assume an active leadership role in all committees and use this to educate other matrix players; share information/help interpret.

• Prepare more thoroughly before entering any key negotiation than you would in nonmatrix situations; and use third-party experts more than normally.

• Strike bilateral agreements prior to meetings to disarm potential opponents.

• Emphasize and play on the supportive role that each of your matrix bosses can provide for the other.

Organizations of the future will depend less upon coercive power and more on competence—on a strong management team. Once organizations are able to process information effectively and quickly, the basis of influence will shift. Power will not be able to get anything more out of an organization than will brains and human commitment (unless the organization is inflexible and unable to respond to competence). In an open, trusting organization the power for action will come from having the right knowledge at the right time, and with each executive assisted by his colleagues.

Organizations of the Future

Changing the base of effectiveness from power to competence will not only narrow the use of power; it will also significantly alter the very design and makeup of organizations. The key qualities of the new organizations will be the adaptive, rapidly changing, temporary nature of the systems. People will be organized around specific skills.

For example, a matrix organization is designed less around power and more around who has the relevant information. A project team is created to solve a particular problem. It is composed of people representing all the relevant managerial functions

Continued on next page

- If all else fails:

    a. You can consider escalation (going up another level to the boss-in-common).

    b. You can threaten escalation.

    c. You can escalate.

Before traveling this road, however, consider your timing. How much testing and negotiating should be done before calling for senior support? Does the top leadership want to be involved? When will they support and encourage your approach? Does escalation represent failure?

To be effective in the context, the two-boss manager must be very flexible. But he must also remember that he is not without considerable power himself. This type of organization can be extremely productive, especially at the middle management level. Nevertheless, after years of experience with a matrix some organizations find they can dispense with its contradictory architecture and revert to the simpler pyramid. What this regression to hierarchy argues is that the matrix diamond is

(e.g., marketing, manufacturing, engineering and finance). Each member is given equal responsibility and power to solve the problem. The members are expected to work as a cohesive unit. Once the problem is solved, the team is given a new assignment or disbanded. If the problem is a recurring one, the team remains active. In many cases, especially in defense programs, the project manager is given full authority and responsibility for the completion of the project, including rewarding and penalizing team members. An organization may have many teams. This results in an organization that looks like a matrix:

Representatives of:	Project 1	Project 2	Project 3
Manufacturing			
Engineering			
Marketing			
Finance			
	Team 1	Team 2	Team 3

unlikely to become the basic architectural module of American organizations. Nevertheless many managers will spend some time playing one of the roles in the matrix diamond.

Costs and Benefits

The matrix organization has costs and it has benefits. The costs may take the form of increased overhead, of management time spent focusing on interaction, changing roles, or the ambiguity professionals may feel when faced with shared responsibility and mutual interdependence. Since the matrix form is designed to operate in an interactive environment, the team leader must create and maintain a climate for effective problem-solving activity. Naturally the matrix requires that various team members assume leadership from time to time as questions arise in each person's area of specialization; and all members are essentially on an equal level. However, specialists in a particular field

Organizations of the future will be a combination of both the old and new forms of organization. The old pyramidal forms will be more effective for the routine, non-innovative activity that requires little, if any, internal commitment by the participants. However, as the decisions become less routine, more innovative, and as they require more commitment, the newer forms such as the matrix organizations will be more effective.

The future executive, then, must have two interrelated skills: He must be able to differentiate clearly between the old and new forms, and he must know the conditions under which he will use the different organizational forms. Moreover, he will need to become skillful in several different kinds of leadership styles, each consistent with a particular form.

may react negatively to the vagueness of specific task responsibilities inherent in the matrix, and too much ambiguity may create tension and anxiety and impede problem-solving effectiveness.

Yet the benefits of the matrix organization seem to outweigh its costs. This organization differs from the project organization in that the team members join or leave the team as required, whereas in the project organization members are permanently attached. In the matrix concept, projects are organized to take advantage of the resource utilization efficiencies of the company's functional organization and at the same time to have the focused attention of project organization. The primary advantage of the matrix type of organization is its ability to create job enrichment by allowing larger work packages and introducing shared responsibility.

CONTINGENCY OVERVIEW TO ORGANIZATIONAL STRUCTURES

Organizational structure consists of much more than an organization chart. Organizational design is concerned with marrying strategies, structures, information, and decision processes to the reward system. The well-educated manager approaches the problem of selecting the organizational design with great care. As Jay Galbraith points out,

165

Box 7.6: The Project Management Team

Project groups of task forces are brought together to solve particular problems that are unusual, that demand considerable technological or organizational innovation, and that the company's normal management would have considerable difficulty in solving.

Typically the chief executive picks the project leader, who then bypasses the regular chain of command and reports directly to a member of top management. The project leader is usually given carte blanche in selection of his staff. If he is experienced he will also ask for terms of reference to be carefully spelled out. Such important matters as office backup staff, computer resources, consultancy support, and expenses are usually documented. The project manager typically chooses his staff according to the following criteria:

1. general problem-solving capability;
2. technical knowledge of a particular problem—usually a technocrat who has worked in the specific field;
3. ability to contend with cliques and cabals;
4. ability to enlist help of people not on the team;
5. computer skills—usually a mathematician or statistician;
6. literary skills—someone to write the final report; and
7. endurance—someone who is willing to work long hours.

The project manager spends most of his time working on the team's goals and demands for scarce resources.

Organizational design is concerned with decision process to bring about a coherence between the goals or purposes for which the organization exists, the patterns of division of labor and interunit coordination and the people who do the work. The notion of strategic choice suggests that there are choices of goals and purposes, choices of different organizing modes, choices of processes for integrating individuals into the organization, and finally a choice as to whether goals, organizations, individuals or some combination of them should be changed in order to adapt to changes in the environment. Organization design is concerned with maintaining the coherence of these intertwined choices over time.[4]

The classical school focused on the structure, paying particular attention to such concepts as authority and motivation, hierarchy, and line-staff relations. Classical designers allow managers to choose between centralization and decentralization. Human relations designers focus on the personal aspect of the problem. The systems approach is essentially

[4] Jay R. Galbraith, *Organization Design.* Copyright © 1977 by Addison-Wesley Publishing Company, Inc. Philippines copyright 1977 by Addison-Wesley Publishing Company, Inc., p. 5.

166

concerned with understanding decision-making processes. The contingency approach assumes that there is not one best way to organizing and not all ways are equally effective. The contingency approach tries to link task uncertainty to organizational design.

REVIEW AND RESEARCH

1. What are the functions of classical organizing? Are they still relevant? Why or why not? Why don't people study actual jobs? How do they get their information about jobs?

2. Describe a job you have actually done. How was the work organized? How could it have been improved?

3. What are the problems of U.S. automobile assembly-line organizing? Why are they so difficult to treat?

4. Why is human relations organizing effective in a supermarket? How does the customer organize the lives of the sales clerks?

5. Explain the success of the Volvo Plant at Kalmar. Are Swedish employees different from American? What is the American work ethic?

6. What is project management? In what setting could such a concept be employed? Why?

7. Find out how the faculty of your business school or university is organized.

8. How does labor organize? Do unions use different principles of organizing from those of business firms?

9. "Hierarchy is being replaced by peerarchy." Do you agree with this statement? Explain your answer.

10. How do John Morse and Jay Lorsch decide between Theory X and Theory Y?

CODETERMINATION AT VOLKSWAGEN

Under the German law of codetermination, seven labor representatives sit on the 21-member Volkswagen supervisory board. Codetermination is the mainspring of labor relations in West Germany. Volkswagen, which employs 90,000 workers and produces 2 million cars a year, has developed a joint decision-making process that connects the shop floor to the top management. In 1975 the supervisory board helped Volkswagen overcome its serious economic problems by developing a proposal for staggered cutbacks among its employees. The union representatives attend 6 or 7 board meetings a year with bankers, businessmen, and politicians. This system of codetermination works very well in West Germany.

Under new legislation, labor's 7 out of 21 votes on the Volkswagen board will rise to 9 out of 20. While there is a certain amount of political positioning in supervisory board meetings, most decision making is carried out in a slow, consensus-building way. The question in the United States is how American auto workers are going to adapt themselves to the concepts and hazards of codetermination. British workers of "Chrysler of United Kingdom" are seeking and probably going to get some kind of representation at the top management level. The United Auto Workers are now asking for a similar sort of representation on Chrysler top management decision making in the United States. Can codetermination work in the United States?

8

Staffing:
Hiring,
Firing,
and
Evaluating
Executives

OBJECTIVES YOU SHOULD MEET

Describe how companies recruit
and select their managers.

Outline the interviewer's strategy
in terms of his search for a stereotype.

Develop an effective job-hunting strategy.

Develop a guide
for using psychological tests.

Describe the various steps
in the assessment center process.

Describe how phased-out managers
can be given a new start.

Empathize with the executive
who has been fired.

List the principal performance
appraisal techniques.

Outline how appraisal can be
made more effective.

Three aspects of staffing (hiring, firing, and evaluating) are considered in this chapter. We begin by reviewing the problems of socialization that arise when a person attempts to take up his role in the organization. The presumption here is that most firms recruit junior managers from without and find their middle and senior managers from within their own organizations. We discuss the principal elements of the staffing process—recruiting, interviewing, and testing—paying particular attention to the interviewer's strategy. Next we will consider the group selection procedure, which is being increasingly used by American companies. After discussing the dynamics of firing, the final part of the chapter deals with performance appraisal. The aim of this part of the chapter is to show the executive how performance appraisal can be made to work.

HIRING

In any organization, one of the most important functions of management is identifying people who are likely to be successful as executives. The executive selection process begins long before the interview. Before we begin the subject of executive hiring, let us review how successful companies identify and recruit managers. Apparently, most firms find senior managers from within, but they recruit some junior managers from universities and colleges.

Although the demand for executives in the sixties was rapidly increasing, evidence now suggests that this demand is leveling off. How does a firm identify its best prospects for managerial jobs?

Identifying the Elite

Most large, successful companies believe in finding middle and senior managers from within their own organizations. When firms do go outside, it is because the right person cannot be found within. At lower levels, managers are brought in from outside. The large, successful, high-growth company typically has "arrangements" with a specific business school (or occasionally several), which keeps an eye open for talent that might be directed the company's way. But once they have attracted good managerial personnel, the policy tends to be promotion from within. This serves the purpose of facilitating socialization and ensuring that middle and senior managers have the necessary technical and organizational knowledge. Box 8.1 describes how a Texas Instrument's manager organized promotion from within by keeping a list of potential leaders.

Psychological tests for the selection of managers are not as common as one might expect from reading newspapers and business magazines. Surveys reveal that between 50 and 70 percent of firms surveyed use mental tests, mainly IQ tests, and a smaller number use personality tests. Many firms are somewhat reluctant to use tests for managerial candidates; and the more senior the appointment, the less likely will there be a test. Firms frequently use test data collected at the time of hiring for an employee's first move into the managerial ranks. The Early Identification of Management Potential (EIMP) test battery, developed at Standard Oil of New Jersey (SONJ) is frequently used for this purpose. A manager's scores are kept in his personnel record but are not available to his immediate superior. SONJ has carried out an extensive validation of the EIMP test. The study and its principal results have been described:

> Each of the managers took a lengthy battery of tests and completed a background survey covering home and family background, education, vocational planning, finances, hobbies and leisure time activities, health history, and social relations. The tests included measures of verbal ability, inductive reasoning, and management judgment (the ability to size up and choose an effective action in different human relations situations); an inventory of managerial attitudes; and personality measures (the Guilford-Zimmerman Temperament Survey). The scores on the tests were correlated with the standings of the managers on the overall success index. In addition, each of the items in the background survey and in the management judgment and Guilford-Zimmerman inventories was examined statistically to learn its degree of relationship with the overall success index. Since many items and even more responses were examined, double cross-validation was used to assure the stability of relationships discovered. The total of 443 managers was divided randomly into two subsamples of 222 and 221. Scoring keys were developed on each subsample and cross-validated on the other sample.

> Finally, the tests and responses showing the highest and most stable correlations with the overall success index were combined to yield a single score on the test and questionnaire materials. The correlation between the composite test score and the overall success index was .70. Figure 8.1 is a theoretical expectancy chart showing the accuracy of the composite test score for reflecting a manager's status on the overall success index.[1]

[1] From *Managerial Behavior, Performance and Effectiveness* by J.P. Campbell, M.D. Dunnette, E.E. Lawler, K.E. Weick. Copyright © 1970 by McGraw-Hill Book Company. Used with permission.

Fifteen years ago, when Patrick E. Haggerty headed Texas Instruments, he was worried about finding the right men to run the company in the future. By pioneering semiconductor technology, T. I. had helped spawn a whole new industry and needed top talent to manage its own explosive growth. Haggerty picked a hundred middle managers he considered "promising," then winnowed them down to fifteen potential chief executives. All in their thirties, with scientific backgrounds, they had performed exceptionally well and had shown prodigious appetites for hard work.

To this day the names on that list are not known—even to the men themselves—though a few have begun to emerge. Seven years ago, Haggerty chose Mark Shepherd Jr., 53, to succeed him as c.e.o. This month, a second name will become obvious. Haggerty, now 62, will retire, Shepherd will move up to chairman, and J. Fred Bucy, 47, will become president. If the directors limit the chief executive's term to ten years or less—as Haggerty has urged—Bucy will be running the corporation within a very few years.

Haggerty's program subjected the young managers to a series of difficult assignments—a kind of trial by fire. He knew the pace would wear down some, and that others would quit for more money elsewhere. Yet Haggerty never tried to outbid competitors for these executives, nor did he tell them how close they were to making

Continued on next page

Reprinted by permission of *Fortune* (April 1976), p. 29.

But SONJ is the exception; a relatively small number of companies do research on recruitment and selection. The interview continues to be the most widely used instrument for selection, in spite of its many imperfections. Firms use a wide variety of different interview techniques, ranging all the way from the highly structured (almost interrogations) to the rather unstructured (chats over cocktails). Executive

Figure 8.1 Expectancy Chart Showing Chances of Being in the Top Half on the Overall Success Index for Standard Oil Managers with Different Composite Test Scores

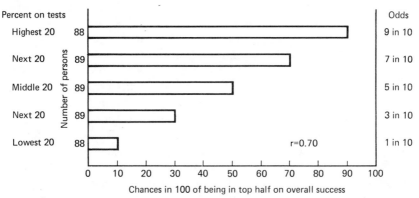

Chances in 100 of being in top half on overall success

From *Managerial Behavior, Performance and Effectiveness* by J. P. Campbell, M. D. Dunnette, E. E. Lawler, K. E. Weick. Copyright © 1970 by McGraw-Hill Book Company. Used with permission.

it at T. I. He simply kept reviewing the progress of those who remained, ranking and reranking them, and planning new tests.

Bucy moved out of research, took charge of government products in 1963, and four years later became head of the semiconductor division. In 1972 he led the venture into calculators—T. I.'s first entry into the consumer field. "When they threw me out to sea," says Bucy, "I made it to shore. And then they'd throw me out again." Reports Haggerty: "Bucy was innately a manager. When there was a crisis, he knew what to do."

After a full day at the office, Bucy carries home not one but *three* briefcases full of papers. Working past midnight, he tapes a dozen or more messages to managers all over the world. His secretary dispatches these "Bucy-grams" when he comes in at 7:30 A.M.

One way or another a good many Bucy-grams deal with what the company is doing to achieve its most ambitious goal: increasing sales sevenfold, to $10 billion—all from internal growth—by the late 1980s. That task is even more challenging than it might seem. For one thing, semiconductor companies stay in business by *lowering* prices, which means that T. I. cannot count on sales rising merely because of inflation. Moreover, T. I. has already grown large in an industry brimful of lively little competitors that are out to beat the giant. It will take a strong swimmer to stay ahead of that pack.

recruiters visiting college campuses use highly ritualized patterned interviews to determine whether to invite the candidate to visit the company for further interviewing. Apparently, in such on-campus interviews, the interviewers look for high grades, good personality, and expressiveness. They are put off by unrealistic goals and insincerity on the part of the candidate.

Most skilled personnel executives make considerable use of the application form. Surprisingly, although nearly all firms have considerable documentary information on the managerial personnel presently employed by the company (that is, they have completed application forms), little research has been done in this area. Firms collect written references but rarely base hiring decisions on them. Increasingly, enquiries are made by telephone, and careful attention is often paid to casual comments introduced by the referee. Occasionally, the whole matter of taking references gets complicated; sometimes the company requires references on the referees. Of course, "minor errors" creep into individuals' curriculum vitae over the years, especially in regard to such matters as dates of employment, education, military rank, age, or reason for leaving a former job. Most minor errors, if uncovered, are overlooked. Nevertheless, there apparently seems to be a small number of senior executives in both Europe and North America whose curriculum vitaes contain major falsehoods about academic degrees and the like. Nevertheless, they go from job to job either undetected or rewarded for their sophistication (or, possibly, exploited through blackmail).

A new selection technique that is being increasingly used is the assessment center. This evaluative method brings together many techniques, including interviews, tests, in-basket exercises, business games, leaderless groups, case discussions, and a variety of simulations to elicit patterns of behavior that have been defined by research as important in the manager's job. In the assessment center, a number of trained managers observe candidates for executive positions, usually for a period of two to three days, and then rate them on their suitability as managers. The assessment center, which draws on T-groups and other management training techniques, is attracting considerable attention and controversy. The controversy arises from the fact that the assessment center not only selects but socializes and trains. The question then becomes, whose values should the candidates be socialized to? Such an issue raises the general question of whether it is possible to separate the selection and training functions.

Executive Talent: Supply and Demand

In the early 1960s the demand for executives by industry, government, colleges, and universities was enormous. The main reason for this gigantic demand was that the job of managing and enterprising was becoming increasingly complex and therefore required an increasing number of sophisticated executives. In 1945, twenty-five of the largest U.S. corporations reported having an average of six vice presidents. By 1965, their number had increased to sixteen. Many were performing such new functions as public relations, tax computations, and government relations.

But the times are changing again. Employment opportunities for executives are likely to be far fewer, and the number of executives graduating from business schools is increasing. As one expert points out:[2]

> In 1964, only 6,000 graduate degress were granted in business administration. In 1976, it is estimated that upwards of 30,000 degrees will be awarded with women receiving some 10% of the total and minority groups receiving 5%. By 1985, it is forecast that the number of graduate degrees in business administration awarded will double this figure, with women making up a whopping 20% of the 60,000 total, or twice the 1964 total.

> It is more difficult to judge how minority groups will fare compared

[2] "The Coming Flood of Young Executives" by Arch Patton, *Harvard Business Review* (September-October 1976). Copyright © 1976 by the President and Fellows of Harvard College; all rights reserved.

to women, but it is generally projected that they will receive less than 5% of the total in 1985. However, this will be almost twice the total number of degrees they received in 1964. Thus not only will the number of highly educated potential business executives increase sharply, but also the effective total—including women and minority groups—will be far greater than might have been projected from reviewing the white male-dominated past . . . Unless the law of supply and demand is abrogated over the next decade, the huge influx of 30-year-olds into the job market will cause starting salaries for executives to decline. At the very least, salaries of young executives will advance more slowly than the compensation of the experienced executive, who will be in increasingly short supply as the decade unfolds.

The availability of women and minority groups as executive candidates is likely to further soften starting salaries. Historical prejudices do not disappear in a generation, whatever the laws prescribe, and both groups have always been paid less than white males.

Because of the change in supply and demand of executives, Patton argues that the manager's self-interest will cause him to consider such new options as professional associations. To cope with these professional associations, companies will have to handle the business of selecting, training, and motivating young executives in a more effective way.

The personnel job will require an executive of broad experience and abilities, who is sufficiently attuned to the company's plans, to hire, train, and provide incentives for the kinds of people the business will need when the future arrives. The personnel manager will no longer be a cast-off line executive or a specialist who never designed, made, or sold the company's products; instead, if this person can deal successfully with the next decade, he or she is likely to be the most promising candidate to be the next chief executive.[3]

The Interviewing Game

Personnel executives have spent a great deal of time and effort improving the rapport between the selector and the candidate. Yet there is no evidence that such an "improved" relationship improves the selection. Interviewees have, of course, invented a counterstrategy to meet personnel interviewers'. Some candidates wear glasses only when they are being interviewed. Dress regulations are developed. In the forties and fifties funeral garb was preferred—dark suits, ties, immaculate fingernails, and recently barbered hair. It apparently does not pay

---

[3] *Ibid.*, p. 180.

to be too good looking. The best bets are athletic, healthy looking men and women with good figures and pretty faces.

Intelligent candidates are ready for such questions as, "Tell me all about your education." They know how to respond to such questions as, "What is your principal disability?" They are not fazed by such questions as, "Where do you expect to be in twenty-five years?"

The trained interviewer usually reserves such open-ended questions until the end of the encounter, after he has worked through the three traditional acts of the interview. These phases are reduction of the superior-inferior relation, establishment of rapport, and termination of the interview. Usually the interview is brought to a close with two quick moves. The final question is, "Do you have any questions you would like to ask us?" which can be met with such disingenuous answers as, "Yes, do you have a planned career trajectory for someone like myself?"

In any case, regardless of the scientific data showing its lack of reliability and validity, its wide use of stereotype seeking, and the superiority of a combination of test data and autobiographical information the interview continues to be widely used. The main reason for its continuing use is that the interview begins the process of socialization, of fitting out the new employee to the rules, roles, and relations of the work group that he or she is about to join. Many executives and personnel specialists have met these "scientific" objections to the interview by recourse to group selection procedure. Group selection, or the assessment center, as it is called today, is a more potent technique for socialization than is the interview because the opportunities for dramatic conversion are so much greater.

Interviewer's Strategy

Instead of following the "oughts" of reducing the superior/inferior relation, establishing rapport, avoiding the halo effect (the tendency to rate a candidate high or low on all traits), and terminating the interview smoothly, most interviewers follow a more practical routine. As E. G. Webster, a well-known industrial psychologist at McGill University, points out, interviewers tend to: 1. develop a stereotype of the right candidate (salesmen have to have the two E's, the big E, ego drive, and the little e, empathy with the other guy), and they set out to match the interviewee to their cliché, even if they have to bend his personality on the way; 2. establish a bias early in the interview, and this bias tends to be followed either by a favorable or an unfavorable decision; 3. be more influenced by unfavorable than by favorable information (for example,

if you tell an interviewer that you left M.I.T. before finishing your
M.B.A. but that you completed the degree at Harvard, he or she is
more likely to consider you an M.I.T. failure than a Harvard success);
4. form a hypothesis early in the interview and then set out to collect
the information to support or refute the hypotheses; 5. have empathy
relations specific to individual interviews; 6. determine their decision
according to demands on themselves; 7. be affected by quota pressures
(having, for example, to recruit ten M.B.A.'s in three days); 8. be
guided by certain biases, for example, people wearing glasses are more
intelligent, or thin people will develop ulcers. Preferred questions
among interviewers seem to be these: Why did you leave your last
company? Why do you want to be a marketing manager? What have we
got that your present company has not? What kind of work do you
enjoy most? Are you good at getting on with other people? What do
you see yourself doing in twenty-five years? Why did you leave your last
job? Have you been having much trouble finding a job? What is your
principal asset/liability? What salary are you looking for?

Interviewee's Strategy

The best bet is wear conservative clothing and have shined shoes,
immaculate fingernails, and clean, combed hair. Don't lounge or sprawl.
Be on time. Wear glasses. Don't be too confident or brash. If you are a
man, do not have a beard or moustache. (If you must, have them
trimmed every week while you are job hunting.) Get fit, start playing
tennis again. If you are overweight, lose ten pounds. Practice smiling.
As *Time* pointed out a few years ago,

> With a vast field of job seekers to survey, some employers now pay
> careful attention to factors other than professional qualifications. "If
> two people are equal," Atlanta Personnel Consultant Neale Traves
> tells his job-hunting clients, "invariably, the employer will take the
> guy with the clean-cut All-American look." A case in point: a former
> clerk in Los Angeles complains that prospective employers have
> demanded that she have her Afro hairstyle straightened and that she
> remove the gold earring from her nose. Overweight people, in
> particular, feel that they are being squeezed out of the job market. In
> a recent study of 1,000 heavies conducted by Dr. Rudolf Noble, a
> San Francisco obesity specialist, 14.2 percent claimed that their
> weight prevented them from landing jobs.[4]

[4] From "Recession Notes," 28 April 1975. Reprinted by permission from *Time*, The
Weekly Newsmagazine; Copyright Time, Inc. 1975.

Guide to Using Psychological Tests

Although business firms still make extensive use of psychological tests, no one can tell whether such a test works unless impartial research has assessed its effectiveness. Psychologists have provided executives with a great variety of tests, including intelligence and personality tests.

In deciding how good a test is, executives should take into consideration three important criteria: reliability, validity, and discrimination. Reliability is the consistency or stability of a measure, regardless of what is being measured. That is to say, a test is reliable when it yields the same scores over and over again, regardless of who is using the testing instrument. The reliability coefficient of an intelligence test, which is the measure of correlation between test scores on one occasion and another, is usually in the region of $+.8$ or $+.9$.

The validity of a test means the degree to which the test measures what it is supposed to be measuring. The presumption of selection tests is that they have predictive ability, that is, the test will be able to discriminate between those who will be good at the job and those who will not. In fact, very few validity studies have been carried out. A lot of companies have been content to settle for "face-validity," which measures the extent to which a test "looks right" to the candidate.

The third criterion that a good test must satisfy is discrimination power, which measures the ability of the test to put people into particular categories. A test that is poor in discrimination is one that everyone passes (or everyone fails). Today the major concern arising from tests is the possibility of discrimination against minorities and members of ethnic groups. According to the government's *Guidelines on Employee Selection Procedures,*

> Evidence of a test's validity should consist of empirical data demonstrating that the test is predictive or significantly correlated with important elements of work behavior which comprise or are relevant to the job or jobs for which candidates are being evaluated.[5]

IQ Tests

On very few occasions are IQ tests for executives justified. Any reasonably sophisticated interviewer can estimate an applicant's IQ from his educational achievement. Nevertheless, job-hunting executives

---

[5] *Federal Register,* 35, 149 (1 August 1970).

will still be faced with IQ tests, especially by executive search consultants. If you are bright and test well, you will have no trouble. If you are worried, develop what the psychologist calls "test sophistication" by taking (and practising on) a number of tests that can increase your test score by anything up to ten points. Any paperback store will sell you a book of tests with such obvious titles as *"Measure Your Own IQ."*

GROUP SELECTION: THE ASSESSMENT CENTER

One of the most effective answers to the question of early selection and identification of management potential is the assessment center. An assessment center is a standardized selection procedure that uses a variety of different techniques, including tests, interviews, and case studies, to evaluate potential managers. Using an assessment center, a company can observe and objectively evaluate a promising young person in terms of his or her managerial potential; it can identify the training requirements of a potential "corporate promotable," and it can reduce high management turnover and develop a rational and sensible plan for the systematic progression of people through the company.

Assessment centers differ greatly in duration, cost, contents, and administration, depending on the objective of the center, the parameters to be evaluated, and the employee to be considered. Furthermore, the method differs from other techniques in that a number of candidates are processed at the same time, trained managers conduct and evaluate the assessment, and a number of exercises are used to evaluate behavior. The candidate's potential success in a specific position is recorded in a two- or three-page report detailing areas of strengths and weaknesses. These reports can be used with current performance information to select the candidates with the best chance of success.

The Assessment Center Process

The assessment center process can be described in five sequential steps:

1. *Identification of job dimensions.* The first step requires the identification and definition of the behavioral variables relevant to success in the management job. This determination can come only from management and may vary depending upon the job to be filled. Theoretically, but rarely in fact, job analysis is used.

2. *Selection and design of the instruments of measurement.* This step requires the selection of the various psychological instruments, such as the interview, the case study, the irate customer, and the in-basket exercise. It also includes deciding which instrument is to measure which behavioral variables.

3. *Observation and reporting.* In a typical center, up to twelve participants who have been nominated by their immediate supervisors take part in the various exercises. Candidates may play a business game, complete an in-basket exercise, participate in group discussions, and be interviewed. The assessors observe and evaluate the candidates' behavior and take notes on specially prepared observation forms.

4. *Evaluation process.* After two or three days of exercises, the participants go back to their jobs. The assessors spend two or more days comparing observations and making a full evaluation of each participant.

5. *Feedback.* A summary report is developed on each participant, outlining potential and, where appropriate, identifying training needs. This information is relayed to the candidate by the personnel director in charge of the assessment center.

Figure 8.2 shows the assessment process.

The Assessment Center as a Selection, Socialization, and Training Process

One of the most intriguing and dramatic developments in executive selection has been the use of T-group technology in the assessment center. The idea behind the concept is objective evaluation of a candidate's potential. Candidates are viewed in social and business situations, theoretically acting out future behaviors. It can be an extremely tense time for applicants, as Box 8.2 shows.

FIRING

A manager's responsibility includes not only hiring people but also sometimes firing some of them. While most managers readily acknowledge that the right to hire and fire is a basic management function, most are reluctant to terminate a subordinate's job.

This reluctance to fire subordinates stems from various factors. At the shop floor level, negotiated contracts provide workers with job

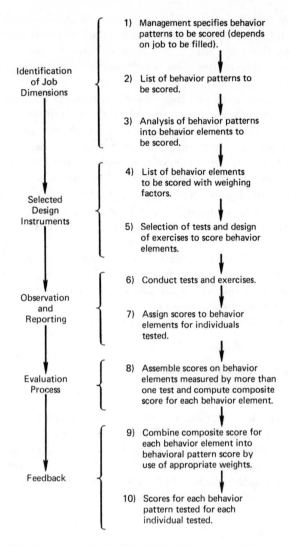

Identification
of Job
Dimensions

1) Management specifies behavior patterns to be scored (depends on job to be filled).

2) List of behavior patterns to be scored.

3) Analysis of behavior patterns into behavior elements to be scored.

Selected
Design
Instruments

4) List of behavior elements to be scored with weighing factors.

5) Selection of tests and design of exercises to score behavior elements.

Observation
and
Reporting

6) Conduct tests and exercises.

7) Assign scores to behavior elements for individuals tested.

Evaluation
Process

8) Assemble scores on behavior elements measured by more than one test and compute composite score for each behavior element.

Feedback

9) Combine composite score for each behavior element into behavioral pattern score by use of appropriate weights.

10) Scores for each behavior pattern tested for each individual tested.

Figure 8.2   Assessment Center Quantitative Measurement Information Flow

protection; in many firms, unless there is criminal conduct, little can be done to dismiss workers. In middle management firing is rare, a more usual method being to force the executive to resign under pressure. The direct method is to inform him that "his work has not come up to expectations," or "things have not worked out." One common method is to give the executive little or no work to do or to omit his name from

Box 8.2: "The White House Fellowship Chase"

A White House Fellowship—a chance to arrive in the precincts of power, to be "among the stars"—this was the prize sought by Miss Beryl Benderly, and thirty other "outstanding young Americans." All had already come a long way, but at this final stage, half of them would be eliminated—and only the other half would become White House Fellows. The question constantly going through Miss Benderly's mind: would she be one of them?

In early fall thousands of brochures had been mailed throughout the country by the staff of the President's Commission on White House Fellows. The criteria for competing were (and still are) that a candidate must be American, between the ages of 23 and 35, and "outstanding." In the winter of 1973–1974, 1,400 completed applications came back, and the filtering out process began: essays, eliminations; essays, eliminations; essays . . . ; culminating in interviews with a regional panel of business and civic leaders. Finally 1,400 became 32 of the most "gifted and highly motivated young Americans" from across the land.

Airlie House, near Warrenton, Virginia, was now the common meeting ground for the finalists—academics or quasi-academics, engineers, urban planners, corporate managers . . . Three days of interviews combined with social gatherings. This time the interviewers were federal judges, former high administration officials, present political appointees, two White House staff men, a dean of a business school, and corporate managers.

Days of interviews primed one to pick words carefully so as to make the best impression possible; evenings of social get-togethers were intended to permit finalists to "associate informally" with commissioners, and on one evening with the current

Continued on next page
Adapted from *The Washington Post,* October 13, 1974. Reprinted with permission.

important circulations. Thus, when executives are fired, it is usually a last resort.

The need for firing starts the moment you hire the wrong person for the job or you fail to describe precisely the job you want done or you fail to review performance.

How to Give Phased-Out Managers a New Start

Several years ago, the Aluminum Company of Canada, Alcan, had to cut back on its personnel because of adverse business conditions. Alcan decided that rather than simply "giving notice," they would not only help dismissed employees to find new jobs but explain why they had become expendable. Like many large corporations, Alcan had provided very secure careers for its people, and the company saw no reason to undermine this happy arrangement. Curiously enough, no performance review procedures existed. Furthermore, most executives

White House Fellows. Yet throughout the entire three days, until the commissioners had finished their last interviews and everyone knew that the decisions had been made (though they would not be announced until the next morning, after the commissioners had departed), there was a never-ending physical and mental competition between the finalists, which naturally led to a state of constant stress and inner tension that could not be dissipated until the competition had ended.

Whether sitting in front of an interviewer attempting to parry intellectual challenges or competing on the tennis court or having cocktails, dinner, and after dinner chat, the pressure always showed. For light relief there was the incident when a finalist who was a champion tennis player was rebuked by a commissioner whose wife had asked him for some pointers; then the evenings when some finalists seemed to be almost bootlicking with commissioners (or was it genuine interest?).

Physical and mental relief came only in the morning when everyone learned the results via envelopes addressed to each finalist. The winners' envelopes contained a letter, the list of winners, and a schedule for the next two days. The losers' envelopes contained only the first two of those items.

The list of winners? All of the tennis players, five of the academics, the sole black, both military heroes, four women. Conspicuous in their absence from the list were the only Chicano and all of the naturalized citizens. One man's comment: "Damn!" But at this stage, there was actually little to be said or done. The winners accepted congratulations with discomfort; the losers lined up for phones. Miss Benderly stood stoically in line.

---

lacked personal career planning, so that neither they nor their bosses had formally identified their strengths or skills. To meet this complex and tortuous situation, a complex and comprehensive termination procedure evolved. (See Box 8.3.)

After managers were informed that they were to be fired, they were given a package of material that outlined the basic dos and don'ts of job hunting. This package included names and addresses of people in reputable management-placement firms in the city and the major personnel-placement people within government agencies. It had basic information about resumé preparation, financial management, and so forth. The line manager then explained to the employee that he would be given a certain amount of money to cover traveling and miscellaneous expenses incurred while searching for a new job.

Money is very important at this stage. A very important part of the termination policy was the financial settlement. Alcan had a generous termination allowance for all its executive managerial and professional personnel. The settlement was usually based on years of service with the company and generally amounted to one month's salary for

Box 8.3: Steps and Timing of the Alcan Termination Process

Identification of redundant employees	Informal—usually three to six months before termination
Internal search for alternate job possibilities	One month before termination
Supervisor's initial discussion with special unit, and preparation of termination letter	One to two weeks before termination
Check of employee's medical history	One week before termination
Coaching supervisor on termination interview strategy	One to two days before termination
Termination interview	Should be held from Monday to Thursday *only*, and early in the day—*never* prior to vacation
Meeting of separated employee with line manager of special unit	Immediately after termination interview
Counselling and process of reorientation toward outside world	Same day as termination interview, continuing for one week, with periodic interviews
Initial interviews with outside consultants and with staff psychologist	Within three days of termination

Continued on next page

the first year of service and two weeks' salary for every year after that. However, the settlement could vary according to age, quality of service, number of years' participation in the pension plan, physical health, and so on.

Alcan's experience showed that middle-aged executives do have marketable skills and that they can find jobs if they look. In fact, 90 to 95 percent of the people using the reallocation services found new jobs in less than four months. Surprisingly, most found new jobs at salaries equal to or better than those they were leaving. Early feedback from "leavers" indicated an existential miasma of success: a sense of restored confidence in themselves and a feeling of performing better for their employers. Though the costs of the program were substantial, going through the process helped management identify shortcomings in the very company policies that had contributed to the massive cutback. Alcan has now instituted career planning programs for its personnel, both groups and individuals. This experience has created an awareness that the company shares in the responsibility for employees' personal development. At least twice a year, performance reviews for all employees identify problems and try to specify solutions. For managers, the experience has created an awareness that their primary responsibility is to themselves and not to the company.

Possible interview with company doctor	Within three days of termination
Beginning of psychological assessment	Within one week of termination
Relocation to new offices	Within one week of termination
Intensive work with consultants to finalize resumés	Within ten days of termination
Consultation with employee benefits staff for advice and clarification of termination policy	Within ten days of termination
Time lag between circulation of resumés and first job interviews	Usually three to four weeks
Counselling with line manager of special unit and with staff psychologist	Continues for two to three weeks and tapers off as the employee gains confidence
Feedback session—results of counselling and assessment	Within two weeks of termination
Time needed for employment interviews	Usually three to four months
New job found	Usually within four months

Being Fired

According to victims, the first thing you feel when you are fired is a sense of disbelief, the feeling that it can't be happening to you. This need for denial forces the firer into heroic efforts and the employee to decide whether to fight or flee. Most flee. A few stand and fight it out. Most leave because they have been set up for being fired by little clues along the way. Then they begin to feel guilty. What are you going to say to your wife?

In general, there are three styles of interpersonal relations: people relate to others by moving towards them, by moving against them, or by moving away from them. When you are fired, you move away; you pull into yourself, withdrawing your attentions and feelings from the external world.

Loneliness, withdrawal, isolation, estrangement, depression, immobilization, alienation, and apathy are all common feelings. People say to you, "You put too much of yourself into your job." And you reply, "I'll never give that much of myself again." You have lost the job, lost a big investment, lost part of yourself. You have suffered a grievous loss. Once your grieving becomes ritualized, things begin to pick up. The urgency, the immediacy of the situation begins to force itself on you. You realize you have a new chance, a fresh start.

Raymond Schiller, a computer specialist who was laid off from a challenging job in his mid forties describes the experience of renaissance.[6]

> One might suppose that this is a fallow period. It is not. The urgency of your predicament develops it into a more profound experience. Daily, your reasoning ability and imagination are stretched; your emotional stability is tried; your spirit is worked to the utmost of its resilience. Then, you discover, one day, you're going to get through it. An exciting regeneration takes place as you find yourself once again contemplating the fundamentals of the human condition. Extraordinary things happen that do not occur in an ordinarily tranquil, well-ordered life. Because of your height of awareness, these experiences become inextricably woven into the fabric of your life.

Slowly the chronic sense of withdrawal begins to diminish. Schiller continues:

> What is it like? Each day is new. Each day brings its hopes; each day brings its disappointments. There is the thrill of anticipation and the wild emptiness of almost-despair. In short, it is life. It is merely an intensified course in the human condition. I am not sorry that I have had this experience. But I hope to hell it doesn't go much longer.

EVALUATING

The Effectiveness of Performance Appraisal

Performance appraisal is a formal evaluation of employee activities. In practice, its effectiveness as a management tool is hindered by a great number of obstacles. In recent years, traditional performance appraisal has been under attack by management theorists, who have offered the alternative assessment tool of "management by objectives" (MBO). Nevertheless, performance appraisal is considered an important evaluation tool by executives and is still widely used. Box 8.4 explains some techniques.

[6] "Too Trained to Be Hired," *The New York Times*, 27 June 1971. © 1971 by The New York Times Company. Reprinted by permission.

Box 8.4: Performance Appraisal Techniques

Essay Appraisal

The rater writes a paragraph or more covering the individual's strengths, weaknesses, potential, etc.

Biggest drawbacks: variability in length and content; difficulty of combination and comparison.

Graphic Rating Scale

Less depth but greater consistency and reliability is achieved by categorizing employees' performance into such levels as: outstanding, above average, average, or unsatisfactory. These categories can be applied to factors such as performance, reliability, cooperation, communication, etc.

Field Review

For the purpose of checking, verify the results of the graphic rating technique by head-office or other impartial parties.

"A member of the personnel or central administrative staff meets with small groups

From "Make Performance Appraisal Relevant" by Winston Oberg, *Harvard Business Review* (January-February 1972). Copyright © 1972 by the President and Fellows of Harvard College; all rights reserved.

In 1975, Alan L. Patz conducted a survey of nineteen companies to determine the extent to which performance appraisal is used. After finding that the process is still widely used, he tried to answer this question: What is performance appraisal supposed to accomplish, and why is the process still widely used in spite of its practical drawbacks?[7]

The survey included two interviews with twenty top managers and eighteen middle managers. Its major conclusions were: "(1) Traditional forms of performance appraisal are still in use, even though many companies have adopted M.B.O. or other development systems, and (2) managers are unwilling to abandon performance appraisal, although they still experience difficulty in carrying out the process."

When asked about the purpose of performance appraisal, all the executives said "they consider it a development technique aimed at

[7] "Performance Appraisal: Useful but Still Resisted" by Alan L. Patz, *Harvard Business Review* (May-June 1975). Copyright © 1975 by the President and Fellows of Harvard College; all rights reserved.

of raters from each supervisory unit and goes over each employee's rating with him to (a) identify areas of inter-rater disagreement, (b) help the group arrive at a consensus, and (c) determine that each rater conceives the standards similarly."

Advantage: more fair and valid than individual ratings.

Disadvantages: very time consuming.

Forced Choice Rating

The purpose is also to reduce bias and establish objective standards of comparison between individuals, without the intervention of a third party.

Most common method: raters choose from among groups of statements those best fitting the individual being rated and those least fitting him.

Statements are weighted and scored.

Drawbacks: in practice, this method irritates the raters, who feel they are not trusted. Recommend describing a better employee when rating a weak or average one.

Because of the difficulty and expense of developing forms, the technique is limited to middle and lower-management levels.

Forms have little or even negative value when used in performance appraisal interviews.

Continued on next page

calling attention to a subordinate manager's flaws in order to improve his administrative ability. In addition, they view the appraisal procedure as a necessary vehicle for answering management potential." As the interviews progressed, other, less explicit reasons for performance appraisal were mentioned: justifying salary, establishing performance standards, determining low-performing subordinates. The most important implicit purpose, according to the author, was to force a large number of unwilling executives to relate the quality of a subordinate's work to actual results. Apparently, although it is easy for an executive to blame or praise an employee in a general way, it is difficult to write an objective statement relating direct action to consequences, and many executives are reluctant to do so.

While nearly all executives understood the purpose of performance appraisal (whether explicitly or implicitly), wide variations appeared in how each company actually implemented the process. All companies had some official performance appraisal form, but the content of these forms differed from company to company, indicating

Critical Incident Appraisal

The author blames the vagueness of the appraisal criteria for the negative effect of negative feedback. Traits like initiative, cooperativeness, reliability, and personality can be difficult to discuss with an employee.

Critical incident appraisal gives the supervisor actual factual incidents to discuss.

Drawbacks: necessity to make notes about each employee. The method may also cause the supervisor to delay feedback to employees by saving up incidents for the appraisal interview.

Management by Objectives

Employees are asked to set or help set their own performance goals to avoid feeling that they are being judged by unfairly high standards.

Drawbacks: at lower organizational levels, employees do not want to be involved in their own goal setting.

a degree of confusion about what is or shoud be focused on in a performance evaluation.

What Hinders the Process

In the interviews, the executives identified two main types of obstacles to successful performance appraisal. First are systematic barriers, obstacles built into either the appraisal evaluation form or the mechanism of the process. Systematic barriers consist of collection obstacles and analysis obstacles. Collection is difficult because much of the information data needed for performance appraisal is qualitative by nature, and no simple and objective method exists to compare one employee with another. Also, when quantitative data is collected a rating scale is usually used. The points in these scales are usually too narrow to allow comparisons among individuals. Interruption of the normal evaluation cycle (such as temporary assignments and transfers) creates situations in which portions of an individual's record may be incomplete

Work Standards Approach

Measured daily work standards are set by some organizations. To be effective, the standards must be visible and fair.

Drawback: difficult to compare. "If people are evaluated on different standards, how can ratings be brought together for comparison purposes when decisions have to be made on promotions or salary increases?"

Ranking Methods

Purpose: to compare people who are working with different supervisors objectively. The two most effective methods of pooling judgment are:

a) alternation ranking: employees' names are listed in random order on the left-hand side of a sheet of paper. The supervisor selects the most valuable employee, puts his name on top of the list in the right-hand side and crosses it off on the random list. He then selects the least valuable employee on the random list, puts his name at the

Continued on next page

or missing. Finally, there is frequently failure to file and follow up the routine work in performance appraisal.

Analysis is difficult for three reasons. First, many executives interviewed have problems analyzing data. Second, a good analysis requires centralized data files, which are seldom available. Third, even when centralized files do exist, virtually no performance appraisals are performed to test more complex manpower policies, such as job rotation or hiring.

Besides systematic barriers to performance appraisal, there are also behavioral obstacles: the fears, concerns, and biases that develop in people being appraised. Behavioral obstacles can be either political or interpersonal. Among political obstacles are first, the fear that the performance appraisal will be falsified so as to work to the supervisor's own advantage, and second, drawbacks of both favorable and unfavorable appraisals. Unfavorable reports expose the subordinate as well as the supervisor to criticism. On the other hand, favorable reports often lead to the loss of the best employees.

Interpersonal obstacles arise because all executives admit disliking

bottom of the sheet on the right-hand side, and crosses it off on the random list. He continues this way until all names are crossed off on the left and appear on the right in the order of their value.

b) paired comparison ranking: each employee is compared with every other employee, and the one who comes out better most frequently ranks first.

Assessment Centers

Purpose: to assess future performance potential.

Individuals from different departments are brought together to spend two or three days working on individual or group assignments similar to the ones they will be handling if they are promoted. They are ranked by one of the above ranking methods by pooled judgment of different observers.

Advantage: possibility for people working in departments of low status or low visibility in an organization to be compared with people from more well-known departments; equalization of opportunity; improvement of morale; increase of the pool of possible promotion candidates.

the face-to-face aspect of appraisal interviews. The consequences of a negative report are uncertain, and the manager might have to continue to work with the subordinate. Furthermore, a negative report might discourage rather than motivate employees.

Making It Work

Taken together, these obstacles present enormous barriers for the effective operation of performance appraisal. Why does performance appraisal still continue to be used, even though management theorists have offered modern alternative techniques? The answer is that executives believe that performance appraisal is capable of serving an important purpose; furthermore, there is a basic difference between performance appraisal and such techniques as MBO. "While performance appraisal has a basic historic orientation—linking past behavior with past results—the basic MBO orientation is to the future—emphasizing present performance and future goals. Futhermore, MBO goal setting is tailored to the individual; performance evaluation attempts to apply uniform standards to all employee behavior." Thus, performance appraisal is still an important managerial tool. Patz suggests four procedures for reducing systematic and behavioral barriers in performance appraisal:

1. Keep it simple. The purpose of a performance evaluation should be to draw a line between above and below average performers; therefore, complex scales measuring subtle differences in individuals should be eliminated.
2. Keep it separate. Performance appraisal should be separate from promotion systems. "Promotion decisions, like all decisions that affect the future, should reflect estimates of management potential more strongly than appraisals of past performance."
3. Keep it contained. Only two items concerning an employee should be centrally filed. First, whether the boss's evaluation is above or below average and secondly, the boss's estimates about the employee's managerial potential.
4. Keep it participative. A superior should listen to the employee's point of view before arriving at an appraisal of performance.

REVIEW AND RESEARCH

1. How do large, successful companies find junior managers? What qualities are they looking for when they recruit management trainees?
2. Are the job opportunities for graduates with M.B.A. degrees likely to increase? What factors affect the supply and demand of executive talent?
3. Why is it a useful cliché to describe the executive interview as "searching for the stereotype"? If interviewing is so lacking in scientific validity, why does it continue to be used?
4. Make a list of prejudices of both interviewers and interviewees.
5. How can the interviewer improve the psychological atmosphere at the interview?
6. Prepare a personal strategy for job hunting with the following headings: target positions, acceptable locations, salary and conditions of employment, personal appearance factors, interpersonal skills, job search strategy, and tactics of accept/reject on receipt of offer.
7. In spite of their lack of validity, psychological tests continue to be used. Why? How can the applicant get ahead of selection tests?

8. Describe the steps in the assessment center process. Explain the statement "assessment centers do more than assess assessees."

9. Management and drama are interlocked. Give examples of how the following dramatic terms can be applied to the managerial work: scenario, script, dialogue, props, actors, entrances and exits, ploys, throw-away lines.

10. There is an analogy between the process of firing and the drama of the movie *The Sting*. Take any movie that you are familiar with, and draw a comparison with a corporate process. Some examples might be *The Godfather* and organizational politics, *China Town* and the corruption of bureaucracy, *Conversation* and the informal organization, and *Paper Chase* and the process of socialization.

11. Why is it important for a manager to have accomplices when he or she takes executive action? Normally, the manager's principal accomplice is his secretary. What complementary roles does his secretary play?

12. Describe the psychological process of being fired. How would you counsel a fired executive?

13. Develop a strategy for the firee.

14. Develop a set of corporate guidelines for an executive layoff in a manufacturing company that employs 1,500 executives.

15. List the difficulties in using performance appraisal techniques. How can these difficulties be overcome?

16. Get in touch with two local companies and ask them to send copies of their performance appraisal forms. Compare and contrast these two methods of appraisal.

17. How can MBO be used as a means of assessing the competence of managers?

18. Why is it necessary to separate performance appraisal from promotion and salary appraisal? Develop an appraisal system for setting out how well your professor of management has done in teaching you management.

GEORGE IS DOING TOO MUCH

You are responsible for the hiring and training of student supervisors at the computer center at Merrimack Polytechnic Institute. It is the student supervisor's responsibility to answer all questions regarding the use of the computer facilities and, when necessary, to demonstrate how to operate the computer terminals.

Four weeks ago, you hired three students. All three are computer science students, and therefore they are very well-informed about the technical aspects of the job.

However, you have received many complaints about George Radkhe. Usually complaints regarding supervisors center around the supervisor's lack of knowledge or continual absence from the office. In either of these cases, your course of action is obvious: you dismiss the student. But George presents a problem you have never previously encountered.

The complaints about George have been that he does too much. The students complain that George not only demonstrates the features of the machines; he actually does the students' work. Also, after students have asked for help, George watches them for ten to fifteen minutes until he is satisfied they are doing it properly. This makes them extremely nervous, but they don't want to tell George how they feel since he is only trying to be helpful. In any event, this situation has created an atmosphere not conducive to learning.

You have been observing George for the past several days, and your observations have borne out the complaints—it is difficult for the students to work while George is around, and he is omnipresent. It seems that George is always in the computer center.

George offers his help to students whether they ask for it or not and whether he is on duty or not. Something has to be done. You don't want to fire him simply because he tries too hard. On the other hand, students stay away from the center when George is on duty, and he is scheduled for more hours than anyone else.

Midterm, the time of year that students most use the computer facilities, is quickly approaching. You must take action immediately. What will you say to George?

9

Executive
Leadership

Diagram the structure, process,
and values of classical leadership.

Explain why the trait approach
continues to be used.

Diagram structure, process, and values
of human relations leadership style.

Explain why effective supervisors
initiate both structures
and show consideration to subordinates.

Diagram the contingency theory of leadership.

Describe the path-goal model of leadership.

Formulate some clues for leading existentially.

The object of this chapter is to introduce the reader to four different views of leadership. The first, the classical view of leadership, is essentially concerned with trying to identify the traits that distinguish leaders from nonleaders. This model of leadership is inspired by the study of great men; its basic presumption is that leadership is found only in the elite, and correspondingly, that most people are content to be followers. In spite of scientific evidence to the contrary, most executives still believe in this trait approach and act accordingly.

The second approach is the human relations leadership style, which is based on the proposition that effective leaders establish a democratic, employee-centered, and supportive environment. While the classical approach employs an individual model, the human relations optic is derived primarily from a group model. This view assumes that leadership is simply the ability to influence others in the group. Therefore, all group members may exhibit a degree of leadership. The leader is the one whose influence predominates at a particular time. Thus, leadership rotates among members of the group depending upon the function to be discharged. Basic to this approach is a notion that a work group requires a task specialist who spells out what the group ought to achieve and a human relations specialist who deals with the emotional problems that arise. A basic issue raised by this group approach is to define the conditions under which the task specialist or the human relations specialist should dominate.

The third theory of leadership is the systems or contingency approach. In this chapter, two contingency theories of leadership will be considered. The first treats psychological distance as a critical variable and argues that a leader ought to vary his psychological distance according to the task, group atmosphere, and power gradient. The second employs a path-goal theory, which is based on the proposition that a leader's job is to define an effective means of clarifying path-goal relations for subordinates. Although they have some empirical foundation, both these theories are difficult for executives to operationalize.

To try and overcome these difficulties, a fourth approach has been suggested. The aim of the existential approach is to try and get beyond the behavioral science aspects of leadership. The basic assumption is that leadership never comes simply in black and white terms but always involves delicate shades of grey. To be effective as a leader, the manager must sometimes be charismatic and must have a considerable tolerance for ambiguity. The emphasis here is on the manager developing an authentic, trusting, positive attitude toward the people he or she must work with. The manager must be able to accept colleagues as they are.

The final part of the chapter is concerned with how to develop a new leadership style. The aim is to help the manager identify the model

of leadership he employs and to examine its relevance to the kind of
work he is doing. The governing variables in this change model are
valued information, free and informed choice, and internal commitment.

TRAIT APPROACH TO LEADERSHIP

The trait approach to leadership is the presumption that leaders have
different, distinct, and indeed superior personalities from followers. At
one time, managers enjoyed drawing up exhaustive lists of traits that
supposedly distinguished leaders from nonleaders. But scientific evidence is not on the side of the trait approach. Towards the end of the
forties, a major effort was made by psychologists to review the studies
of leadership that distinguished leaders from nonleaders. The only
traits that characterized leaders were intelligence, scholarship, depend-
ability, responsibility, social participation, and socioeconomic status. The
most important finding to emerge from these surveys was negative: no
consistent pattern of traits could be used to identify leaders. Yet such
negative findings are very difficult for managers to accept. Indeed,
most assessment center exercises still begin by drawing up a long list,
sometimes consisting of as many as thirty traits, that supposedly characterize the managers to be assessed. (Box 9.1 lists some of them.)
Despite negative results, many managers still believe that intelligence,
supervisory ability, initiative, and self-confidence are important to managerial success.

A search for leadership qualities was a major obsession for psychologists in the thirties, forties, and fifties. Every leader has his own
particular combination of traits. His style has developed out of a matrix
of genetic and environmental factors that stamp his relationships with
his superiors, peers, and subordinates. The effort to identify these traits
is of considerable interest, because it reveals a preoccupation with fixed
talents, which could be spotted, measured, and developed—a preoccupation with the cult of the personality.

The Cult of the Great Man

In this view, leadership is the ability to recognize and exploit the
drama of the moment, hold or steal the floor, and move events in a
direction that allows people to achieve their preordained destiny. The
history of an organization is but the curriculum vitae of great men.

The ideal classical manager has:

1. technical knowledge, with higher degrees, preferably in engineering and business administration;
2. a successful record of achievement;
3. managerial experience;
4. strong organizational abilities and the capability for structuring problems;
5. creativity but ability to be cost conscious; and
6. aggressiveness and the ability to be a self-starter.

Business cannot imagine functioning without a core of task-oriented, tough-minded, hard-but-fair classical managers. *Time* described one of them, a former Lockheed design chief:

Continued on next page

These great men show an infinite capacity for turning the dross of everyday life into dramatic moments of fateful opportunity.

A leader is a person who is willing, indeed eager, to accept publicly the challenge of filling the principal role in the organizational drama, even though some ritualistic denial of seeking greatness in nomination is required. This virginal quality of "If I am nominated I will not run; If I am elected I will not serve," is an integral part of the apparent deception of leadership. But such disclaimers cannot be accepted without a careful examination of the relationship between the leader and the led.

THE HUMAN RELATIONS APPROACH

But there is a necessary relationship between the leader and the led. The leader cannot lead unless he has followers who follow. What is the human relations leadership style?

Structure

Human relations-oriented executives have a continuing, almost obsessive interest in the informal organization, which they believe to be critical in determining both productivity and rewards. Good human relations (or how to work the informal organization) is seen as a kind of

Kelly Johnson may well be the last of a breed of uniquely gifted pioneering jet-aircraft designers who combined theoretical knowledge with wide-ranging practical skills. For example, his early experience in metal machining acquired during summer jobs in auto plants proved invaluable in working the heat-resistant titanium sheets needed for the SR-71's tough skin, which heats up to cherry red temperatures of 630°F. during flight. Johnson deplores the trend toward specialization with the lament of a designer who also knows how to handle machine tools. "Some of the fellows in the Skunk Works never had any cutting oil splashed on them." He expects more and more future decisions to be made by committees of experts with no experience beyond their own specialties. Trouble is, he says, committees "never do anything completely wrong, but they never do anything brilliant either."*

charismatic magic, which baffles brains and logic and bends ears and rules to get things done. Human relations still provides a set of insights about the optional if elusive extra called "informal leadership" and its rules, roles, and relations.

Rules, Roles, and Relations

The human relations manager bases his style not only on the needs of the led but also in terms of the structure and setting within which they interact to achieve particular goals. The situational approach to leadership is the belief that style, structure, and setting are interlocking group variables.

Initiating Structure and Consideration

Therefore, behavioral scientists have turned their attention to the structure and function of groups. Inevitably, whenever two or more people get together, one will dominate. But the form of the leadership depends on group members, the task, and the group ideology.

If leadership is the ability to influence others in the group, then all group members may exhibit a degree of leadership. The leader in the conventional sense is the one whose influence predominates.

* From "A Farewell to Kelly Johnson," 1 December 1975. Reprinted by permission from *Time*, The Weekly Newsmagazine; Copyright Time, Inc. 1975.

The Ohio State Studies

The Ohio State Leadership Studies, which began shortly after World War II, had as their objective the specification of how a given situation affects leadership behavior.[1] The original research took place in military organizations.

The studies found that there are two basic types of group functions: task behavior and human relations behavior. Task behavior stresses the importance of the objective, focuses attention on production, and reviews the quality of the work that has been done. Human relations behavior includes "keeping the group happy," "settling disputes," "providing encouragement," and "giving the minority a chance to be heard." Corresponding to these functions are two dimensions: "initiating and directing" and "consideration." Initiators make sure not only that their role is understood but also that official procedures are followed; they also try out new ideas on members. They are most efficient when the group faces a task problem. Executives high in consideration are group-oriented; they reward good work and invite participation in the setting of group goals.

Leaders who excel in initiating structure make specific work assignments, spell out deadlines, evaluate the quality of work, and establish well-defined work patterns and procedures. They were highly rated by their superiors and generated high performance in terms of productivity; they also reduced costs. But high-production supervisors had higher rates of grievance and labor turnover than their low-scoring colleagues.

Supervisors scoring high on consideration (who were supportive, willing to explain their actions, warm, and friendly had more satisfied subordinates and lower levels of grievance and turnover. The essence of the problem appears to be that superiors and subordinates view the leadership behavior of supervisors from different perspectives. Production supervisors with abilities in both dimensions could get the production out without increasing either the rate of grievances or labor turnover. Figure 9.1 shows these concepts graphically.

The Relationship

The human relations manager does not seek to formalize role relationships but prefers to deal with problems informally. At one level

[1] Ralph M. Stodgill and Alvin E. Coons, "Leader Behavior: Its Description and Measurement," Research Monograph No. 88 (Columbus: Ohio State University, Bureau of Business Research, 1957).

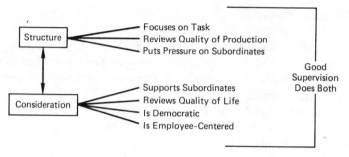

Figure 9.1   Ohio State Studies of "Structure" and "Consideration"

his behavior may ensure good relationships at the expense of efficiency. He prefers informal discussion with his subordinates to regular staff meetings. He is inclined to select his friends from within the firm. Given this desire for finding friends at work, he is frequently accused of trying to dominate and possess subordinates. According to research, he will delegate only relatively minor matters and insists on frequent individual consultation.

His opposite number, the task specialist, tends to formalize role relationships with both superiors and subordinates. He is somewhat more reserved and withdrawn in his relationships within the firm. He tends to take "calculated risks" and prefers formal staff consultation to seeking opinions informally. His most striking characteristic is his acceptance or rejection of subordinates on the basis of performance. Oddly enough, though he is reserved, he still has the ability to ensure smooth interpersonal relationships. He does not develop deep friendships with his colleagues. Being a task specialist, he demands considerable freedom of action from "up top" and usually gets it. Being realistic, he expects his people to make mistakes and plans accordingly. He prefers ambitious subordinates.

The Breakdown of the Human Relations Approach

In 1951, careful work had shown that effective supervisors were perceived by their subordinates to be employee-centered, supportive, and democratic. A little later another study, based on equally careful work, came up with the alarming finding that effective managers consider themselves psychologically distant from subordinates, particularly those who are least productive. How can one reconcile such contradictory statements? They are reconcilable because they are two different perceptions of the same behavioral event. The same event can be classified in different ways by different participants. For example, when a manager describes an interaction as "giving orders," his subordinate may record the event as "receiving advice." What kind of behavioral alchemy is this? Apparently, to be effective, an executive must give orders in such a way that his subordinates perceive his behavior as supportive or at least nonthreatening.

THE SYSTEMS OR CONTINGENCY THEORY OF LEADERSHIP

According to F. E. Fiedler, the effective manager's psychological distance is a function of the situation (power, task structure, and group atmosphere).[2]

To measure psychological distance, Fiedler has developed the LPC (least preferred coworker) scale, which assesses the esteem in which the leader holds his least effective subordinate. Figure 9.2 is such a scale. Typically the questionnaire contains sixteen to twenty items. Fiedler points out

> we visualize the high-LPC individual (who perceives his least preferred co-worker in a relatively *favorable* manner) as a person who derives his major satisfaction from successful interpersonal relationships, while the low-LPC person (who describes his LPC in very unfavorable terms) derives his major satisfaction from task performance.[3]

A leader who describes his least preferred coworker in very negative terms has a strong negative reaction to people he cannot work with. What he is saying, in effect, is, "If I can't work with you, you're no good!"

A leader who describes his least preferred coworker in more positive terms sees the coworker not only as an employee but as a person. The "high-LPC" leader considers close interpersonal relations a requirement for getting the job done.

---

[2] From "The Leadership Game: Matching the Man to the Situation" by F.E. Fiedler, *Organizational Dynamics* (Winter 1976). Copyright © 1976 by AMACOM, a division of the American Management Associations.

[3] Fred E. Fiedler, *A Theory of Leadership Effectiveness* (New York: McGraw-Hill Book Company, 1967), p. 45.

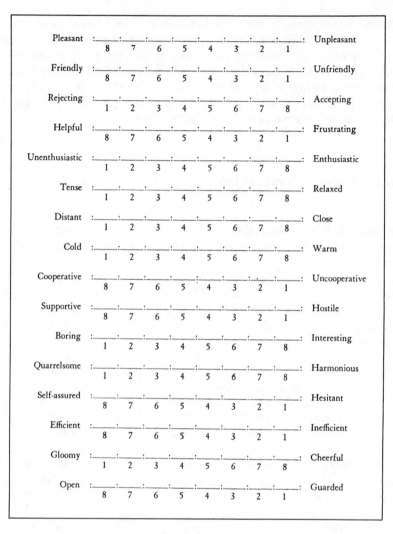

| Pleasant | :___:___:___:___:___:___:___:___: | Unpleasant |
| | 8   7   6   5   4   3   2   1 | |

Figure 9.2   Least Preferred Co-worker Scale

Reprinted by permission of the publisher, from "The Leadership Game: Matching the Man to the Situation" by F.E. Fiedler, *Organizational Dynamics* (Winter 1976). Copyright © 1976 by AMACOM, a division of the American Management Associations. All rights reserved.

Situational Aspects

A major factor in Fiedler's theory is "situational favorableness," which specifies the degree to which the leader has authority and influence and therefore feels he can determine outcomes. Situational favorableness is measured by three subscales: leader-membership relations, task structure, and position power. Fiedler is arguing that the leader has more control and influence if his subordinates support him, he is technically fluent, and he controls the reward and punishment structure. Fiedler concludes that

> This relationship has now been found in well over 50 different studies; in fact, a carefully controlled experiment by Chemers and Skrzypek showed that the contingency model accounted for 28 percent of the variance in task performance. The model is most easily described by the schematic drawing in Figure 9.3. The vertical axis shows the group's or the organization's performance. The horizontal axis indicates "situational favorableness"—that is, the degree to which the situation provides the leader with control and influence. The solid line shows the performance of high-LPC leaders, and the broken line the performance of low-LPC leaders. As can be seen, the high-LPC, or relationship-motivated, leaders generally perform best in situations in which their relations with subordinates are good but task structure and position power are low. They also perform well when their relations with subordinates are poor but task structure and position power are high (both situations of moderate favorableness as defined in Figure 9.3). Task-motivated leaders perform best when all three factors that define their control and influence are either high or low.
>
> It should be clear that we can improve group performance either by changing the leader's motivational structure—that is, the basic goals he pursues in life—or else by modifying his leadership situation. While it is possible, of course, to change personality and the motivational structure that is a part of personality, this is clearly a difficult and uncertain process. It is, however, relatively easy to modify the leadership situation. We can select a person for certain kinds of jobs and not others, we can assign him certain tasks, give him more or less responsibility, or we can give him leadership training in order to increase his power and influence.[4]

Leadership and Cognitive Complexity

One of the most interesting findings to emerge from Fiedler's work is that leaders who are high on cognitive complexity are more flexible in terms of leadership style. High-LPC leaders used not only more information but also more complex information-processing procedures for selecting their leadership style. Highly effective leaders,

---

[4] Fiedler, "The Leadership Game," pp. 11–12.

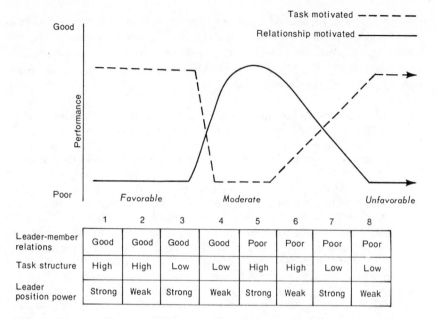

Figure 9.3   Schematic Representation of the Performance of Relationship- and Task-moti-
vated Leaders in Different Situational Favorableness Conditions

apparently, need more information to deal with problems of low task
structure or high role ambiguity than do less effective leaders.

A Critical Evaluation of Fiedler's Theory

Fiedler's contingency theory of leadership has been widely tested
in a variety of different occupational milieus. Statistical critics have
shown that the empirical validity of the model is questionable and that
a number of the correlations on which it is based lack statistical
significance.

The more fundamental difficulty is that the Fiedler contingency
theory of leadership has no explicit paradigm to guide managers in
selecting a leadership style. His theory produces no process explanation
of leadership that can tell the ordinary hard-pressed manager what to
do, with whom, where, and when. In brief, Fiedler's theory of leadership
is disconnected from the world of motivation (and this is precisely the

208

point of departure for House's path-goal theory of leadership, which we discuss next). For example, Fiedler does not question whether an individual manager is capable of developing a variety of different leadership styles. Most managers find the idea of having to select a leadership style from a whole portfolio of choices very threatening. They seem to prefer to develop a leadership style that is both consistent with the integrity of their basic personality structure and still meets the exigencies of the situation.

PATH-GOAL THEORY OF LEADERSHIP

The new concept for leadership, the path-goal theory developed by Robert J. House, attempts to link leadership with motivation.[5] It attempts to define a more effective means of clarifying path-goal relations for subordinates so that they can get the work done and still meet their own needs. The objects of the path-goal theory are to identify subordinates' expectations, determine what satisfies them, and then organize their choices so there is a high probability they will act in a way that maximizes both organizational performance and their own personal satisfaction.

House argues that individuals can make probability estimates about whether:

1. they can do the job,
2. the boss will notice that they have done it,
3. if he notices it, he will reward them, and
4. the rewards can be used to achieve personal satisfaction.

Having worked out these probabilities, the individual estimates the path his behavior might take: "If I start here, can I get there?"

The manager's job is to study and estimate his subordinates' perceptions of these path-goals. The manager then decides which parts of the path-goal network requires classification. For example, House has shown that some systems already have highly structured attempts to clarify paths and goals. Further structuring may be seen by subordinates as redundant. Such efforts may increase performance but only at a price of decreased satisfaction.

[5] Robert J. House, "A Path-Goal Theory of Leader Effectiveness," *Administrative Science Quarterly* (September 1971), pp. 321–38.

There is some evidence to support the view that managers who consistently accomplish a lot are able to adapt their style to the situation. Wickham Skinner and W. Earl Sasser describe the manager who is a low accomplisher as having a tendency to give inappropriate attention to details, to be unable to develop priorities, to be unable to move fast enough, and to be lacking in boldness, nerve, and self-confidence. Ineffective managers are also tolerant of ineffective subordinates unwilling to seek advice or help, and unaware of their own blind spots. Skinner and Sasser illustrate a classical dilemma in which a subordinate has to deal with an inconsistent and somewhat incompetent boss:

> "How do I deal with a boss who, while brilliant and held in esteem at high levels in the industry, won't sit down long enough to plan objectives and strategy, or even read his mail. He says, 'Don't write it, tell it.' But when you talk with him, he's easily distracted. When you're discussing one problem, his mind jumps to another and he usually doesn't listen well. When you are trying to reason with him, he extends your argument to an absurd extreme, argues rhetorically, with unrealistic 'what ifs,' or makes totally unreasonable 'principles' out of points you have raised.
>
> "He makes sudden, impulsive, and sometimes angry decisions based on little data and mostly on intuition. In making these hasty, long-postponed decisions, however, he often fails to consider their inevitable second-order implications. He doesn't keep me informed and seldom levels with me about what is on his mind or concerns him. We never set clear objectives or goals. He forgets from one time to the next what we've talked about or decided. Sometimes he tells me the same thing two or three times. We have few staff meetings when we can discuss our problems and plan together.
>
> "When we do meet, we ramble around and reach few clear decisions unless he suddenly and sometimes angrily lays down the law. He is successful and technically competent, but as a boss he's a disaster. All I get is specific criticism or vague praise. He has no idea really, in any depth, of what I do."

But this manager cannot be content to merely blow off steam and criticize his boss. He must learn somehow to find out what the organization and the boss need from him; he must assist the boss in the boss's own way to do some planning; he must learn to get through to him. He cannot blame things on the "disastrous boss" for he will usually be the loser if the relationship is poor and he's kept in an information vacuum. He is the one who will be criticized when things aren't letter-perfect, even if expectations are vague and never made explicit. The management of the relationship upstairs is often the responsibility of the subordinate. It's his neck; he must make the relationship work.[6]

For the effective managers the best formula seems to be "it all depends." These highly effective managers engage in careful analysis of the situation to get at the facts, to ascertain cause and effect relationships, and to grasp strategic realities. They develop new operating strengths, which are reviewed every six months. They make wide use of a variety of techniques. But they are also able to recognize classical dilemmas and to come up with solutions to them.

LEADING EXISTENTIALLY: A MODERN EXECUTIVE STYLE

Call it what you may, leading, taking the initiative, making the first move, or acting as a resource person is an integral part of organizational life. We know a great deal about leadership from two sources, the lives of great leaders and our own personal experiences. By studying the lives of effective leaders, some executives appear to be able to draw inspiring insights, which apparently invoke analogies in their experience.

Reviewing one's own experiences is an essentially existential exercise, and if the process is carried through in a perceptive way, it can be a revealing self-encounter. To illustrate the existential approach it may be useful to set out some principles of existential leadership.

1. Leaders are charismatic visionaries who respond to crises. They have an acute sense of history and their own personal destiny. They consider themselves to be the personal embodiment of an institution, organization, or state.

2. Existential leadership never comes simply in black and white terms. It always involves the delicate shades of grey. Dealing with such dilemmas as quality versus quantity, equality versus individuality, task achievement versus human satisfaction, and ecology versus economy requires a peculiar personal style. The ability to achieve a set of conflicting and frequently mutually contradictory ends, is a necessary executive skill that can be developed.

3. Executives must have a tolerance for ambiguity and the capacity to live with other team members who have different roles, are governed by a different set of rules, and generate a different set of relationships.

[6] "Managers with Impact: Versatile and Inconsistent" by William Skinner and W. Earl Sasser, *Harvard Business Review* (November-December 1977). Copyright © 1977 by the President and Fellows of Harvard College; all rights reserved.

Table 9.1 Leadership Styles

Variables	Classical	Human Relations	Systems	Existential
Structure	Formal	Informal	Informational	Depends on situations but always charismatic
	Hierarchical	Personal Peerarchical	Sapiential Adhocratic	
Process	Consensus formulation	Participation, using the informal group	Varying psychological distance in clarifying path-goals	Historical and personal destiny
	Risk syndication			
	Zone of indifference			
Values	Traditional: Dominance	Employee-centered	Cool	Sacramental: Accepting people as they are
	Legalistic By precedent	Democratic	Calculating	
		Supportive	Suboptimal	
Model of Man	S-R Man	S-O-R Man	P-G Man	E-Man

Most executives are not comfortable discussing power or its dynamics. This is particularly true of American executives, who have typically grown up in an environment that is suspicious not only of the misuse of power but also of power itself. Nevertheless, power has to be exercised if goals are to be accomplished. Usually managers are happy enough to exercise formal authority, usually through persuasion. But the uncertainty of the modern environment compels the manager to exercise power with people on whom he is dependent.

One of the first things the effective manager has to recognize is that he or she is dependent upon many colleagues. These dependencies inevitably make the manager vulnerable. As a manager moves up the hierarchy, the extent to which he or she is vulnerable increases, and the nature of the vulnerability becomes more complex. John Kotter argues that managers who are successful in acquiring power share a number of characteristics:[7]

1. They are sensitive to what others regard as the legitimate exercise of power.
2. They have good intuitive insight into varieties of power.
3. They develop career goals that allow them to acquire and use power.
4. They use all their wit and resources to "invest" in power so that it will give them the highest payoff.

[7] "Power, Dependence, and Effective Management" by John P. Kotter, *Harvard Business Review* (July-August 1977). Copyright © 1977 by the President and Fellows of Harvard College; all rights reserved.

212

5. They rarely use power in an antisocial way.
6. They are comfortable exercising power.

Table 9.1 shows the views of the major leadership styles regarding the structure, process, and values of leadership.

REVIEW AND RESEARCH

1. Compare and contrast the leadership styles of Presidents Eisenhower, Johnson, Kennedy, Nixon, Ford, and Carter. List a set of traits for each. Classify them according to whether you think their main style of leadership was classical, human relations, systems, or existential. Give reasons for your choices.
2. Why did the cult of personality catch on in the Soviet Union? Were there corresponding personality cults in the West? Why?
3. Describe the trait characteristics of a successful leader with whom you have worked. Compare and contrast your list with those of the other members of your class. What conclusions can you draw from this small experiment?
4. Characterize the experience of putting human relations into action in any situation. What can go wrong?
5. Compare and contrast Fiedler's and House's theories of leadership.
6. What has Fiedler to tell us about management?
7. Why is it difficult, if not impossible, to develop a science of leadership?
8. What is the executive dilemma?
9. Prepare a plan of action to develop your own existential leadership style.

TIM BABCOCK AS MANAGER*

When young Tim Babcock was put in charge of a division of a large manufacturing company and told to "turn it around," he spent the first few weeks studying it from afar. He decided that the division was in

* "Power, Dependence, and Effective Management" by John P. Kotter, *Harvard Business Review* (July-August 1977). Copyright © 1977 by the President and Fellows of Harvard College; all rights reserved.

disastrous shape and that he would need to take many large steps quickly to save it. To be able to do that, he realized he needed to develop considerable power fast over most of the division's management and staff. He did the following:

- □ He gave the division's management two hours' notice of his arrival.
- □ He arrived in a limousine with six assistants.
- □ He immediately called a meeting of the 40 top managers.
- □ He outlined briefly his assessment of the situation, his commitment to turn things around, and the basic direction he wanted things to move in.
- □ He then fired the four top managers in the room and told them that they had to be out of the building in two hours.
- □ He then said he would personally dedicate himself to sabotaging the career of anyone who tried to block his efforts to save the division.
- □ He ended the 60-minute meeting by announcing that his assistants would set up appointments for him with each of them starting at 7:00 A.M. the next morning.

Throughout the critical six-month period that followed, those who remained at the division generally cooperated energetically with Mr. Babcock.

10

Managing Information for Control and Evaluation

OBJECTIVES YOU SHOULD MEET

Define control in terms of comparing actual with predicted performance.

Diagram information flow and control to show how feedback works.

Explain the statement, "information can be measured by the logarithm of the number of available choices."

Summarize the computer analogy whereby an organization can be seen in terms of six subsystems: sensor, data processing, decision-making, process, control, and memory subsystems.

Illustrate what is meant by the term *critical decision variable* by looking at the control system of International Supplies Inc.

List the four steps in budgetary control.

Restate in your own words the meaning of dysfunction.

The central problem of control is one of obtaining a desired result in the face of adverse conditions. The control function is closely tied to the planning function. The fact that plans have been established does not mean that the desired results will necessarily follow. Deviations of the actual from the planned can occur. Control is concerned with detecting such deviations and correcting them.

Control is the final step in the management process. The control system compares actual against planned performance. The object of control is to check, regulate, verify, and keep performance within the limits of the plan. For control to be operational, the manager must analyze past and present performance and devise a standard. Once such standards have been established, one can specify the tolerance for each relevant variable (that is, how far away from the standard each is allowed to go). Exception reports then identify deviations that exceed these tolerances.

A control system operates by establishing a feedback of information about performance at different stages of the product's or service's development. This feedback information, or control data, facilitates both more realistic planning and closer adherence to established plans. Secondly, the control system prevents excessive deviations from established standards that can cause a breakdown in coordination. To be effective, a control system should operate at a number of different levels within the process. Box 10.1 gives an example of control in action. The problem is how to control the use of the office copier.

CONTROL AND CYBERNETICS

Control is linked to cybernetics, which is the study of self-regulating systems. Cybernetics is essentially concerned with the ways in which the outputs in a dynamic system can be maintained in a more or less steady equilibrium. A simple example of a cybernetic system is a house furnace controlled by a thermostat. The effector of the heating system is made up of a thermometer, control circuitry, and switches. The effector influences the environment by heating it or refraining from doing so. The environment influences the furnace by communicating a temperature to the thermometer. The thermometer activates the control circuitry, which switches the furnace off or on depending on whether the temperature is lower or higher than the setting. The point of the cybernetic system is that it transforms the problem of heating the house into a self-controlled system.

As many cost-minded managers are acutely aware, the ubiquitous office copier is just as handy for duplicating Aunt Tillie's strudel recipe as for running off copies of business mail. Now Manitou Systems Inc. of Bensenville, Ill., is offering a way of preventing office workers, as President Paul Leopold puts it, from "thinking of the copier in the same way they think of the water fountain." The company has developed a device, easily attached to any copier, that switches the machine on only when the user inserts a plastic identification card issued by his employer. The apparatus is hooked up to a computer that "reads" the cards and keeps a running tab on who has been using each copier—and for how many copies.

Manitou claims customers who have tried out the system, which costs about $60 per installation plus a $60 monthly rental fee, have been able to cut copying costs by as much as 50%. The University of San Francisco found some professors were duplicating whole books instead of buying them. Some employers, among them Levi Strauss, use the system primarily to monitor department-by-department copying costs, but Leopold sees it mainly as a money saver. Says he: "Companies don't leave the petty-cash box sitting in the lobby, but each time the copier is used, it takes another nickel off the bottom line." Then again, bosses eager to save those nickels may have to reflect that many employees would accept controls on copiers about as eagerly as they would meters on the water fountain.

From "Copy Cut," 19 April 1976. Reprinted by permission from *Time*, The Weekly Newsmagazine; Copyright Time, Inc. 1976.

The same kind of logic can be applied to the control of management systems. The basic idea is to interlock three steps in the process: planning, decision making, and controlling.

FOUR STEPS OF CONTROL

In business, as one expert has explained,

> To plan is to make decisions. Control is the evaluation of decisions, including decisions to do nothing, once they have been implemented. The process of control involves four steps:[1]
>
> 1. Predicting the outcomes of decisions in the form of performance measures.
>
> 2. Collecting information on actual performance.
>
> 3. Comparing actual with predicted performance.

[1] Russel L. Ackoff, *A Concept of Corporate Planning* (New York: John Wiley & Sons, 1970), p. 112.

4. When a decision is shown to have been deficient, correcting the procedure that produced it and correcting its consequences where possible.

All decisions, whether they are made in planning or process operations, must be subject to control. As we shall see, control and decision making are closely interrelated and are subsystems of what Ackoff calls the management system. It is only for the purpose of analysis that we consider the control subsystem separately. In practice, control must be considered along with both decision making and managing the information system.

INFORMATION FLOW AND CONTROL

In a self-regulating management system, the key element for control is feedback.

Figure 10.1 describes a simple production process. An input of material, information, and energy goes through some sort of transformation process, which adds value to the product. When the system has a control element, the procedure involves a constant monitoring of the output, a comparison of the output with the standard, an evaluation of any discrepancy, and a flow of information concerning the degree of deviation back to the production system.

Figure 10.2 describes a closed-loop type of system. In a closed system, which is often described as "information-tight," the control mechanism has the capacity to affect the processor to achieve the desired result. Closed control systems include the Watt's governor, the controlling of engine speeds, and the thermostatic control of air temperature. Open systems do not have information-tight control subsys-

Figure 10.1   The Process Subsystem

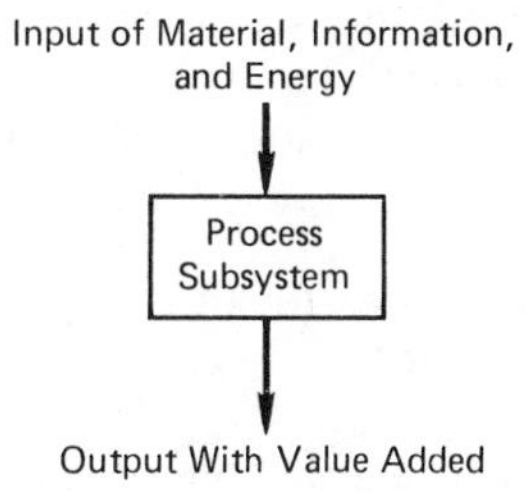

Input of Material, Information, and Energy

Process Subsystem

Output With Value Added

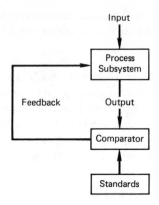

Figure 10.2   A Closed Loop System

tems. In an open system, the relationship among the subsystems is affected by changes in the environment. Business organizations are examples of open systems.

The Environment as a Flow of Information

The environment can be viewed as a flow of information that crosses organizational boundaries. Thus, to control the organization, managers must develop an intelligence-gathering operation to monitor these informational aspects of the environment. Decision making about control evolves from the analysis of this intelligence. Warren B. Brown has argued that there are:

> ... three traditional levels of decision-making in organizations: (a) the institutional level for strategic planning, i.e., those concerned with general company objectives and the broad problems of the position of the organization in its environment; (b) the managerial level which focuses on the gathering, coordinating, and allocating of resources for the organization, e.g., planning budgets, formulating personnel practices, and deciding on routine capital expenditures; and, (c) the technical level, involving the acquisition and utilization of technical knowledge for operational controls, e.g., production scheduling, inventory controls, and decisions concerning the measurement of workers' efficiency.[2]

Figure 10.3 shows the interlocking aspects of decision making, production process, and control.

[2] Warren B. Brown, "Systems Boundaries and Information Flow," *Academy of Management Journal,* 9 (1966), 318–27.

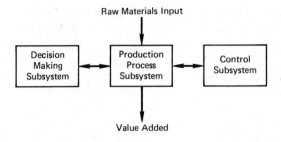

Raw Materials Input

Decision Making Subsystem ⟷ Production Process Subsystem ⟷ Control Subsystem

Value Added

Figure 10.3   Interlocking of Decision Making, Production Process, and Control

INTEGRATION OF INFORMATION: DECISIONS AND CONTROL

To develop an adaptive management system, management must integrate information, decisions, and control. A complete analysis of the adaptive management system requires consideration of six systems: a sensor subsystem, a data processing subsystem, a decision making subsystem, a processing subsystem, a control subsystem, and a memory subsystem.

The sensor subsystem's function is the collection of information about the environment. When the information has been collected it is passed to the data processing subsystem. The data processing subsystem is normally programmed to collect information about a particular category. In the decision making subsystem, a major effort is usually made to do three things:

1. identify symptoms of deviation, i.e., variations from the norm,
2. diagnose the problem, and
3. develop a prescription.

As Ackoff points out:[3]

A complete technology is available for defining "normality" of a system's behavior and for detecting deviations from it. The technology is that of *statistical quality control*. It is normally applied to performance characteristics of production subsystems, but it need not be so restricted. By statistical analysis of past performance of a system it is possible to define a range of "normal" behavior. Behavior outside this range is very unlikely to occur unless the system has changed in some fundamental way. Hence such behavior is taken as a symptom

---

[3] Ackoff, *A Concept of Corporate Planning*, pp. 124–25.

221

of something wrong. The probability that something is wrong when a symptom occurs can be set at any level that is desired.

By applying statistical techniques to a wide variety of performance measures of a system we can detect when something has probably gone wrong, and direct diagnostic attention to it. Once the symptom-identification procedure has been developed (e.g., one that uses a statistical control chart), its use can be computerized. On receipt of information about actual performance from the data bank the computer can carry out the necessary analyses and report any deviation from normal behavior.

Symptoms are obtained not only by comparing current behavior of the system with its past behavior but also by comparing its current behavior with that of similar systems; for example, with that of competitors. A company that is not growing as fast as are most of its competitors has something wrong with it. Such comparisons can also be programmed for the computer.

The Process of Integrating Information and Action: The Computer Analogy

Systems theory has pushed this idea of the integration of information, decision making, and action to its logical conclusion: any organism (an individual, a group, or an organization) can be treated as if it were a computer.

A good way of understanding the computer analogy is to look at an example of its application. Let's describe how a doctor treats a patient.

The Sensor Subsystem

The sensor subsystem receives and recognizes information. A patient with no symptoms reports for his annual checkup. The doctor notices irregularities in the chest x-ray. The x-ray plate is not clear. The doctor and the patient move to the next step in the process.

The Data Processing System

The data processing system breaks information into terms and categories that are meaningful and relevant. Let us presume the doctor has three categories for diagnosis: T.B., a fungal infection, and lung cancer. The patient has two categories: it is lung cancer, or it is not lung cancer.

The Decision Subsystem

In the decision subsystem actual choices are made. Skin tests, further x-rays, and clinical histories are developed. Let's presume the patient has a tubercular spot on the lung. The physician has the following options:

1. benign neglect
2. hospitalization
3. chemotherapy
4. treatment at home
5. surgery
6. any combination of the above

The doctor may decide to take any of these options.

The Processing Subsystem

The processing subsystem integrates information, energy, and materials to implement decisions, accomplish tasks, and produce output. It can be conceived of in a number of different ways. At one level it is the patient who has the bacillus and who is receiving the drugs. The patient's self-regulatory or homeostatic process has been disturbed by the presence of the tubercle bacillus. The process may be further complicated by introducing drugs into the treatment.

So far we have discussed the system as if the patient were the whole system. Other answers can be worked out if the system is the physician and the patient. Then a major consideration would be the physician's anxieties, his avoidance or acceptance of his role. A larger system would be the clinic staff: the nurses, x-ray technicians, radiologists, lab technicians, cleaners, matrons, and so on. In this system, a major criterion of efficiency becomes the throughput, the sheer volume of business. Elaborate procedures have to be developed to keep the patient at a distance.

The Control Subsystem

The control subsystem ties the whole system together with a set of feedback loops. In this particular case, the critical data can be extracted from x-ray pictures, sputum analysis, weight, and other critical information. These loops incorporate the equations of the critical decision variables (area and depth of infection).

The Memory Subsystem

The final stage is the memory subsystem, which stores and retrieves information. There is an ongoing analysis of demographic data with a view to ascertaining who gets T.B., where, and when.

The Critical Decision Variable

For control systems to operate effectively, one must identify the critical decision variable (CDV). This can be a tricky process, for the CDV may change. An American car manufacturer may decide to increase his share of the market by offering a five-year warranty on the engine. If the other manufacturers do not follow suit, his increased share of the market may be offset by the costs of repairs at service stations. Now the control may shift to the management of the warranty. Staff will have to be increased and training given to reception clerks in the service stations. After the automobile manufacturer has secured his share of the market, he will normally try to change the CDV again, for there is a limit to what you get out of any variable in control.

INTERNATIONAL SUPPLIES, INC. (ISI)

The way organizations process information to maintain control can be illustrated by an example. International Supplies, Inc., is a medium-sized company. In the twenty years since its establishment, ISI has grown to a $9-million-a-year operation with branches in all major cities in the Northeast.

ISI sells a comprehensive line of printing supplies, including specialty papers and inks. Paper sales make up 60 percent of total sales dollars. ISI has no manufacturing operations but buys in quantity from various established suppliers. With few exceptions, customers are other companies who buy from ISI either for their own consumption or for raw materials to be incorporated into products ultimately sold to the consumer.

Examination of how customers' orders are actioned (often called "the order entry system") gives us the opportunity to examine a control system in action. Since customers' orders are necessary for survival and growth, the effectiveness of the order entry system has a direct influence on the company's success. The six subsystems depend heavily on the design of the order entry system.

In Figure 10.4 we depict the ISI order entry system and identify its six subsystems.

Orders are received at the sales desk by telephone or mail. A customer order form is prepared and orders for established customers within their credit rating are sent to the inventory desk. Orders exceeding credit limits or for new customers are referred to the credit department for credit checking. At the inventory desk, the order is checked against stock records. For items in stock, the order is sent to the warehouse, from which the order and the goods are sent to shipping. For items out of stock a back order is raised (to be filled when goods become available) with notice of the "back-order condition" sent to the purchasing department and the customer.

After preparing the goods for transmission to the customer, shipping advises the invoicing section of the controller's office. Here prices, credit terms, and so on are checked, an invoice is forwarded to the customer, and entries are made to the customer's account and other accounting records. This data enables companies to formulate operational budgets.

OPERATIONAL BUDGETING

The budget is an integral part of the management control process. A budget can be used in any business; it is implicitly, though perhaps not overtly, used in every household. Budgeting is the control process by which managers assure that resources are obtained and used efficiently and effectively to accomplish the organization's objectives. We shall be especially concerned with operational budgets, which essentially deal with and link expected sales, projected production, budgeted selling expenses, and budgeted administrative expenses. Budgets tie together four different aspects of management: planning, coordination, training, and control.

Planning

Based on financial plans for a longer period (for example, five years), a short-term or annual budget is prepared to cover all financial

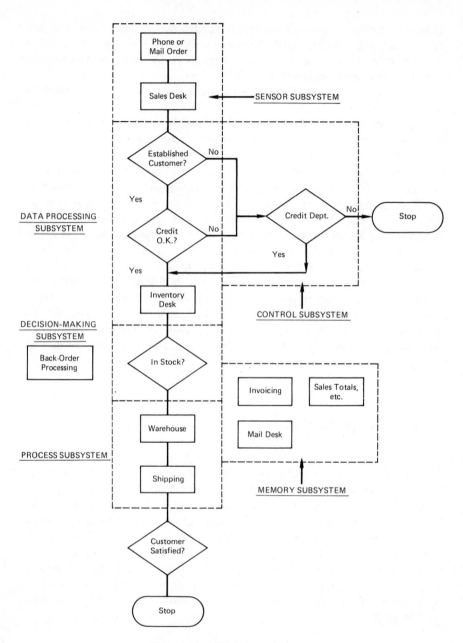

Figure 10.4   ISI's Information System

226

aspects of the organization's operation. If a new product is coming out next year, for example, the budget must cover such questions as: What equipment will be needed? When? Where? How many people need to be hired and trained? What costs will be involved? Where? When?

Coordinating Activities

Part of planning is to coordinate the activities of the different departments so that they can work in balance toward a common goal. Effective budgeting reaches into the details of every phase of the business so that planned activities in interdependent departments mesh. For example, as a minimum, sales forecasted by the sales or marketing department must be coordinated with manufacturing capacity, inventory policies, purchasing, and labor and cash requirements.

Training

The process of budgeting is a form of training in management responsibility and commitment as well as a possible source of motivation. Department heads ask supervisory personnel under them to prepare detailed budgeting reports for their respective segments, which the department heads then consolidate. The budget, in effect, becomes a model of the firm's activities in which each manager can see his contribution.

Control

Budgets create a powerful basis for control that is grounded in principles of management. Management reports highlight those aspects of actual performance that deviate from expected or planned performance.

Budgetary control, viewed as a process, consists of four stages, which are shown graphically in Figure 10.5. The first stage involves setting objectives for the budget period (usually one year) based on forecasts, standards, and expectations that are in line with organizational goals. The second stage includes monitoring actual performance to the planned performance objectives: profits, costs, machine speeds, scrap losses, labor output per hour, etc.

The third stage requires comparing actual with planned performance to determine if any variance exists. Analysis of variance is essential

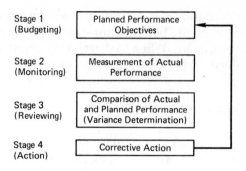

Stage 1 (Budgeting)	Planned Performance Objectives
Stage 2 (Monitoring)	Measurement of Actual Performance
Stage 3 (Reviewing)	Comparison of Actual and Planned Performance (Variance Determination)
Stage 4 (Action)	Corrective Action

Figure 10.5   Budgetary Control as a Process

to determine whether any corrective action is necessary in the final stage. This final stage and the analysis associated with it provide feedback that is used to correct performance that is out of line with expectations. If actual performance cannot be improved, it may be necessary to modify the planned performance in stage 1.

Stage 1: Budgeting

Sales budget

The sales forecast is crucial since the reliability of other budgets is dependent on its accuracy. A sales forecast and budget give a detailed analysis of sales in units, dollars, products, sales areas, types of customers, size, quality, and so forth. Normally the forecast is made for the next financial year, which is broken down into monthly or four-week periods. It involves the participation of many managers (primarily those in marketing) at various levels, each contributing information pertinent to the accuracy of the budget. The following should be considered in forecasting sales:

1. historic sales performance and trends,
2. findings of any relevant market research,
3. likely impact of controllable expenditures (advertising, new products, pricing) and uncontrollable expenditures (general business conditions, fashions, competition, government intervention),
4. experience of competitors and expert opinion, and
5. reports from sales representatives.

Manufacturing and expense budget

Production details are then calculated. These are based on demand for product units by sales in specific periods of time, allowing for the depletion or build-up of inventories in line with management policy. Next, production in units is multiplied by the standard quantities and costs for raw materials and labor to arrive at the "prime" (materials and labor) costs of production. The other component of manufacturing cost, overhead, is a total of the variable and fixed overhead components. The variable overhead (e.g., power, miscellaneous supplies) cost per unit times the number of units gives the total for variable overhead. The fixed component (e.g., rent, production supervision, depreciation, etc.) is added to give total overhead.

Such costs as direct labor, direct materials, and overhead are arranged under appropriate departments, but such other costs as general administrative and selling expenses are totalled for the entire plant. For control purposes, the budget is broken down by departments or areas of responsibility. Usually managers who are to be held responsible for a particular area or acticity are given the opportunity to participate in setting their positions of the budget.

Purchase budget

The sales, manufacturing, and expense budgets provide the source documents for calculation of purchase requirements. Raw materials purchases are determined and, by means of inventory models (allowing for any inventory policies), economic order quantities and stock levels are determined. Other purchase requirements include consumable supplies for office and factory, maintenance spares, new plant and equipment, and miscellaneous overhead items. Standard prices are set for important materials in manufacturing; these are periodically compared with actual prices to determine any price variance.

Financial budgets

Finally, a cash budget based on the previous budget can be prepared. It shows cash balances, receipts and disbursements, and the need, timing, and cost of any borrowing during the coming period. A gross profit budget is prepared for various divisions or product lines, and a balance sheet, net income statement, and funds statement are also completed.

Stages 2 and 3: Monitoring and Reviewing

The process results in budgets for all activities before the new accounting period starts. At the close of each time period (daily, weekly, or monthly), actual materials used, labor hours, and costs are assembled, recorded, and compared to budgeted forecasts to determine any variances. The time period depends upon the nature and importance of the particular item under review. For example, purchases bought at a price above standard should be reported as soon as the invoice is received, not when the goods are taken from a storeroom to be used. Production losses from defective units or scrap in a machining operation may be reported hourly to minimize losses from dull cutting tools or accidental changes in machine settings.

The final control reports are statements showing material, labor, and overhead for each product by departments (or responsibility areas) with variances between budgeted and actual costs. The variances may be favorable (performance on usage below budget) or unfavorable. These variances are then classified as either controllable or uncontrollable, depending on whether they can be influenced by the manager on whose report they appear. Managers should be held responsible for variances only when they can control or significantly influence the causes of the variances.

Responsibility accounting

The formation of departments, processes, or certain activities into responsibility centers is an extension of budgetary control. The organization is divided into a hierarchy of responsibility centers, each the responsibility of one manager, with each manager reporting to a superior until the center under the top manager is reached. The budget and performance data for lower centers is aggregated into the performance reports of superiors.

Responsibility centers may be of three types:

1. Cost centers, in which the manager is responsible for costs only;
2. profit centers, in which the manager is responsible for both revenue and expenses; and
3. investment centers, in which the manager is responsible for assets, revenues, and expenses.

A responsibility accounting system may include one type of center or a mixture of two or all three types.

Stage 4: Corrective Action

The main advantage of the control system is the use of feedback for corrective action when actual performance significantly differs from budgeted performance. This corrective action requires an extensive information and reporting system to focus attention on variances and to facilitate determination of the causes of the variances.

Zero-Base Budgeting

Zero-base budgeting is a new management technique, which instead of taking last year's budget as its starting point requires that all the company's activities and priorities be reviewed every year. With zero-base budgeting, each year a company reviews its priorities with a view to developing a better set of allocations for the upcoming budget year. Zero-base budgeting requires each department to propose a budget that makes no reference to previous budgets.

Zero-base budgeting has three steps:

1. Specify each discrete organizational activity in a "decision package,"
2. evaluate and rank these packages according to some cost-benefit approach, and
3. allocate financial resources accordingly.

Management can evaluate, rank, and approve or disapprove the decision package. Decision packages usually use the following headings: objective, cost, personnel, measures of performance, alternative choices, and an evaluation of the consequences of performance and nonperformance.

Experience with zero-base budgeting has been mixed, as is pointed out by two experts:[4]

> If you are dissatisfied with your present budgeting system, or are uneasy about the magnitude of some or all of your administrative programs, you will find that zero-base budgeting provides you with a systematic method of addressing your problems.
>
> It, like all programs, requires top-down support and sensitivity. The program requires training, lots of time, lots of paperwork, and changes in budget preparation behavior. It requires hard-nosed decisions by

---

[4] "Where Does Zero-Base Budgeting Work?" by James D. Suver and Ray L. Brown, *Harvard Business Review* (November-December 1977). Copyright © 1977 by the President and Fellows of Harvard College; all rights reserved.

people knowledgeable about the goals and operations of the entire organization. And, to be most effective, the system requires output measurements in order that every decision package can be ranked on a cost-benefit scale.

Thus, there is good and bad in zero-base budgeting. Only you know the budgeting problems of your organization; whether you need to really dig into program costs; whether you have the talent to meaningfully review the budget; and whether the operating environment of the organization would be receptive to a zero-base program.

OPERATIONALIZING CONTROL

Most business students, especially those who have never worked on the production shop floor, regard the subject of control with distaste. Yet control, which is concerned, essentially, with moving from "the actual to the desired," is something with which every student is familiar. A college examination is a form of control arranged by the professor to test the knowledge of the student with a view of measuring his performance.

In organizational life, as in college life, the form of control that is used is a major factor in determining what kind of work is done in which areas. Whoever controls the policing and definition of criteria determines what eventually happens.

Dysfunctions

When setting up a plan of action, it is very useful to allow for dysfunctions. *Dysfunctions* is a technical term that describes unanticipated outcomes that injure the interests of the organization. One of management's main functions is avoiding or minimizing dysfunctions.

A good example of dysfunctions is the unanticipated consequences of introducing copying machines into many offices. These machines are used not only to copy important office documents but also "employees' homework": tax returns, children's homework, political propaganda, and scores of other nonbusiness papers. In addition, secretaries commonly make more copies of business papers than specified. It might almost be possible to argue that the dysfunctions exceed the eufunctions—the "bads" exceed the "goods."

Planning and control can often have immense dysfunctional con-

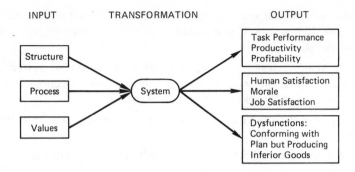

INPUT   TRANSFORMATION   OUTPUT

Figure 10.6   Model with Dysfunctions Added

sequences. Often, meeting dysfunctions with tighter control can generate even larger and more convoluted dysfunctions. General Motors' trouble with the small Chevrolet Vega illustrates how dysfunctions can develop.

When the Vega was introduced in 1971, it was meant to compete with imports, and the price was held to around $2,000. To make money at that price, G.M. had to cut costs, which in turn meant taking copper out of the radiator and removing a planned stainless-steel gasket. This gasket was located between the iron cylinder head and the aluminum engine block. These two savings worked against one another; the engine began to overheat and consume inordinate amounts of oil. To meet this situation, G.M. had to extend the guarantee for five years or 60,000 miles, the longest guarantee in the industry, and replace thousands of engine blocks. A cost-cutting operation ended up generating very large costs. To keep this dysfunction in balance, managers have to be realistic. They must try to guess what dysfunctions might occur. A good concept to keep in mind is Murphy's law: "Anything that can go wrong, will go wrong." Figure 10.6 updates our management model by including dysfunctions.

REVIEW AND RESEARCH

1. How do universities control performances of (a) students, (b) faculty, and (c) administrators? What are the dysfunctions of that system? How can they be overcome?

2. How does the manager of your local automobile service station control performance and stay on plan?

3. What are the purposes of budgeting? What is a "critical decision variable"? How would you establish the critical decision variable for an automobile assembly plant?

4. If you were assessing the effectiveness of a control system in a company, to whom would you want to talk, what documents would you need, what things would you want to see?

5. Discuss the dysfunctions of introducing a copying machine into an office.

6. What dysfunctions did G.M. run into when they introduced the Vega?

7. Why do employees begin to audit the audit?

"SMALL IS BEAUTIFUL"

A growing body of evidence argues for two changes in production arrangements. The first, promulgated by E. F. Schumacher in his book, *Small Is Beautiful*, urges the employment of intermediate technology that is labor-intensive and energy-saving rather than energy-intensive. The second proposed change is participative democracy, which can generate high productivity and enhance an employee's self-respect. Unfortunately, it is extremely difficult for people brought up in our industrial society to adapt themselves to democratic procedures. Although democratic organizations have developed in Yugoslavia, Cuba, and China, the two super powers of the world, the U.S. and the U.S.S.R., continue to rely on hierarchically organized factories.

According to L. S. Stavrianos' *The Promise of the Coming Dark Age,* low-paid workers in the Soviet Union are resentful of the privileged upper layers of Soviet society and react against the system by taking it easy on the job, doing sloppy work, and even sabotaging factories. As Stavrianos points out, even highly paid American factory workers, who are closely supervised from above, are reluctant to give of their best, use drugs on the job, drink at lunchtime to make their work tolerable, occasionally sabotage the product, and steal whatever they can. Stavrianos argues that our industrial society should switch to local initiative, intermediate technology, and democratic organizations. Already in the U.S. we have a considerable number of autonomous communities, communes, with their own units of production that are geared to a survival that does not pollute the environment. Do you think such communes are realistic? Why or why not? What other solutions can you offer for this "workers' malaise?"

11

Decision
Making

Understand why managers do not always act rationally when making decisions.

Define problem solving in terms of diagnosis, evaluation, and implementation.

Develop a ten-step plan for problem solving.

Illustrate how evaluation involves both selecting a solution and selling that decision.

Describe the four steps in implementation.

List the four steps in the creative process.

Construct a simple break-even chart.

Illustrate how bottlenecks in the flow of work can be broken by using queuing theory.

Develop a formula useful for planning inventories.

Diagram a simple network technique that helps in planning.

State the advantages of linear programming.

List some important principles of quantitative decision making.

The truth, the central stupendous truth, about developed countries today is that they can have—in anything but the shortest run—the kind and scale of resources they decide to have . . . It is no longer resources that limit decisions. It is the decision that makes the resources. This is the fundamental revolutionary change—perhaps the most revolutionary mankind has ever known.*

"Decide or Die" might well be the motto of managers, for their business is essentially the process of converting information into action for a profit. This is done solely by making decisions. Decision making, the core of planning, is a continuous requirement for the manager.

INFORMATION DECIDING ACTION

The decision-making process begins with information. But the manager does not consider all the information available to him. He takes only information that is readily available and that he considers credible and relevant. Furthermore, he digests only enough of it to feel sure he has found a viable answer to a specific question. The manager is governed by rationality.

The Model of "Rational" Decision Making

The rational decision-making model is based on the assumptions that:

1. it is possible to have an accurate and complete understanding of the multiple goals relevant to the problem;
2. the decision maker has some method of accurately, precisely, and relevantly sequencing the problems in order of their importance;
3. the decision maker has complete knowledge of all feasible alternatives open to him and a reliable way of predicting the consequences of each alternative;
4. the decision maker is capable of assigning a measurable value, usually in terms of utility or profit, to each of these choices; and that he can construct a complete and unambiguous preference order, which will allow him to select the "best" alternative;

* From *"The Long Wait"* by U Thant, former Secretary General of the United Nations.

5. the decision maker is free to choose the alternative that maximizes his outcome;
6. The cost of gathering information is zero; and
7. decision criteria can be expressed as unidimensional variables.

Reality Decision Making

Rational decision making as we have described it is rarely employed in the complex and convoluted life of corporate society. To understand why, we must consider some important findings promulgated in the mid-1950s by H. A. Simon.[1] Simon and his colleagues argued that the decision-making process is made up of three steps:

1. searching the environment for problems demanding a decision—basically an intelligence activity;
2. processing data so that concepts, figures, and information are manipulated to suggest alternatives—essentially a creative process; and
3. selecting an alternative—a somewhat irrational, intuitive process.

Simon found that managers are guided by "bounded rationality." This concept means, essentially, that there are limits to the information-processing capacities of the mind. The capacity of the human mind to formulate and solve problems is relatively small compared with the problems themselves. What managers do is collect sufficient information to enable them to find a solution that will work. Managers, restricted by bounded rationality, engage in directed research; to avoid uncertainty they make maximum use of routine procedures. Further, when they have to choose among alternatives they employ a rather simple "rule of thumb" guideline; they actively stop searching when they reach the first satisfactory alternatives.

In brief, managers satisfice rather than maximize: they make "good enough" decisions. The basic rules of satisficing are:

1. In terms of return generally, take just a little more than you need; don't be greedy because greed mobilizes the opposition.
2. Give a certain amount to the stockholders, a certain amount to the government, and a little bit to the consumers.
3. Make sure the losers within the firm are paid off.
4. Keep some resources in reserve by increasing inventory or hiring more

[1] H.A. Simon, *Administrative Behavior*, 2nd ed. (New York: Macmillan, 1957), p. 284.

staff (especially secretaries, consultants, and specialists) who can be let go if necessary.

HOW FIRMS MAKE DECISIONS

A good example of how firms typically make decisions can be seen in the case of a small data processing firm. The sequence of events might be something like this: the firm is getting behind in servicing the data processing needs of its client firms. After several crises, the president appoints a task force to identify the problem and make a recommendation. The task force recommends that the company buy a larger computer.

The president sets up a search committee chaired by the executive vice president, to recommend what computer to purchase. He allows them three weeks to come up with an answer.

The executive vice president't group invites computer manufacturing firms to tender and sets up a process of judging among the contending computer companies. All this information is carefully organized, structured, and finally presented to the president.

The president scans the report, sifts the essential information regarding the capacities, capabilities, and costs of the different computers; and perhaps calls the top people in the computer firms. They, in turn, make various accommodations. In a couple of hours, a decision has been made.

What is important to note about our example is that executives set out in a realistic way to find viable answers to immediate problems. Basically, they try to simplify problems, so that they can bring the problems within their own capacity for perception, analysis, and decision.

THE PROBLEM-SOLVING PROCESS

Surprisingly, modern classical management owes a considerable debt to the young Karl Marx who argued that the point of life is to change it, not merely to understand it. By producing simplified versions of reality, modeling allows an executive to get to the heart of a problem so he or she can solve it.

As shown in Figure 11.1, problem solving has three phases: diagnosis, implementation, and evaluation.

Diagnosis

Identify the problem

The first step in the decision-making process is to list the problems requiring solution. Since it is sometimes possible to solve problems in groups, it is useful to arrange the list according to either importance or similarity (of resources to be used, for example). Often there is one problem of such importance that it must be solved first.

One way of ranking problems is to attack first those with the most stringent time limitations or those that are likely to become more difficult with the passing of time. Another sorting procedure is to categorize problems according to whether they can be postponed and/ or how clearly the problems can be articulated. A threefold category is usually employed:

1. top priority—requires immediate action;
2. second priority—useful to solve but can be postponed;
3. third priority—important but requires further clarification.

Once the problem has been selected, it must be carefully defined in terms of its broad objectives and constraints, the nature of its environment, and the factors affecting the problem. The result should

Figure 11.1   Problem-solving Stages

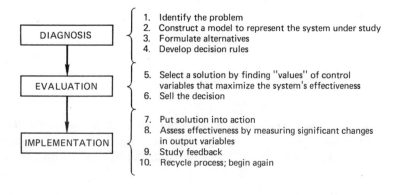

be a short, clear statement, setting out the objectives of the problem situation, the quantitative and qualitative factors of the situation, and the consequences of both solving and failing to solve the problem.

Construct a model

The next stop after defining the problem is constructing the model. Constructing a model helps the manager put the complexities and uncertainties of the problem into a logical framework that is suitable for analysis. A properly constituted model clarifies alternatives and anticipated effects, specifies the data that is relevant for analysis of alternatives, leads to the collection of information, and suggests conclusions. The model, in other words, translates the verbal definition of the problem into a mathematical framework that relates the factors of the problem to measures of effectiveness.

In operations research, a model is almost always mathematical; in the latter part of the chapter we shall examine a number of quantitative methods that can help managers solve problems. The important thing to keep in mind is that a model is always a substitute representation of reality. By simplifying details, it helps managers think about problems in systematic ways.

Once the model has been developed, experimentation and validation make sure the model corresponds to the reality of the problem. Here we get down to the nub of the problem. The manager must decide on proper data inputs and appropriate information outputs and then carry out some kind of analysis to see whether the inputs are related to the outputs. The major part of analysis consists of determining the sensitivity of the solution to the model specifications. For example, a manager in the automobile industry could construct a model with the following variables: the selling price of the car, the volume of production, total sales, inventory size, and level of advertising budget. Using his model he could set out, for example, to determine how demand is correlated with price changes.

Formulate alternatives

Executives tend to be people of action. They are therefore reluctant, once they have identified and defined the problem, to spend time generating alternatives. Nevertheless, this is one of the important objectives of systematic problem solving. If a president of an automobile company finds that one plant is operating below expectations, he could consider the following alternatives:

1. close down the plant,
2. replace the general manager,
3. reduce the price of the automobile,
4. increase the advertising budget,
5. introduce consultants,
6. change the method of production,
7. change the model to be manufactured, or
8. some combination of the above.

A more systematic analysis of the problem may suggest an even wider range of options, including:

9. extend the car warranty, and
10. restructure the channels of distribution.

Develop decision rules

Setting up decision rules allows you to select the best alternative. Generally, such rules have certain superrules, e.g., (a) we must not win everything (and bring down the government) and (b) we must not lose our shirt. To experienced executives the business of optimizing is not all that difficult. Given a choice, you back all the horses in the race. For example, if an oil company has $100 million to spend on buying squares in the North Sea, which, say, has a thousand squares, it buys outright forty good bet (good evidence of oil or gas) squares, then forty half shares of the next best, then two hundred of one-tenth shares of the next best, and so on.

Evaluation

Select a solution

Having got your rules together, you now make the decision. All decisions are equally attractive to you as long as they apply your decision rules. Accept the first alternative that meets the minimal level of acceptability in the complete range of criteria.

It is useful to keep in mind that

An alternative is *optimal* if: (1) there exists a set of criteria that permits all alternatives to be compared, and (2) the alternative in question is preferred, by these criteria, to all other alternatives. An alternative is *satisfactory* if: (1) there exists a set of criteria that describes minimally satisfactory alternatives, and (2) the alternative in question meets or exceeds all these criteria. . . . Finding that optimal alternative is a radically different problem from finding a satisfactory alternative. . . . To optimize requires processes several orders of magnitude more complex than those required to satisfice.[2]

Sell the decision

Japanese business management behaves in a singularly different fashion from Western management, American or European. Japanese institutions make decision by "consensus." They debate a decision throughout the organization until there is agreement on it. Only then do they make the decision.

By Western thinking, this method appears to be slow and to lead to an innocuous compromise. The key to this misconception is that the Westerners and the Japanese mean something different when they talk of "making a decision." In the West, all the emphasis is on the *answer to the question*. Indeed, we have been taught to try and develop systematic approaches to giving an answer. To the Japanese, however, the important element in decision making is *defining the question*. The critical steps are deciding whether there is a need for a decision and what the decision is about. It is in this step that the Japanese aim at attaining consensus.

What can we learn from this process? In the first place, the Japanese method enhances speedy and effective decisions. We in the West make the decision first and then spend years selling it and getting people to act on it. Too often, either the decision is aborted by the organization or it takes so long to make it effective that the decision becomes obsolete. The Japanese, by constrast, spend absolutely no time on "selling a decision." Everybody has already been presold. If there are any dissenters, there is plenty of time to persuade them without violating the integrity of the decision.

In the West, we are moving in the direction of "task forces," "long range plans," and "strategies." But we do not build selling into the work of these task forces. This helps explain why so many of the brilliant reports of these task force planners never develop into action. At the same time, we expect these task forces or long-range planners to come up with recommendations and commit themselves to one alternative. To the Japanese, however, the most important step is understanding the available alternatives. They are disciplined not to commit themselves

---

[2] James G. March and Herbert A. Simon, *Organizations* (New York: John Wiley & Sons, 1958), pp. 140–41.

until there is agreement on what the decision is all about. Because they obtain consensus to bring out the full range of alternatives, they are far less likely than we to become prisoners of preconceived answers.

Box 11.1 considers one approach to selling decisions.

Put solution into action

Once the alternative has been selected and sold, it must be implemented or put into action. Today, executives make a conscious and deliberate effort to implement decisions. In terms of objective setting, planning, and especially control, a well-defined program must be developed. Each stage of the decision program must be implemented to be meaningful. If an executive means business then he must be ready to accept responsibility for his decisions by being prepared if necessary to police the implementation. Thus, the meaning of the decision is its implementation.

Assess effectiveness by measuring significant changes in output variables

In recent years, many managers have attempted to state actual output or end product variables in quantitative terms. (Box 11.2 shows one way of doing this.) Behavior must be carefully monitored to insure a substantial measure of correspondence between performance and plan. We must measure the capacity of the organization to produce the qualitative and quantitative measure of output that the environment demands and for which it is willing to pay. Measures of production include profit, sales, market share, documents processed, passengers carried, students graduated, patients cured, and the like. The human aspect can be measured by assessment of morale, which in turn can be derived from measures of labor turnover, absenteeism, sickness, number of grievances, and accidents.

So far we have only discussed short-run criteria of organizational effectiveness. Another approach is the measurement of organizational effectiveness. This considers the factor of time and employs the concepts of adaptiveness, development, and survival (see Figure 11.2). Adaptiveness is the extent to which the organization can and does respond to externally and internally induced changes. Development is the organization's capacity to grow to meet changes in the environment. Survival is the capacity of the organization to exist over a long period of time in the face of changes. Thus, when managers talk of optimal balance they are referring to the art of balancing the organization's performance

Box 11.1: Can Decision Selling Be Taught?

The most common approach of the manager is to try to persuade his subordinates to adopt the solution he has in mind, as contrasted with the approach of posing a problem and requesting the workers' participation in finding a solution. When he has a preferred solution in mind, there is a strong tendency for him to reveal a bias. It is also found that leaders usually fail to share data with workers. But trained people do share data, do sell before the decision. Maier and Sashkin carried out an experiment involving two groups:

- A trained group consisting of students in undergraduate courses in industrial psychology who had been exposed to concepts of group decision, case discussion, and role play; and
- An untrained group consisting of students in introductory psychology courses.

A case method approach was used. The case was "Changing Work Procedure," in which the foreman and three assembly workers were experiencing a conflict. Following role play, the students were asked to complete brief questionnaires pertaining to the type of solution reached, estimates of production, the foreman's discussion approach,

Continued on next page
From N.R.F. Maier and M. Sashkin, "Specific Leadership Behaviors that Promote Problem-Solving," *Personnel Psychology*, Vol. 24, No. 1 (Spring 1971), pp. 35–44.

over time and the proper relations among the criteria within the given time period.

Feedback

Management has to police performance, and it does so through feedback. To achieve this feedback, information and control systems

Figure 11.2   Criteria of Organizational Effectiveness

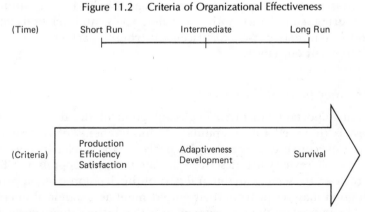

From James L. Gibson et al., *Organizations* (Dallas, Tex.: Business Publications, Inc., 1976), p. 65. © 1976 by Business Publications, Inc.

and the sharing of data in the foreman's possession. In their solutions, the trained group was less inclined to persuade and more inclined to pose a problem; the untrained group had opposite inclinations. Nearly half of the untrained group presented their own solutions; just one in the trained group did so. The trained leaders were also more inclined to share data than were the untrained leaders.

Training also increases the frequency with which integrative solutions are developed. In the foreman's discussion approach, the trained group scored their foreman's approach more integrative than did the untrained group. The results of this experiment show the benefit of training in which the leader:

a. Poses a problem and the group generates the solution, versus
b. Poses a solution and persuades the group to adopt it.

However, Maier found that even after training, most leaders still sold, although they seemed somewhat more inclined to listen and entertain objections. Leaders familiar with the concept of group discussion were significantly more inclined to initiate group discussion with a problem-solving approach.

must be set up that allow the manager to police the results of his decision. It is at this stage that the manager can get a first glimmering of whether he has made the correct choice. But such control systems can be dysfunctional. As we noted in Chapter 10, control refers to how a business monitors performance and polices behavior and attitudes. But securing compliance with the rules, roles, and relations of the control system may cause a displacement from the achievement of real and important objectives.

Recycle process; begin again

An important but often neglected point of the decision-making process is the need for recapitulation, for moments of tranquility so that the executive can examine the process as a whole. In periods of anxiety such reviews are described as "agonizing reappraisals." But if such reviews are seen as an integral part of the decision-making process, much good may result from their employment as a standard operating rule. The important thing to remember is that history does repeat itself, but only if you are not paying attention.

The decision tree is a diagram of decision possibilities, drawn horizontally for convenience. The trunk of the tree is the beginning decision point and its branches begin at the first possible events. The beauty of the decision tree method lies in its simplicity and its ability to consider probabilities.

Let us consider a typical business decision and "grow" the related decision tree in order to see how these trees work.

The sales manager at Emperor Products Inc. (a manufacturer of electronic components) was recommending the addition of a fifth production unit to meet increasing sales demand. While the company treasurer conceded that the existing four units were operating at full capacity he cautioned, "Maybe . . . I say, maybe . . . we can get a 20 percent sales increase. But with present tax and inventory prospects we have to cover ourselves in case sales drop."

To settle the discussion the president asked for a joint estimate and the two groups agreed that while there was a 60 percent likelihood that sales would increase there was a 40 percent chance they could drop as much as 5 percent. The president then called for figures on the possible dollar consequences for the next year, considering two decision alternatives to increase capacity: new equipment or overtime. The net cash flow figures he got were:

Continued on next page

MAKING CREATIVE DECISIONS

To be efficient decision makers, executives have to think creatively. Unfortunately, many executives who come into management via engineering have been trained to think in linear terms. Linear, or logical, thinkers work towards answers in a kind of A→B→C sequence. Nonlinear thinking, on the other hand, is the ability to think of new options, to make new and daring connections, to take on problems that other people have passed up because they are difficult to identify, categorize, and quantify. Nonlinear, creative thinking involves four steps: preparation, incubation, illumination, and verification.

Preparation

Preparation is the process of arming one's mind with all the information and data necessary for making a decision. Preparation

247

Events		New equipment		Overtime
Sales rise 20%	+	$460,000	+	$440,000
Sales drop 5%	+	340,000	+	380,000

The president needed an analysis which would take the probabilities of the events into account. Therefore, he drew a beginning decision tree to start his analysis.

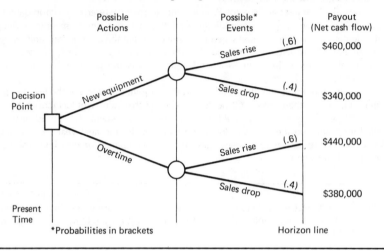

involves mulling over various concepts, conclusions, and facts and trying to get them to fit a variety of explanations.

One useful technique to employ is synectics. Developed by Williams J. J. Gordon, synectics gathers a group of experts to discuss a particular topic. They are encouraged to express ideas off the tops of their heads in a nonevaluative, spontaneous atmosphere. Another technique is lateral, or zig zag, thinking, which is described in Box 11.3.

Incubation

Once preparation has been completed, the next step is to relax, to pass the problem over to the unconscious. Creative people have a particular cognitive style that allows them to engage in other, playful activities while their unconscious carries on the hard work. What it amounts to is that creative people can not only digest large volumes of information, but they can also take risks with their thinking. Creative people are wide categorizers who frequently appear very disorganized

This diagram sets out the decision and the data provided to the president. In order to determine the better composite value of payout-as-modified-by-probability, or "expected value," he multiplies each event branch cash flow by its related probability. This analysis yielded the following:

	New equipment	Overtime
Sales rise 20% (60% probability)	$276,000	$264,000
Sales drop 5% (40% probability)	136,000	152,000
Total expected values	$412,000	$416,000

The president had to explain to his subordinates what these composite figures or expected values meant. They were not the actual cash flows that would result if either event occurred, but rather a weighted average of the forecast results with the probabilities used as weights. Thus, the expected value of $416,000 for overtime showed it as the preferable alternative based on the adds-weighted probabilities. Of course, if the overtime alternative were chosen and the forecasts accurate, actual results would be either a net cash flow of +$440,000 or +$380,000, depending on which event (sales rise or drop) actually occurred.

The treasurer decided it might be worthwhile to extend the decision tree another

Continued on next page

to their colleagues. They tend to be of an iconoclastic disposition; that is, they are not reluctant to smash images of either the status quo or established doctrines.

Illumination

Once incubation has been gone through, it is not unusual for the solution of the problem to come like a bolt from the blue. The dramatic effect can be an extremely illuminating experience. Most creative people can recall instances when solutions came to them, fresh and new, perhaps as they were taking a bath or stepping off a bus.

Verification

The final phase is verification, in which the manager sets out to establish the reliability and validity of his solution.

year forward to see if the overtime option would remain the better choice. He obtained new sales estimates and probabilities for the second year and, using the basic method illustrated earlier, extended the chart. Upon computing the expected values he found that over the two year period the option of new equipment produced the largest expected value and, therefore, became the preferable option. Thus, he recommended purchase of the new equipment as the better way to increase capacity considering the growth forecast for the second year.

This example is simple enough so that, given the background information, most (but not all) executives would intuitively have made the option chosen by the treasurer. What decision trees do, even in a relatively simple situation, is to clarify what would have been debatable—and debated—in most companies.

THE NUMBERS GAME: MODELS

Since the end of World War II enormous advances in decision making have been made in quantitative disciplines. This new field is called operations research (sometimes management science). It began in the Second World War, when groups of scientists studied logistics and such specific problems of war as convoy routings, bombing tactics, bomb explosions, and bomb damage. After the war, OR grew in scope and complexity as it received fresh impetus at major university research centers.

Gradually it became evident that many OR techniques could be applied to problems in industry. An enormous acceleration and broadening of applications and methods occurred and is still continuing. The spread and general acceptance of EDP (electronic data processing) equipment has coincided with and assisted in the growth of OR.

Today, most big decisions emerge after a problem has been analyzed and filtered by subordinates who possess technical OR expertise. Thus, there is pressure on decision makers to be able to state their problems in a numerical form, which facilitates computer handling.

Both lateral and vertical thinking are concerned with effectiveness. Whenever a solution is found by lateral thinking one can always, in hindsight, see how it could have been arrived at by vertical thinking. But looking back in hindsight is quite different from actually finding the solution by that route.

From the operations research field comes the well-known story of the skyscraper that was built with too few elevators. The office staff became very impatient waiting for the elevators at the beginning and especially at the end of the day, and began to quit. Various ways of dealing with the problem were considered: putting up new elevator shafts outside the building or driving a new shaft through the floors; speeding up the elevators or arranging them so that they stopped only at certain floors; staggering working hours to reduce demand at either end of the day. In short, there were lots of ideas on how to increase the supply of elevators or how to utilize them better. Then the operations research people came up with a rather simple answer: they suggested putting mirrors around the entrances to all elevators. As a result, the staff became so preoccupied with looking at themselves (or surreptitiously at others) that no one noticed the long wait for the elevators anymore.

Vertical Thinking
You cannot dig a hole in a different place by digging the same hole deeper—and

Continued on next page

From Edward deBono, "The Virtues of Zig-Zag Thinking." Reprinted by permission from THINK Magazine, published by IBM copyright 1969 by International Business Machines Corporation.

Requirements Before Quantitative Techniques Can Be Applied

Most quantitative methods require the following:

1. the problem must be expressed numerically in some form,
2. the goal must be well-defined,
3. the decision maker must have a set of alternatives, and,
4. the constraints that bound the solutions must be formally defined.

Uses of Models

In OR, models are used extensively. Business uses models to

1. improve systems by comparisons to alternative options,
2. design systems or outputs for optimal performance,
3. clarify objective and tentative plans,
4. train personnel by means of business games (simulation), and
5. forecast effects of changes in various variables.

vertical thinking is digging the same hole deeper. You start from what you have and go straight ahead, using any one of the many effective information-handling techniques available. Vertical thinking is the highly esteemed (and rightly so) traditional method of thinking that has proved immensely effective, especially in technological matters. It has three basic characteristics. Vertical thinking:

1. is a stepwise process. Each step follows on from the previous step in an unbroken sequence.
2. must be correct at every step. (This is perhaps the very essence of the process.)
3. selects and deals with only what is relevant, e.g., computer programming.

Lateral Thinking

What is lateral thinking? Instead of digging the same hole deeper, lateral thinking digs a hole in a different place. As the name implies, lateral thinking is thinking sideways: not developing a pattern but restructuring a pattern.

QUANTITATIVE TECHNIQUES

Sampling

Applications

To make descriptive inferences about a large quantity of items or data (called a population) used in market research, work sampling, inventory control, auditing, and so forth.

Inputs

Sample information is obtained by using randomized techniques applied to a small percentage of the total population with specified degrees of reliability.

Assumptions

The samples have all the characteristics of the total population from which they were selected.

Outputs

Within specified degrees of reliability, characteristics of the total population can be inferred: averages, variances, probabilities of type of occurrences, and so on.

Notes

Sampling enables the user to obtain information that cannot economically or practically be gathered by examining 100 percent of the population.

Inventory Models

Application

To determine how much of an item to keep on hand and when to reorder it, while minimizing total costs.

Inputs

Historical information or estimates, often on a daily basis, on the behavior of each item in inventory that is to be controlled.

Assumptions

Past behavior is an adequate basis for future predictions; that is, that the demand, delivery delays, and costs can be estimated probabilistically using past and present information.

Outputs

Reorder points and order quantities for each inventory item so that the possibility of a stock-out (item unavailable when demanded) and the total inventory costs are at acceptable levels.

Notes

Varying degrees of sophistication from simple models of certainty to complex integrated probabilistic computer models.

In many businesses, both large and small, cash shortages have been caused by carrying too much inventory in relation to current and anticipated sales. On the other hand, insufficient inventory results in lost sales or idle production facilities. Present inventory levels in industry influence production activity in subsequent periods. Inventory levels are the combination of two elements: the amount of goods needed for the regular turnover (expected usage) plus a safety stock or reserve against the unexpected.

The proper reorder point depends upon lead time (the delay between order and delivery), usage, and the optimum order size (the economic order quantity, or EOQ) for each item. Lead time requirements are often built into safety stock levels.

Some inventory basics:

1. Inventory levels can be either too high or too low; inventory control consists of establishing and maintaining the optimum level.

2. Many inventory costs (for example, profits and customer good will lost by being out of stock) are not available in the regular accounting records. In cases where they are available, they must be analyzed to determine the portions applicable to inventory (clerical costs, transportation and storage costs, etc.).

3. In some companies, inventories are purchased as a hedge against or in anticipation of price increases. The gamble is that the increased carrying costs for the excess inventory will not exceed the savings from the lower purchase prices.

4. Supplier delivery reliability is important, since uncertainty about delivery increases costs through larger safety stocks and a higher occurrence of stock-outs.

Queuing or Waiting-line Theory

Application

To prevent flow-of-work, customer, or material bottlenecks through particular points in order to maximize the throughput efficiency over time.

Inputs

Rate of arrival of things or people at the checkpoint, the rate at which they can be processed, and the cost of idleness.

Assumptions

Optimal allocation of resources based on balance between service levels and service costs.

Outputs

Alternative service and cost levels enabling optimal decision making.

Notes

A typical example is the determination of the number of cash registers and cashiers at a supermarket. Queuing is used primarily in production and distribution problems and in such trafficking problems as aircraft landings and takeoffs.

Queuing problems involve customers (or any entity that is to pass through a process) waiting to be served at specific times. The arrival time is the instant a customer joins a queue. The time between arriving and receiving service is the queuing time. Queuing theory provides answers to questions such as: If we want to reduce to less than 10 percent the number of customers who must wait more than 1 minute, how many servers are necessary? Can costs be reduced by separating servers into separate groups? Should we increase space or use more servers? Variance in arrival rate or in processing (queuing and servicing) time will have what effect on servicing time at peak periods?

Correlation Techniques

Application

To determine the degree of functional relationship between variables when the unknown can be better known by looking at other variables. It is used extensively in forecasting and market research.

Inputs

Statistical techniques of regréssion analysis, correlation coefficients, and scatter diagrams.

Assumptions

These vary with the method, but they generally assume that the patterns of relationship remain constant.

Outputs

Estimated value of one or more variables based on the value of one or more correlated variables.

Notes

Very often correlation provides a technique of indirect measurement.

Network Techniques

Application

Aid in planning, scheduling, and controlling projects and complex activities that take place over time.

Inputs

A plan of necessary steps or stages in a process, a definition of objectives, and time and cost considerations.

Assumptions

Under conditions of risk and uncertainty, a small number of operations control or limit completion time or performance of the total activity. Concentration on these critical activities allows true management by exception.

Outputs

Probability of achieving targets, highlighting critical stages, and optimum schedules.

Notes

Many varieties of networks exist. The best known are CPM (critical path method) and PERT (project evaluation and review techniques). PERT is explained in Box 11.4.

PERT and CPM are used for planning, scheduling, and controlling the utilization of manpower, materials, and facilities. One way to understand their use is in terms of the basic management functions to

BOX 11.4: PERT: How to Meet a Deadline

What do retailing and building missile-carrying submarines have in common? Well, managers in both areas face deadlines and can use a common management tool—PERT—to plan and control performance to deadlines.

The credit for developing PERT goes to the U.S. Navy's Special Projects Office (SPO). The Navy used PERT to accelerate its Polaris missile program and hit its target date nearly three years ahead of time. Since the Navy's SPO shared this technique with industry in the early 1960s, PERT has become a standard tool for planning and controlling projects. It became practical for complex jobs with the advent of the computer.

You probably have employed PERT concepts without calling them by name. For example, a young couple who decide to marry and set a wedding date will inevitably PERT the task. They know, or will learn, that certain events must occur sometime between their decision and the day of matrimony: parental permission, engagement, marriage license, preacher, ushers, church, flowers, reception, guest list, etc. It is obvious that these events are interdependent, that some cannot occur until others have been completed, and that each takes a certain amount of time. Of course, in a very complex task such as building a missile-carrying nuclear submarine the network of events cannot be readily integrated and processed by the mind.

Continued on next page

From Howard Simons, "PERT: How to Meet a Deadline." Reprinted by permission from THINK Magazine, published by IBM copyright 1962 by International Business Machines Corporation.

which they contribute. To perform the planning function, one must resolve such questions as:

1. What tasks must be accomplished to attain the end objective?
2. How will the tasks be accomplished?
3. Who will perform the work required to accomplish the task?
4. How much time will be required to perform the task?
5. What relationship exists between the various tasks?

PERT is a means of achieving objectively planned programs, realistic predictions of program progress, measurement of program progress, better application of available resources, predicted impact of alternatives, and timely accomplishment of program schedules.

Simulation Techniques

Applications

To imitate an operation or process prior to actual implementation or as a learning device for students and managers. Applications exist in

PERT is deceptively simple. Essentially, events that must take place to meet a target date are tied together sequentially by the estimated times it takes to move from one event to another. Progress, or the lack of it which affects the program, is computed by electronic data processing and then made available graphically (in a network) for all to see and act upon. The network is continually updated to reflect change, trouble, potential trouble, and achievement. The approach is repeated until the project is completed on time.

Here, in six steps, is how PERT works:

1. select and identify every significant event which must occur to realize the end objective;
2. establish the interdependencies among the events;
3. put three time values on each activity: (a) optimistic, (b) most likely, and (c) pessimistic;
4. compute the expected time for completing each activity using the formula:

$$\text{time} = \frac{\text{optimistic time} + 4(\text{most likely time}) + \text{pessimistic time}}{6}$$

virtually every area of business activity. Most simulations are more complicated models that require computers to handle the calculations.

Inputs

A model that represents some part of reality and alternative decision choices to be tested.

Assumptions

Existence of an adequate model of realities.

Outputs

Effects taking long periods of time in real life can be simulated in very short periods, thus allowing the decision maker to test decision alternatives before implementing one of them.

5. using a computer, total the expected times along every possible path of the network to determine the "critical path"—the longest distance in time between beginning and end;
6. use the printout to focus management attention on those areas where corrective action is most needed and can do the most good.

PERT techniques have been extended to include the management of dollar activity in PERT/Cost. This is a mirror image of PERT with the exception that only one dollar estimate is made against three time estimates for PERT. But unlike PERT itself, PERT/Cost offers information so that the best plan or allocation of resources which will yield the lowest cost can be determined.

PERT's proponents claim much for their system but they are the first to admit it is not a panacea. "To apply PERT unreasonably," says Commander Daniel, who was head of the SPO Program Evaluation Branch, "is to invite a lot of trouble. PERT puts a powerful tool in the hands of executives, but it does not replace sound management. The boss must want to use it and even then it will be effective only if its capabilities and limitations are understood, all management levels cooperate and it is used for decision—the manager must decide, the computer won't do it for him."

Cost-Volume-Profit Analysis

Application

To illustrate the changes in costs and profits as sales volume varies.

Inputs

Basic ingredients are a revenue function and cost function.

Assumptions

Relationships are linear (they can be realistically represented by straight lines) over the volume range, and either a single product is sold or sales mix (the relative sales percentages of products with different profit percentages) is constant.

Outputs

Determination of a break-even point, profits or losses at different volumes, and marginal contributions to income stemming from changes in volume.

Notes

Most useful in situations of limited change in the relationship between variables. Under conditions of change and uncertainty more sophisticated simulation techniques can be used.

Break-even charts contain a great deal of information about interrelations. Cost and profit at various sales levels can be read and the effects of changes in the cost structure can be readily demonstrated.

Decision Techniques for Situations of Total Ignorance

Application

Deals with situations in which there is total ignorance of probabilities of various results stemming from different decisions.

Inputs

Alternative results (states of nature) to alternative strategies, estimated impact of each strategy in each state of nature, and a decision rule.

Assumptions

A decision rule that provides a suitable guideline (for example, the minimax technique, which determines the worst possible outcome for each alternative and then selects the alternative that minimizes maximum loss).

Outputs

An optimum solution based on the adopted decision rule.

Notes

Other alternative decision rules are available that are optimistic, pessimistic, or in between.

Linear Programming

Application

The use of mathematical techniques to allocate limited resources among competing demands to either minimize total cost or maximize contribution margin; that is, to yield an optimum solution.

Inputs

A function to be optimized, the resources available, the work or service demands, and resource restraints or limitations.

Assumptions

Variables are assumed to be linear and to be relatively certain over time.

Outputs

The optimum solution(s).

Notes

Solutions can be arrived at mathematically, or such specific methods as the transportation method or computer programs can be used. Box 11.5 describes how a particular problem was solved by linear programming.

Tips on Quantitative Decision Making

1. If a thing can be quantified, quantify it.
2. Even when a phenomenon is quantified, we don't know everything about it.
3. Remember that managers have different cognitive styles. A sales manager thinks in quite a different way than does a manager of research and development.
4. Keep in mind that the main reason management science models are not used is because they are too complicated.
5. Learn to distinguish among certainty, uncertainty, and risk.
6. Systems managers employ this sequence: planning, allocation of resources, operations, and measurement.
7. Remember that the best operations research teams are made up of a mix of professions. Typically, they include physical scientists, biologists, social scientists, and managers.

Box 11.5: A Case in Point

Here's how one supervisor used the services of a mathematician to help him solve an important problem:

Production manager Fred Halloway had to make a production schedule for the coming week. He asked one of the operations-research people for some help. This is how he phrased the problem: "The B-26 turret lathe is down and the QC (quality-control) boys have frozen the last shipment of castings so that they can do some additional testing. Since we can't use those castings, we can switch over to the base plates for the McElwain contract, catch up on our housings production, or finish the X-101 gear covers. Should we try to do some of each to keep the sales department off our backs?"

The operations-research analyst didn't know what Fred was talking about. "Look, Fred," he said. "Let's sit down and try to work this thing out. Could you explain it in a different way?" After discussing the problem with the mathematician, Fred came up with this definition: "The company must allocate scarce resources (labor, materials, machines) to meet several competing needs (products) in a way that will maximize the total contribution—first to overhead and then, after overhead costs are met, to profit."

To Fred, it was a production problem; to the mathematician, a problem in linear programming. After receiving pertinent data from Fred, the operations-research analyst translated the problem into these symbols:

Reprinted by permission of the publisher, from "Quantitative Decision Making" by William A. Ruch, *Supervisory Management*, vol. 19, no. 1 (January 1975). Copyright © 1975 by AMACOM, a division of the American Management Associations. All rights reserved.

8. Cautions
   a. Remember GIGO—garbage in, garbage out. Analysis or prediction is only as good as the data input.
   b. Ultimately, quantitative aids are just that—aids. They cannot replace the decision makers.
   c. Rarely do quantitative techniques encompass all the variables that affect human behavior and motivation.
   d. Most business decisions are multidimensional and involve tough-to-quantify tradeoffs, which may be too complex to model completely. Thus, the manager should balance the gain in prediction against the cost of calculation.

REVIEW AND RESEARCH

1. Review a decision with which you are familiar. How was the decision made? How extensive was the search for information? How effective was the decision?

- □ Max Z + 5.00A + 2.00B + 1.00C
- □ Subject to:
- □ R: 3A + 5B + 4C ⩽ 2,700
- □ S: 1A + 1B + 0C ⩽ 1,800
- □ T: 3A + 2B + 0C ⩽ 3,000
- □ Solution: Z = $4,600
- □ A = 800   R = 0
- □ B = 300   S = 700
- □ C = 0   T = 0

Fred, of course, didn't understand the mathematician until he translated the symbols into Fred's language. The mathematician explained that A, B, and C were the real products, which contributed $5.00, $2.00, and $1.00 per unit to overhead and profit. R, S, and T were the available resources, expressed as 2,700 hours of labor, 1,800 square feet of material #1, and 3,000 gallons of material #2.

The equations expressing the restraints imposed by the available resources also indicate how much of each resource is used in making each product. So, 3A + 5B + 4C ⩽ 2,700 means that each unit of Product A requires 3 units of labor; each unit of

Continued on next page

2. List three steps in problem solving. Interview an executive about an important decision he has made recently. Try and match your data to the framework.

3. Why is decision making so often nonrational?

4. Find out more about the Kepner-Tregoe method of problem solving and explain it.

5. Use lateral thinking to figure out ways and means of making flying to Europe more attractive.

6. Use synectics to produce a set of viable projects that could generate cash for you if you used your university business school facilities.

7. Find out what PPBS is. Explain it.

8. What is probability?

9. Draw up a list of points that will help you to communicate more effectively.

10. Why do managers have to spend so much time communicating with peers?

11. What is the point of the parable of the spindle? Explain either (a) how

Product B, 5 units of labor; each unit of Product C, 4 units of labor; and that the total labor used must equal or be less than 2,700 units. This is information that Fred gave the mathematician.

The solution to the *model?* Producing 800 units of Product A, 300 units of Product B, and none of Product C would yield the highest profit contribution: $4,600.00. All labor and all of material #2 would be used, but 700 square feet of material #1 would be left over.

Fred carefully considered this information. Then he decided to produce a minimum 100 units of Product C because of a special order that was coming in, adjusted the rest of the production schedule accordingly, and released it to the shop.

Neither Fred nor the operations-research analyst could have solved the problem alone. Each made a contribution to the problem-solving process—Fred at the beginning and end, the mathematician in the middle. The critical links in the process—where the operation came closest to failure—were the points at which the language of one discipline were translated into the language of the other.

Fred's approach to mathematics from the viewpoint that it was a specialized discipline, written in a foreign language, minimized much of his irrational—but natural—aversion to using math in solving managerial problems.

air traffic controllers function or (b) how the reception desk in an automobile service station acts as a spindle to control and manage the flow of information and events in their environments.

12. Describe the production, planning, and control system for any organization with which you are familiar (for example, an automobile service station, a hospital, or registration at a university) and show how it can be analyzed into these six steps: sensor, data processing, decision-making process, control, and memory subsystems.

13. We know that different managers have different ways of thinking about corporate problems. Using a model, set out the difference between the cognitive processes of management scientists and line managers.

ON WORKING HOURS

Mr. Jacobs, president of a large manufacturing firm, has overheard several comments lately on the tardiness of office staff in the firm. He himself has noticed people arriving a few minutes late for work and has almost been knocked over on several occasions in stairwells by the mass exodus just before official quitting time. He also has heard that employees have extended their 30-minute lunch hour to nearly 1 hour.

The company is presently on summer hours which will end the second week of October. These hours are: Monday, 8:15 to 4:00; Tuesday to Thursday, 8:00 to 4:00; and Friday, 8:00 to 12:00. Lunch hour is 30 minutes with no lunch on Fridays.

The regular working hours before summer hours started were 8:15 to 4:00, 5 days a week, with 30 minutes for lunch. The 30-minute lunch hour was reduced within the last 2 years from 1 hour. It was decided then to shorten the lunch hour since the firm was located in an area where there were few places nearby for lunch and most of the employees ate in the company cafeteria. The end of the workday was then changed from 4:30 to 4:00, allowing people to return home earlier.

There was speculation at the beginning of the summer, as during past summers, that summer hours would be extended to year-round, going with the trend of shorter work weeks.

Although the office is not under any sort of union, the contracts signed by the plant union have always applied to the office in terms of total hours worked over the year. The plant's hours are scheduled differently over the year, but in total their hours have equaled those of the office. A new contract has just been signed with the plant union, and the hours to be worked have not been changed.

Mr. Jacobs is contemplating these points before sending out the official reminder of the return to regular working hours.

Develop a decision track for Mr. Jacobs. Start with the definition of the problem and its factors. List the alternatives. Make a choice. Develop a plan for implementation.

III

VALUE
VARIABLES

12

The Changing Value Set

OBJECTIVES YOU SHOULD MEET

Define values.

Categorize classical, human, systems, and existential values.

Illustrate how superiors create moral problems for subordinates.

Explain how society today is holding the executive responsible for his or her company's actions.

Specify the behaviors of "a reasonable, prudent person," who is an executive.

The aim of this chapter is to discuss the concept of managerial values. In a general sense, values are the social glue that hold a structure in position and allow the process to run on track. Values are necessary because structure and process cannot be precisely defined to meet every operational contingency that may emerge. Values are needed to help managers and other employees make choices among competing objectives, especially when the issues do not emerge in black and white terms.

Everybody has values; those of other people may be difficult to recognize because they are different from one's own. Managers, like everybody else, need moral frames of reference within which they can exercise choices and thus commit themselves to a course of action with some underlying moral rationale.

A value is a set of beliefs about what is desirable or "good." We can classify value systems according to management theory. Classical values emphasize rationality, causality, integrity, independence, deferred consumption, and hard work. But the classical value system is now under attack from a number of different viewpoints. One reason classical values have been attacked is developments in technology and their attendent value systems. Another major force for changing traditional values is future shock, which describes the stress and disorientation people experience when they are overexposed to change. As a result of future shock, there has developed a new consciousness among business people.

THE CLASSICAL VALUE: RATIONALITY

The Birth of Modern Bureaucracy

While bureaucracy is often denigrated today, it is worthwhile to review briefly how, why, and when bureaucracy reappeared in its modern form. As we know from biblical records, forms of bureaucracy have existed from man's earliest times.

The development of railways, steamships, and telegraphs paralleled the evolution of bureaucracy. To run a railroad at the turn of the century demanded not only such hardware as locomotives, wagons, track, and signaling systems, but also a particular attitude. Managers, employees, passengers, and suppliers learned to live by the clock. In some industries, such as shipyards, the men were issued tokens telling when they were allowed to visit the lavatory. Time was money. The very idea of coffee breaks was anathema to the owners and directors of companies. The hourly paid operative had arrived on the scene.

Rationality and Perfectability

In Europe at the turn of the century, the more powerful a country was industrially, the more pervasive was its bureaucracy, Germany leading in both aspects. It was Max Weber, the German sociologist, who developed the theory of bureaucracy as the ideal way of organizing.

The conventional discussion of bureaucracy usually focuses on such structural matters as fixed duties or offices (specialization) defined hierarchy, promotion on merit, tenure of appointment, guidance by precedent, and right to appeal decisions. Concurrently with this structure there emerged a particular value system. The most important single value underlying bureaucracy was a deep, pervasive belief in rationality and perfectability. People lived with a Newtonian sense of certainty. In Germany, the enlightened and informed person saw order reigning all around him, not only in the physical sciences, but also in the new science of psychology.

Knowledge was presumed to be finite, and people could master most of it, if not all of it. The faculty doctrine assumed that the mind was made up of a number of faculties—memory, understanding, consciousness, and will—and these faculties, like muscles, could be strengthened by exercise. It was just this type of rational certainty that pervaded the institutions of Western Europe and the United States. Adam Smith's paradigm of the pin factory permeated not only business but education, the military, hospitals, and government and municipal institutions. Bureaucracy, as it was felt, was not only efficient; it was fair. The great engines of state and commerce required an educated, healthy, happy proletariat. Legislation was enacted accordingly, although perhaps too slowly for most social critics. The First World War was the first real test of modern bureaucracies, but for a long time it was a stalemate.

Modern Views of Bureaucracy

Today bureaucracy is being attacked at every turn. The main reason for this is the emergence of the new technologies and their attendant value system. In *The New Industrial State*, John Kenneth Galbraith defined technology as the systematic application of scientific or other organized knowledge to practical tasks. Its key characteristics are the division and subdivision of tasks into component parts to facilitate the focusing of organized knowledge as applied to performance. According to Galbraith, as technology began to pervade society, the technocrats lost sight of society's values and purposes. They became preoccupied with the structures, processes, techniques, and values of their specialty. The state of the art became more important than the ends of the state.

Future Shock

The rate of technological change is so rapid and so pervasive that many people in our society are suffering from what Alvin Toffler has called future shock, the cataclysmic stress and disorientation people experience when they are exposed to too much change too rapidly. Somehow or other, we have been conditioned to accept a level of novelty, arousal, and anxiety that barely enables us to make the transition from the horse and buggy era to the railroad age.

The tempo of human evolution is continually being accelerated. The rate of change since the time of Newton and Galileo has been increasing all the time. In this century, the throttles have been opened so wide that only "the exaggerations," as Warren Bennis put it, "seem to be there." Population explosions, exponential growth of knowledge, rapid GNP growth seem to be the order of the day. The world's population is growing too fast for the food supply. Urbanization is proceeding at such a rate that there are more than 140 cities with populations over a million. According to Alvin Toffler,

> What such numbers imply is nothing less revolutionary than a doubling of the total output of goods and services in the advanced societies about every fifteen years—and the doubling times are shrinking. This means, generally speaking, that the child reaching teen age in any of these societies is literally surrounded by twice as much of everything newly man-made as his parents were at the time he was an infant. It means that by the time today's teen-ager reaches age thirty, perhaps earlier, a second doubling will have occurred. Within a seventy-year lifetime, perhaps five such doublings will take place—meaning, since the increases are compounded, that by the time the individual reaches old age the society around him will be producing thirty-two times as much as when he was born.[1]

But this corporate growth has been bought at a terrible moral cost.

---

[1] Alvin Toffler, *Future Shock* (New York: Random House, 1970), pp. 24–25.

Human Relations

As the growth of pseudoreligions, cults, and self-help manuals prove, many people feel neglected and powerless in our technological age. The human relations approach we have discussed realizes that people:

1. want to be needed;
2. want to be in groups with rules, roles, and relations;
3. want physical contact with other people;
4. need more meaningful rituals as rites of passage mark the events of their life cycles: birth, puberty, marriage, menopause, retirement, death;
5. want a philosophy that transcends their lives. People need purpose, process, and meaning that transcend immediate events;
6. want the quality of life improved even at the expense of quantity of goods;
7. are prepared to fight the system to regain quality.

What are management theorists and corporate executives doing about these needs? Modern systems theory presumes that people will assimilate the organization's task and thus achieve commitment. It assumes that the sociotechnical system fuses social and technical constraints to achieve its purpose; people will sort themselves out optimally. In theory, yes; in fact, no. Why? Because any organization cannot be all things to all people.

Human Relations Values

The human relations approach proceeds from certain assumptions. These include:

1. a presumed superiority of feeling over thinking. The essential idea is that to understand something, it must be personally experienced.
2. an expanded awareness of oneself and other people;
3. a new spirit of openness, which demands an increasing authenticity in interpersonal relations;
4. communication as more than words. Nonverbal forms of communication, especially expressing feelings through sight and touch are emphasized;
5. a breakdown of conventional authority patterns, which have been replaced by a cooperative and interdependent style with superiors and colleagues;

6. a new approach to conflict management and confrontation. There is a realistic acceptance of conflict as an integral element of groups and organizations.

SYSTEMS VALUES: BLACK BOXES WITHIN BLACK BOXES

Structure

Modern organization theory is systems theory. In terms of structure, organizations are a hierarchy of systems. All human organizations have a clearly hierarchical structure; they have parts within parts. The different parts of a system are known as the subsystems. These subsystems are linked in such a way that the various inputs are transformed into outputs. A system may deal with only one output, as does a management information system. The structure of a system is defined by the way in which inputs are transformed into outputs. The boundary of the system is defined arbitrarily; the modern practice is to include the environment as part of the system study area. At some point in analyzing the system, the system analyst ceases to be interested in the structure of a component as such. When the transformation between input and output is known, but the internal structure is unknown, the component is called a "black box." Thus the structure of a system consists of a set of elementary tasks, which are treated as black boxes; the structure describes the manner in which the elementary tasks are arranged hierarchically.

Coupling and Decoupling

For the system theorist, the need for hierarchy springs not from the need of an authority but from the need to reduce the apparent complexity of the system. Thus, in system design, a plan must be developed to reduce interactions and make those that occur salient and productive. To achieve this selective separation, decoupling devices are used. They reduce the need for coordination. The spindle, for example, is a decoupling device that holds orders in a short-order restaurant and selectively disconnects the waitresses from the cook. Decoupling can also be made conditional, as happens when a subordinate contacts his superior only when something unusual happens. The determination of structure, the hierarchical arrangement of tasks and the degree of decoupling (amount of autonomy) always require a tradeoff between coordination and independence.

TOWARDS EXISTENTIAL VALUES:
THE MYSTIQUE OF THE BLACK BOX

Viewing the organization as a system has a distinct effect on member values, although these are somewhat difficult to categorize. Systems people put great stress on selective openness and are apparently willing to receive a great number of inputs. These inputs are selectively transformed. The ability to transform inputs or questions is a major systems activity, which is ultimately based on the proposition that no assumptions (value judgments) are sacrosanct.

If systems people are utterly skeptical about all assumptions, how do they maintain equilibrium or control their level of surprise? Many have developed a taste for challenging, intriguing, and exciting problems, which requires them to travel from problem to problem, place to place, technology to technology. Their mobicentric values become ends in themselves, and change is welcomed for the sake of change. Performance is measured by the rate of change, not by the actual milestones or stations reached. This can raise questions of executive ethics, especially for young managers who were radicals in the sixties.

The Students of the Sixties as Managers

A fair number of former radical activist students are now business executives. Their reception in business, presumably after they have made some adjustments, has been positive. As one ex-radical, who is now a senior associate of a Manhattan-based management consultant firm, put it,

> The former radicals are an asset to business. They are aggressive as hell, they're by and large well educated, they have stamina. Business is a rigorous area in which to channel the same kind of energies we had then. And it's damn satisfying to see the results of your work on a balance sheet.[2]

_____

[2] From "The '60s Kids as Managers," 6 March 1978. Reprinted by permission from *Time*, The Weekly Newsmagazine; Copyright Time, Inc. 1978.

These new executives present some unusual challenges to their bosses, who have had to accommodate themselves to new lifestyles. Many of these new managers believe that their college experiences have improved their effectiveness as managers. They question decisions, and they are not afraid to confront power. These young managers place a high value on their lives away from the job. But at the same time, they must be prepared to put in long hours to finish projects or enhance their chances for promotion. All this has led to changes in values:

> Differences about the work ethic have led to friction between generations. Terrence Thompson, 36, a 1970 graduate who is a senior financial representative at Bechtel, says sweepingly (and with a touch of the arrogance that veteran executives criticize in the juniors): "The older group seeks recognition for patriotism. Judeo-Christian morality, prudence, thrift and loyalty. Younger managers value creativity, energy, sensitivity and candor. If I don't get present-day satisfaction, I won't stay. I won't work for the future. Nobody is going to guarantee its arrival."[3]

EXECUTIVE ETHICS

The ethics of U.S. executives are of interest because as managers have begun to control many aspects of society, they have become increasingly vulnerable to corruption. Twenty years ago the main questions about managerial morals concerned receiving gifts, gratuities, and bribes.

But the moral questions of management go far deeper than these issues would suggest. In the 1960s several managers in the electrical equipment field were sent to jail for engaging in collusion and price fixing. In response to this scandal, managers began to scrutinize their behavior more carefully. But when managers examine their consciences they begin to realize that few business issues can be starkly black or white. The ethical dilemma is between being an efficient, profit-conscious, performance-oriented manager and an ethical person. One survey into executive values, norms, and conduct found that apparently, relations with superiors are the primary source of ethical conflict. The authors cite the following examples:[4]

---

[3] *Ibid.*

[4] "Is the Ethics of Business Changing?" by Steven N. Brenner and Earl A. Molander, *Harvard Business Review* (January-February 1977). Copyright © 1976 by the President and Fellows of Harvard College; all rights reserved.

The vice president of a California industrial manufacturer "being forced as an officer to sign corporate documents which I knew were not in the best interest of minority stockholders."

A Missouri manager of manpower planning "employing marginally qualified minorities in order to meet Affirmative Action quotas."

A manager of product development from a computer company in Massachusetts "trying to act as though the product (computer software) would correspond to what the customer had been led by sales to expect, when, in fact, I knew it wouldn't."

A manager of corporate planning from California "acquiring a non-U.S. company with two sets of books used to evade income taxes—standard practice for that country. Do we (1) declare income and pay taxes, (2) take the "black money" out of the country (illegally), or (3) continue tax evasion?"

The president of a real estate property management firm in Washington "projecting cash flow without substantial evidence in order to obtain a higher loan than the project can realistically amortize."

A young Texas insurance manager "being asked to make policy changes that produced more premium for the company and commission for an agent but did not appear to be of advantage to the policy holder."

Executive Values and Corporate Corruption

In the mid-70s, evidence became available of massive American payoffs overseas. A great number of American executives find it morally difficult to accept these payoffs. As Charles Percy, formerly president of Bell and Howell, pointed out some time ago, "Corporate corruption is the dry rot of capitalism."

Not everyone feels this way, however. Unfortunately, scarcely a day goes by without further allegation of corporate bribes, payoffs, and kickbacks. Apparently, this corporate corruption is not generally perceived by executives as necessarily immoral. A 1976 Conference Board study found that about one half of the 73 executives it surveyed defended this form of payoff as a normal way of doing business. On the other hand, many corporate leaders have expressed their public concern about this erosion of business ethics. The *New York Times* editorially complained on February 15, 1976,

The powerful role which American society has assigned to its free enterprises dictates a far higher and broader sense of social ethics than many corporations have shown up to now. The narrow self-interest of an independent entrepreneur, to maximize sales and profits, is simply not good enough. If the dry rot is to be stopped, it is the business community itself which must have the power—and the self-interest—to stop it.[5]

But some business executives argue that the federal government is at least tacitly aware of what is happening and is guilty to some extent of implicitly endorsing some of these "unusual forms of payments." Some executives go further, arguing that the bribes are consistent with the objectives of American foreign policy.

In any case, publicity exposing overseas payments and kickbacks has weakened the image and standing of executives, many of whom have been acting irresponsibly. (See Box 12.1 to find out how people rate executive honesty.)

Corporate Culpability

Increasingly, the blame for corporate law breaking is being placed on the executive, who is held personally responsible and, if tried and found guilty, fined or even jailed. In 1976, six workers were killed and fifty-five others seriously injured in an explosion in a Long Island chewing gum plant. Following the investigation, five company executives were charged with manslaughter and criminally negligent homicide.

Clearly, the senior executive is considered a responsible officer, even when he must delegate responsibility and even when he cannot personally supervise all operations. The same policy is being pursued in other areas of corporate operations. Conduct is considered to be negligent when the harm it causes could be anticipated by "a reasonably prudent person." Executives' credibility in the eyes of the public is at an all-time low; the public wants white-collar crime brought under control.

The inescapable conclusion of any discussion of executive ethics is that managers are and will be held morally responsible for their actions. At first sight, this runs contrary to the modern view of organizational decision making, which argues for consensus formation, risk syndication, and operation within the zone of indifference of subordinates. The reality of the matter is that while decision making is decentralized, responsibility is centralized.

Managers constantly need to remind themselves that they are the

[5] © 1976 by The New York Times Company. Reprinted by permission.

Box 12.1: Rating the Honesty of Business Executives

Many more people esteem the honesty and ethical standards of medical doctors than the standards of business executives, labor union leaders, and advertising executives, according to a 1976 Gallup poll. The survey results indicated an antibusiness and an antiunion leader sentiment, as shown in the survey results:

Medical doctors 55%
Engineers 48%
College teachers 44%
Journalists 33%
Lawyers 25%
Building contractors 22%
Business executives 19%
Senators 19%
Congressmen 14%
Labor union leaders 13%
Advertising executives 11%*

people who will be held responsible and that they must act accordingly. In brief, they should not allow or encourage irresponsible participation.

To maintain this approach, a wise business executive should be guided by the following considerations:

1. Business and society are subject to the same laws, moral and legal.
2. The moral law may not always be clear; legality can be defined more precisely.
3. When in doubt, act like "a reasonably prudent person."
4. There is a high probability today that one's decisions will be challenged.

EXISTENTIALISM AND THE SYSTEMS APPROACH

There is a curious alignment of interest between the systems approach and existentialism. Just as the systems approach is antireductionist (it believes that all behavior cannot be reduced to stimulus-response bonds) and is based on the proposition that the whole system is not completely knowable, likewise existentialism rejects destructive, competitive power relations and the supremacy of science as an explanation of all aspects of life.

* From "High Rating Given to Doctors in Poll," *New York Times*, August 22, 1976. © 1976 by the New York Times Company. Reprinted by permission.

Existentialism argues for a return to ethical values and to genuine contact between human beings. Science's presumption of the existence of value-free facts has created an environment of assumed objectivity, which has generated an atmosphere characterized by arrogance. This "objectivity" is a direct outcome of the "certainties" of Newtonian physics; it creates the illusion of an absolute truth.

Both the systems approach and existentialism presume that the world is not completely knowable, that it is given meaning only by imposing one's own meaning on it. Existentialism believes that one should refuse to choose between alternatives when neither is acceptable.

REVIEW AND RESEARCH

Categorize these sayings into four categories: C for classical theory; H for human relations; S for systems theory; and E for existentialist.

1. The difficult we do today, the impossible tomorrow.
2. People count; people matter.
3. People should have meaningful dialogue.
4. Offense is the best form of defense.
5. Don't let the best become the enemy of the good.
6. Efficiency is doing things right, effectiveness is doing right things right.
7. Today is the first day of the rest of your life.
8. Turn on, tune in, and drop out.
9. Two-way communication is always best.
10. Good guys come last.
11. Conform with instructions or nominate your successor.
12. Don't bend, spindle, or mutilate.
13. What's good for General Motors is good for the United States.
14. Make love, not war.
15. Nothing human is alien to me.
16. Be firm but fair.
17. I relate well.
18. There is the $n^{th}-1$ option; you can quit.
19. A happy ship is an efficient ship.
20. Workers are lazy, unambitious, and need to be led.

21. You have nothing to fear but fear itself.
22. Optimal organization is not a function of personality.
23. Management style is a function of the situation, task characteristics, and power distribution.
24. Do your thing.
25. Workers work best in a supportive, democratic environment.
26. An optimal level of conflict is good.
27. No man is an island.
28. Treat others as you would like to be treated yourself.
29. If something exists, it must exist in quantity and is thus capable of measurement.
30. Organizational logic is based on brilliant insights that are made to work by consensus formation and risk syndication by the top people who work within the "zone of indifference" of lesser people.
31. Everybody's got something—it's just a case of finding it and developing it.
32. People often act irrationally; therefore a mature person is someone with a weak superego.
33. Lose your mind and find your senses.
34. Work hard; play hard.

PROBLEMS OF ADJUSTING TO FREEDOM

A growing number of the existential generation who reached maturity in the sixties and who are now approaching their thirties are experiencing problems of adjustment. Robert Lindsey, writing in the New York Times (February 29, 1976), points out that

> According to dozens of specialists who counsel young people, interviewed in 14 cities across the country, large numbers of the men and women who grew up in the 60s are now experiencing a generational malaise of haunting frustrations, anxiety and depression.
>
> The malaise, they say, is reflected in an increase in the number of people in their late 20s and early 30s receiving psychiatric help; by a rise in suicides and alcoholism in this age group; and a boom in the popularity of certain charismatic religious movements, astrology, and

pop psychology cults that reflect part of this generation's search for contentment.

The reasons cited for its problems range from disillusionment following the Watergate scandals, to disorientation caused by new sexual freedom, to the failure of life to fulfill the expectations established for themselves and society during the idealistic 60s.*

This new generation appears to be facing a crisis of values. Whereas in the sixties young people were trying to learn intimacy and to be authentic, they are now confronted by a social and economic reality where such skills have only limited advantage. Many of these young men and women were not prepared for work in a world that can be cruel. Lindsey illustrates this point by quoting the experience of psychiatrists and social workers.

"You'd be amazed at the number of young people who put themselves through college working as barmaids, bunnies, selling marijuana, working at anything to achieve their goal—which is to graduate; and when they reach the date and can't find a job, that's really a big wipe-out," said Betty Spencer, a clinical social worker at the Pontchartrain Mental Health Clinic in New Orleans.†

The conclusion seems to be that young people are slowly becoming more conventional as they face the realities of corporate life. Do you agree? Why, or why not?

* From "High Rating Given to Doctors in Poll," *New York Times*, August 22, 1976. © 1976 by the New York Times Company. Reprinted by permission.

† *Ibid.*

IV

MANAGING PEOPLE AND BEHAVIOR

13

Human
Motivation

OBJECTIVES YOU SHOULD MEET

List four models of man.

Describe how behavior modification can be used to improve performance.

Define perception.

Diagram the VANE model, which shows how values, attitudes, needs, and expectations affect behavior.

Integrate three theories of motivation.

Diagram and illustrate the path-goal theory of motivation.

List the characteristics of the existential personality.

What Is Man?

"A self-balancing, 28-jointed adapter-base biped; an electrochemical reduction plant, integral with segregated stowages of special energy extracts in storage batteries for subsequent actuation of thousands of hydraulic or pneumatic pumps with motors attached; 62,000 miles of capillaries . . . the whole, extraordinary complex mechanism guided with exquisite precision from a turret in which are located telescopic and microscopic self-registering and recording range finders, a spectroscope, etc.; the turret control being closely allied with an air-conditioning intake-and-exhaust, and a main fuel intake . . . "*

The crucial question in this chapter is a simple one. Why do people behave as they do? To try and answer this question, we must explore personality and motivation. Personality is a crystallizing focus around which the individual's behavior, attitudes, and motivation form a unified and integrated system. To function properly, an executive must have some insight into how his personality works, especially if he wishes to mobilize his energies and resources and focus them in a productive way. Let us look at personality from a number of different perspectives which are summarized in Table 13.1.

S-R (STIMULUS-RESPONSE) MAN OF CLASSICAL THEORY

Behavioral theory began in nineteenth-century Russia with the work of Ivan Pavlov. Pavlov studied conditioning, the process of controlling and modifying behavior by managing the environment. Pavlov discovered that a response that is customarily elicited by a given stimulus (food, for example) can result from a substitute stimulus, provided the latter is presented repeatedly just before the former. Working with dogs, Pavlov found that he could stimulate salivation by ringing a bell when the dogs began to associate the bell's ringing with the food's arrival.

Pavlovian conditioning was the epitome of objectivity. Pavlov had developed procedures that allowed the psychologist to study how changes in the environment stimulate behavioral responses. A new

Table 13.1 Four Models of Man

Ethic	Model of man	Management theory	Characteristics	Effects of dysfunction
Scientific ethic	S-R man	Classical	Rational, Responsible, Autonomous	Overdependency
Therapeutic ethic	S-O-R man	Human relations	Irrational, Interdependent, Creative	Tendency to consider oneself neurotic
Computer ethic	P-G man	Systems	Choice, Calculative, Numerate	World too clinical
Existential ethic	E man	Existential	Choice and Chance	Need to be reconciled with best features of other three theories

form of psychology was emerging, which was to have tremendous consequences for the development of American psychology.

By the early twentieth century, this "objective" psychology had reached the United States. J. B. Watson, an animal psychologist at Johns Hopkins University, began the objective study of behavior. He taught that since behavior could be seen, it could be measured in experiments that other psychologists could repeat.

In time, Watson's mantle of leadership passed to Burrhus Frederick Skinner, professor of psychology at Harvard University. Skinner showed that rats and pigeons could be conditioned to various forms of behavior provided they were put on the right reinforcement schedule. If the rats pressed the right lever at the right time, they got a reward, a pellet of food. If the rat pressed the wrong lever, it got an electric shock—the basis of aversion therapy.

Even though "rats aren't people," Skinner's ideas achieved very wide currency. Out of his work has come not only aversion therapy but also behavior modification, which has been used in industry to produce more appropriate patterns of work activity.

Behavior Modification

Following the ideas of B. F. Skinner, some years ago Emery Air Freight Corporation made extensive use of behavior modification to increase effectiveness. Emery used "positive reinforcement" as a means of getting daily feedback on how employees were achieving company goals and standards. Disappointed with traditional sales training methods, an Emery executive became convinced that sales calls had to be made more productive. He asked the customer in any sales interaction to take some kind of action to indicate his intention to use one of Emery's services. In 1968, the application of behavioral modification at Emery produced a dramatic jump in sales. Sales jumped from $62 million to nearly $80 million, a gain of almost 28 percent.

Engineering Behavior

Such sales programs are based on positive reinforcement, the idea that behavior can be engineered or shifted by a carefully controlled system of rewards. In Emery's customer service department, for example, the goal was to respond to customers' queries within ninety minutes. Although department employees thought they were meeting the standard nine times out of ten, the research study showed that they were meeting the goal only 50 percent of the time. Emery asked each operator to mark on his sheet whether each call had been answered within ninety minutes. The results were dramatic. Performance in the first "test office" jumped to a score of 95 percent. Using a relatively simple positive reinforcement technique (in this case, actually marking down calls answered in the specified time), Emery was able to make significant savings in cost and significant improvements in performance.

Evaluation of Behavior Modification

To be effective, behavior modification must begin with a statement of goals. Secondly, a specific plan must be developed for reaching those goals. The plan must include a positive reinforcement, or reward, which employees receive when they practice the right behavior. Behavior modification minimizes employees' options for individual choice.

S-O-R (STIMULUS-ORGANISM-RESPONSE) MAN: THE HUMAN RELATIONS MODEL

People make choices. A person is more than a bundle of stimuli and responses. A good number of executives find the S-R psychologist somewhat unhelpful. To their mind, corporate life is too complex for behavioral theories to be of much use. Human relations believes that people's response depends not so much on the stimulus as on how people *perceive* the stimulus.

"You Describe What You See; You See What You Describe"

A central proposition of the S-O-R model is the notion of "feelingful awareness." "You describe what you see and you see what you describe." Perception describes the process of how a person becomes aware of the outside world in relationship to himself. It involves, essentially, information getting and information decoding. But human perception is not a camera; the information that is fed through the senses is decoded by the brain. Knowledge enters the brain in the form of structures. This means that people cannot perceive a "thing" as something unless they have a category system in their heads to which they can allocate the "thing." Perception is thus an act of categorization. People who have been blind since birth and then have their sight restored cannot recognize the world in our terms; their perceptions must all be relearned.

But perception involves more than categorization. It also requires a transaction between the stimulus and the category system. Technically, some of the qualities of the object are derived from the perceptual set (or classification system) and tried on the object for fit. This concept can be explained by Gestalt psychology.

Gestalt: The Whole Is More than the Sum of the Parts

Gestalt, a German word meaning *configuration* or *shape,* describes a school of psychology that came into prominence about 1912.

The central Gestalt proposition is that *the whole is more than the sum of its parts.* This proposition is at variance with the simpler behavioristic proposition that complex sensory events are no more than the sum of individual nervous impulses.

Max Wertheimer, one of the founders of Gestalt psychology, showed that people perceived something, in one case motion, when nothing had moved. Wertheimer had demonstrated this perception with the motion picture. The eye perceives motion, although it has actually received a number of discrete "still" photographs. Wertheimer used two slits, one vertical and the other inclined 20 or 30 degrees from the vertical. If light was directed through one slit and then 60 milliseconds later through the other, movement was perceived. In other words, the brain was apparently adding something to the input. The whole, or the Gestalt (perception of movement) was more than the sum of its parts (two stationary lights).

The Principles of Perception

Gestalt psychologists were arguing that the brain had the capacity to organize sensory data in certain well-defined ways. In 1923, Wertheimer set out the principles of organization that determined perception. These principles included proximity (dots close together in space or time tend to be perceived as a group), similarity (identical dots are grouped—for example, stars and stripes in the U.S. flag are seen as two separate groups), and *pragnanz* (the more "pregnant" or closed picture is perceived).

From Gestalt psychology behavioral scientists have taken the view that human beings as such supersede the sum of their parts. People cannot be understood as organisms in an empty space; modern psychology is concerned with people in their human context as they relate to other people. Further, the manager focuses on the fact that people are aware, and that some of this awareness is unconscious. Modern behavioral theory adds to behaviorism two other human attributes, choice and intention.

BASIC NEEDS

No matter where you start, when you try to deal with a problem in an organization, you end up dealing with people. You puzzle over "what makes them tick," what it will take to make them do what you want. Making them do what you want is what motivation is all about. But first you must know what it is that you want.

What do we want? Basically, everyone wants and needs the same things, and they can be arranged in order of importance. Figure 13.1 shows the hierarchy of needs.

Figure 13.1   Basic Hierarchical Needs

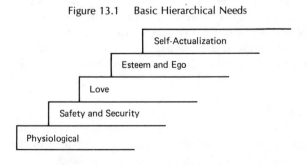

Physiological Needs

Physiological needs include food, drink, warmth, shelter, sex, and so on. People can be trapped at a particular level so that they try to meet all their needs at that level—through, for example, eating ("living to eat rather than eating to live"). Sex can be another fixation level.

Safety and Security

Once a person has satisfied his physiological needs, his thoughts turn to getting things organized. People have a strong need for "law and order," for an environment that is structured in a safe, predictable way.

Love

People need love and affection. They need to believe that somebody cares about them at a primitive, unsophisticated level. They need to be stroked, and beyond that they have a deep and pervasive need to belong, to be on someone's team.

Ego and Esteem

As every manager knows, people not only have a tremendous need to be loved; they also have a significant need to be in good standing. At its lower limit, this need for esteem manifests itself in a desire for respectability. But at a higher level, it is a desire to be held in high regard by one's professional colleagues or peers. Integrating these esteem needs is a powerful ego, which somehow or other welds the need to belong, the need for esteem, and the need for positive self-regard into an identity. The presumption of modern personality theorists, exemplified by Erik H. Erikson, is that identities are necessary in particular stages in an individual's personal development; not only must they be formed, but they must be reformed, in fact, renewed.

Self-Actualization

Self-actualization is the integrating capstone need of the hierarchy. In its most terse form, self-actualization is embodied in statements like,

"What I can be, I must be." Self-actualization is a psychic perpetual motion machine that somehow allows an individual and a society to work together for the individual's good. Self-actualization means a deeper personal insight into the existential notion of personality, to which we will turn in a moment. To get a quick look at how to put self-actualization into action in business, we turn now to Herzberg's motivation-hygiene theory.

Herzberg's Motivation-Hygiene Theory

No discussion of contemporary motivation theory is complete without considering Frederick Herzberg's two-factor theory ("Motivation versus Hygiene Factors"). Herzberg's theory is worth considering in some detail not because it is scientifically correct but because it has been so widely used by managers as a means of changing the organizational climate.

The quickest way to getting an insight into the Motivation-Hygiene Theory is by comparing it with the traditional view of dissatisfaction and satisfaction.

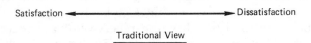

Satisfaction ◄─────────────────────► Dissatisfaction

Traditional View

Herzberg begins by rejecting the traditional notion that dissatisfaction and satisfaction are opposites on a single continuum. The motivation-hygiene model rests on the notion that satisfaction and dissatisfaction are on two separate continuums.

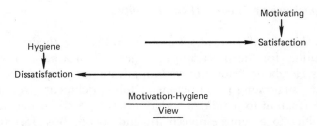

Motivating
↓
Hygiene   ─────────────► Satisfaction
↓
Dissatisfaction ◄──────────────

Motivation-Hygiene
View

In essence, the motivation-hygiene theory states that it is necessary to look at motivation twice. The first look is to find out what is causing dissatisfaction. This cause can be "treated" by giving the person some "hygiene," for example, better working conditions. According to Herzberg, this treatment removes dissatisfaction and takes the person back to the zero point on the scale.

Hygiene Factors	Motivation Factors
Company policy administration	Achievement
Relations with superiors, peers, and subordinates	Advancement
Working conditions	Recognition
Job security	Responsibility
Salary	Opportunities for personal growth
Personal life	Work itself

To get satisfaction, the firm must get the worker motivated. Herzberg is arguing that people in our society do not live by bread alone but are seeking personal growth and development. Personal growth and development can be achieved only through meaningful work.

Herzberg's research technique is of considerable interest. Herzberg asked his subjects to think of times when they felt exceptionally good and exceptionally bad about their jobs. He recorded the details of the good times and bad times. This use of the critical-incident technique has been widely criticized by other behavioral scientists, who have argued that subjects tend to respond to Herzberg's question by (1) taking the credit when things are going well (motivators) and (2) blaming the environment when things go badly (hygiene). The theory has also been criticized by other researchers who have repeated Herzberg's method but have come up with different results. While these objections seem warranted on the basis of purely scientific evidence, they seem to miss the nub of the matter in regard to Herzberg's motivation-hygiene theory.

Motivation-Hygiene Theory: High in Utility

The beauty of Herzberg's motivation-hygiene theory is that it is high in utility for the practicing manager. When a hard-pressed executive asks Herzberg, "How are we to motivate our people?" he is able to respond by suggesting job enrichment. Job enrichment gives employees more information to handle, a wider variety of tasks to perform, more opportunities to accept responsibility, and so on. Box 13.1 tells more about job enrichment.

Unfortunately, job enrichment is used on a microscopic scale in the United States (see Box 13.2). An extremely small number of firms are willing to engage in this type of innovative job structuring; and in any case, many American shop floor workers are not particularly

Box 13.1: Positive and Negative KITA

Most managers today recognize that the surest, simplest way of getting someone to do something is for you to kick him in the pants, or, as it is better known, KITA, of which there are three known forms:

- Negative physical KITA—a literal application that is inelegant, contradicts good behavior, and could result in negative physical feedback.
- Negative psychological KITA—has some advantages over negative physical KITA in that there is no visible cruelty, the possibility of physical retaliation is lessened, there are more areas to attack, the person administering the blow can remain aloof and let the system do the dastardly deed, and there is a certain amount of ego satisfaction for the administrator.

Unfortunately both of the above lead to movement, not to motivation.

- Positive KITA—a reward system in which one receives something (promotion,

Continued on next page

From "One More Time: How Do You Motivate Employees?" by Frederick Herzberg, *Harvard Business Review* (January-February 1968). Copyright © 1967 by the President and Fellows of Harvard College; all rights reserved.

enthusiastic about job enrichment. It demands a degree of involvement they are not always willing to give.

Job Enrichment in Action

One of the best examples of job enrichment has been provided by Robert N. Ford, personnel director in charge of work organization and environmental research at the American Telephone and Telegraph Company.[1] From 1965 to 1968, Ford directed a group of researchers at AT&T, in a formal field study of nineteen experiments in job enrichment. Ford learned that the "life-saving" elements of many jobs can be expanded, and conversely the boring, unchallenging aspects can be reduced. The researchers at AT&T found that employees are saying more than, "Treat me well"; they are also saying, "Use me well."

The AT&T research team moved beyond such high level concepts as self-actualization, need for achievement, and psychological growth to deal with three aspects of the job itself:

[1] "Job Enrichment Lessons from AT&T" by Robert N. Ford, *Harvard Business Review* (January-February 1973). Copyright © 1972 by the President and Fellows of Harvard College; all rights reserved.

wages, etc.) for doing a certain deed. Instead of pushing by a KITA the manager is pulling.

While positive KITA is looked upon by management as an acceptable form of motivation, it fails in that successive increments of reward must be put forth to continue the motivation. Motivation is being able to kick yourself and get yourself going to do the job that has to be done.

Next Herzberg deals with the positive KITA personnel practices that were developed to try to instill motivation. The first is the reduction of work hours, which does not work because motivated personnel seek more hours for work. Second, spiraling wages, which seem only to motivate the employee to look for the next increase. Third in the list of practices are fringe benefits. These, however, are now taken for granted by the employee. Fourth is human relations training, which was once thought to be a way to motivate the employee but is now a casualty of employee sophistication; employees require their supervisors to act acceptably. Fifth is sensitivity training, which failed to instill motivation because the employees did not understand what the

---

1. designing the module of work,
2. controlling the module,
3. feedback signaling when something had been accomplished.

Beginning with such boring tasks as compiling telephone directories the research team found ways to enrich the jobs. At AT&T good modules were described with pride in the following terms.

- □ "A piece of turf" (especially a geographic responsibility).
- □ "My real estate" (by engineers responsible for group of central offices).
- □ "Our cradle-to-grave modem line" (a vastly improved Western Electric switching-device production line).
- □ "Our mission impossible team" (a framemen's team, Long Lines Department).

Jobs were redesigned so that employees were given authority to perform a wide range of tasks, including such delicate matters as setting credit ratings of customers, canceling credit for nonpayment, making one's own budgets, and calling directly to repairmen and suppliers to negotiate services within the budget. In terms of feedback, jobs were redesigned to make the control responsibility self-monitoring.

What the research team found at AT&T was that enriching

managers were offering. This opened the field for six, communications, which also failed and led to seven, two-way communications.

Herzberg differentiates between horizontal job loading and vertical job enrichment, which stimulates the motivating factors better. Certain steps must be taken to ensure that job enrichment is successful, and they include:

1. Select a job conducive to change;
2. Approach the job with a positive attitude toward the change;
3. Brainstorm a list of changes;
4. Screen the list, eliminating those involving hygiene;
5. Screen the list for generalities;
6. Screen for horizontal loading;
7. Avoid the participation of the one whose job is to be enriched once the ideas are in;
8. Initially set up a controlled experiment to monitor progress or problems.

Job enrichment will come to be a management function, and it must be monitored continuously.

existing jobs pays off; that job enrichment requires a different managerial style; that to be enriched, jobs have to be dealt with in sets; that a maintenance function to keep the program moving must be part of the plan; that unions welcome this type of effort; and that new technology can be used to break free from old work habits.

Is job enrichment widely used? Survey research studies suggest that the majority of firms do not employ job enlargement techniques. While most executives have read books and articles about behavioral science and attended seminars dealing with job enrichment, few applications have been made.

Critics of job enrichment argue that the case for it has been dramatically overstated and overgeneralized. They feel that not everyone coming to work expects to find fulfillment there. Many employees' reaction to their work is the opposite of what behavioral scientists predict. A considerable number of shop floor workers reject involvement in work, seeking fulfillment outside their work. Why isn't job enrichment used more extensively in shop floor jobs? Perhaps because most factory workers are not high achievers in the work situation; they do not expect to be satisfied at work.

While this explains part of the reason job enrichment is not widely used, the major reason is still the problem of job design.

... job enrichment is not presently widely used or accepted in industry; an analysis of its base in motivational theory indicates that part of the problem lies in the oversimplification and overgeneralization of the two-factor theory; and a process motivational theory seems to lead to better understanding, but its applicability is limited. However, the situation is not hopeless. There are many tools already in existence that can be developed to more effectively manage human resources. Participative techniques that involve employees in the decision-making process will play a role. Specific training techniques, such as the Managerial Grid®, the T-Group, and team building, also will continue to play important roles in organizational development. The same is true of management by objectives. Mutual goal setting and appraisal by results promote compatibility between personal and organizational goals. New tools, such as one developed by the senior author called Organizational Behavior Modification, or O.B. Mod., may also have important applications in management practice. And job enrichment has an equal, though not necessarily more important,

P-G (PATH-GOAL) MAN: THE SYSTEMS MODEL

The systems approach uses the P-G (path-goal) model. The path-goal approach is a cognitive theory of motivation; the presumption is that people can identify goals, set paths to these goals, and choose among paths and goals to reflect their interests.

The Path-Goal Model

The concept of P-G man received its initial thrust from the work of Victor Vroom, an organizational psychologist at Yale, who made information and decision making central concepts in his theory. Vroom argues that performance is a multiplicative function of motivation and ability:

$$\text{Performance} = F\ (M,A)$$
$$\text{where } M = \text{motivation and } A = \text{abilities}$$

Motivation to perform varies with the utilities of the outcomes and the instrumentality (belief that performance and outcome are linked).

300

future role to play in organizational development and human resource management.

The survey evidence . . . certainly indicates that job enrichment is still in the experimental stage and at this point is, indeed, more fiction than fact. On the positive side is the fact that 29 firms (23 percent of the respondents) stated that they intended to initiate programs in the near future, and 30 percent of the respondents are currently practicing J.E., on at least an informal basis. Management itself is the key, in terms of both opportunity and obstacles, to the further development and implementation of job enrichment. It must become more knowledgeable about the potential of job enrichment, but by the same token, management should not think of J.E. as the panacea for all its behavioral problems now or in the future. Job enrichment is but one of many tools in the manager's O.D. bag. Like the others, job enrichment should be applied contingently in those situations where the social, organizational, and technological factors are favorable to its effectiveness. The biggest challenge to the future development of job enrichment will lie in spelling out these contingencies in depth and detail.

P-G theory argues that management must determine what employees' expectancies, utilities, and instrumentalities are and then meet or change them.

Job Design and Expectancy Theory

Edward E. Lawler makes use of P-G theory to facilitate job design. Lawler defines the path-goal attitudes of the employees, that is, the type of behavior they feel provides a path to the rewards that they value.

Lawler argues that the importance of money to managers has virtually no relationship to how hard they work. Only those managers who place a high value on money and link it to high performance are prepared to exert greater effort for money. Lawler contends that job design mainly affects the instrumentality of good performance by clarifying and increasing the rewards.

People Differ in Their Needs and Strengths

Lawler has put forward a number of useful propositions about individual work behavior. He takes as his point of departure the notion that people differ in meaningful ways. All individuals do not respond to job enrichment with higher satisfaction, productivity, and quality. Recent findings have shown that individuals differ in the strength of their needs. A worker from a rural background has stronger higher-level needs, such as self-actualization, competence, and self-esteem, and responds well to job enrichment. Many workers from urban backgrounds prefer highly paid but unchallenging work. Lawler summarizes his findings:

> What seems to be needed is an organization theory based upon assumptions like the following, which recognize the existence of differences among individuals:[2]
>
> 1. Most individuals are goal-oriented in their behavior, but there are large differences in the goals people pursue.
>
> 2. Individuals differ both in what they enjoy doing and in what they can do.
>
> 3. Some individuals need to be closely supervised while others can exercise high levels of self-control.

For organizations to deal with individual differences it is necessary to develop selective job enrichment schemes. What Lawler is pushing for is the individualizing of organizations and work through the development of a motivating work climate.

Motivation for Performance

Expectancy theory has become a popular approach to motivation among behavioral scientists. We are still confused by the fact that there is no simple relationship between satisfaction and performance. Nor do we know the conditions that affect the magnitude and directions of the relations between these two factors.

We do know, however, that motivation is highest among top managers and that highly motivated managers prefer open-minded, approachable bosses. Furthermore, managers who get to the top have a very high need for power.

Money is still an important motivator. Most behavioral scientists believe that money can provide positive motivation. But money's instrumentality is a function of an individual's background. E. E. Lawler has found that keeping executive salaries secret is dysfunctional: executives

---

[2] From Edward E. Lawler, "The Individual Organization: Problems and Promise." © 1974 by the Regents of the University of California. Reprinted from *California Management Review*, volume 17, number 2, p. 35 by permission of the Regents.

overestimate the pay of their subordinates, underestimate the pay of their bosses, and generally feel underpaid. Most pay systems violate the principles derived from reinforcement theory, because pay increases are given at predictable times without differentiating between good and bad performance. A number of firms are now experimenting with performance-based bonuses. If goals are defined shrewdly, are widely known, and result in the payoff of performance, they can be strong motivators. If the goals are set too high, they become a constant discouragement; if they are set too low, they fail to mobilize energy.

As Leidecker and Hall show, goal attainment is not just a means of reducing internal tensions.

The path-goal framework suggests persons will behave in a manner which will lead to the attainment of a goal which they value and which they expect they can achieve. This framework identifies, for the manager, three criteria which are important for the motivational process (tension reduction):[3]

1. *Goal availability.* For example, within an organization, some goals may not be perceived as available to the employee.

2. *Goal value.* How likely is it that the reward offered by the organization provides the means to satisfy a goal valued by the employee?

3. *Perceived effort-reward probability.* How likely is it that a given amount of effort will result in the attainment of a valued goal? Does the organization consistently reward the behavior it desires?

M. Scott Myers and Susan S. Myers have made an important contribution to understanding this changing work ethic.[4] According to their view, a person may approach his work in one of the following ways:

a I prefer work of my own choosing that offers continuing challenge, and requires imagination and initiative, even if the pay is low.

b I am responsible for my own success, and I am always on the lookout for new opportunities which will lead to a more responsible position and a greater financial reward.

c I don't like any kind of work that ties me down, but I'll do it if I

[3] Joel K. Leidecker and James J. Hall, "Motivation: Good Theory—Poor Application." Reproduced by special permission from the June 1974 TRAINING AND DEVELOPMENT JOURNAL. Copyright 1974 by the American Society for Training and Development Inc.

[4] M. Scott Myers and Susan S. Myers, "Toward Understanding the Changing Work Ethic," *California Management Review* (Spring 1974).

have to in order to get some money; then I'll quit and do what I want until I have to get another job.

d I have worked hard for what I have, and think I deserve some good breaks. I think others should realize that it is their *duty* to be loyal to the organization if they want to get ahead.

e The kind of work I usually do is o.k., as long as it's a steady job and I have a good boss.

f I believe that doing what I like to do, such as working with people toward a common goal is more important than getting caught up in a materialistic rat race.

Each of these six responses represents a legitimate point of view about work, each response is a reflection of a different set of values.

E (EXISTENTIAL) MAN:
THE EXISTENTIAL PERSONALITY

A new view of people is emerging which recognizes that we are both intractable and potentially better than we are. Part of this new vision reflects the old notion that people have an undeniable core of evil; the other part recognizes our ability, if we are properly reinforced and held accountable for our own actions, to develop a higher moral level.

Existentialism is essentially concerned with how people can become a more active force in shaping their own destiny. Such a conception directs the executive to discover his potential for greatness and good (and for evil) and to focus on the notion of will. The idea of freedom, the need for choice, the capacity to control (or at least to influence) the key decisions of one's life is the central desire of the existentialist. The "will to meaning" is stronger than the "will to pleasure."

REVIEW AND RESEARCH

1. Which theory of personality (S-R man, S-O-R man, P-G man, E-man) do you prefer? Why?

2. Describe how behavior modification could be used to stop someone from doing something.

3. How was behavior modification put into action at Emery Air Freight? Can you apply these principles to a business with which you are familiar? How?

4. Spell out the principles of perception (give examples of each). Explain how "movies" work from "stills." Using an introductory text in psychology as a source, draw diagrams of three illusions. What do illusions tell you about perception?

5. How did American psychology benefit from the rise of the Nazis in Germany?

6. Describe the VANE model. Fill in your own VANE.

7. What are the basic needs? Which one is most important to you?

8. Why is Herzberg's motivation-hygiene theory so widely used?

9. Apply P-G theory to the most recent decision in your career.

10. How far are you on the way to becoming an existentialist?

"OLD JIM IS OUT AGAIN DOING THE HOUSEWORK"

Bill Jones, maintenance manager of the Turner Company, has struggled to get supervisors and employees alike to accept the principle that the organization cannot and will not tolerate absenteeism. Persistent absenteeism is now considered grounds for discharge. For the past year, James Allen, a highly skilled maintenance repairman, has been absent without notice once or twice a month. Having been with the company for six years, he has the reputation for high quality work, for accepting almost any assignment unquestioningly, and for working overtime when necessary.

When confronted with the facts (and he has received one disciplinary layoff already), he always promises to do better. Although he is a very quiet, uncommunicative man, it is known that he has family problems. His wife is a rather disorganized homemaker; they have six children, one of whom is always ill.

The company does not like to contemplate losing this skilled man, yet fellow employees are beginning to talk, and whenever he fails to show up for work, one hears comments like, "Old Jim is out again doing the housework."

Bill Jones is waiting for James Allen to come into his office to explain his latest absence. How should Bill Jones deal with this interview?

14

Managing
Groups

List the roles in a group.

Define group dynamics.

Describe several kinds of meetings.

Specify the duties of the chairman of a committee.

State the three steps in discussion leading.

Understand the T-group.

Diagram the managerial grid identifying five different types of managers.

List the six stages of the grid.

How should we think about the relation between individuals and groups? Few questions have stirred up so many issues of metaphysics, epistemology and ethics. Do groups have the same reality as individuals? If so, what are the properties of groups? Can groups learn, have goals, be frustrated, develop, regress, begin and end? Or, are these characteristics strictly attributable only to individuals? If groups exist, are they good or bad? How *should* an individual behave with respect to groups? How *should* groups treat their individual members? Such questions have puzzled man from the earliest days of recorded history.*

Group dynamics is the study of the structure, process, and values of groups. It is especially concerned with the changing patterns of intragroup adjustments, tensions, and conflicts. In more popular usage, group dynamics are experiments carried out in small groups. One of the most important findings to emerge from group dynamics is that people are aroused by the group context. An individual's motivation appears to be heightened in a group. Secondly, people tend to make more risky decisions when in groups than they do when they are working on a problem alone. Figure 14.1 shows some kinds of groups and classifies them according to type, and Box 14.1 discusses a group that is familiar to almost everyone—the Beatles.

MANAGING GROUP MEETINGS

We know from behavioral studies that managers spend up to 80 percent of their time talking. A fair proportion of this interaction time is spent with more than one other person. Some critics argue that managers spend too much time in committee. Complaints often take such forms as, "The committee is a meeting called to design a racehorse, but it ends up producing a camel"; "Minutes are kept and hours thrown away"; "The ideal number for a committee is three with two in absentia"; "Meetings should be held only at 5:00 P.M. in a room with no table or chairs."

How valid are such criticisms? Before attempting to answer this question in general, we might consider the various kinds of committees and meetings that managers must often manage.

* D. Cartwright and R. Lippitt, "Group Dynamics and the Individual," *International Journal of Group Psychotherapy*, Vol. 7 (1957). Reprinted with permission.

One group that most students are familiar with is the Beatles. Even a quick glance at the Beatles reveals the principle that a group is more than the sum of its individual parts. Leadership in the group, if one can use such a term with the Beatles, was shared by McCartney and Lennon. The group's popularity was at its height in the early sixties; once they stopped touring in 1966, the members began to go in different directions. It may be of considerable interest to the student of management that a major reason the group folded was that they could not manage their success. Another reason for the disintegration of the group was that individual members began to reach out to other people, and these new members introduced tensions that the primary group could not cope with. The person often held responsible for this breakdown is Linda Eastman, who joined Paul McCartney in 1967. Yoko Ono similarly interested John Lennon. Soon the group was beset by doubts, recriminations, and bitterness.

Kinds of Meetings

A good way of reducing confusion about meetings is to classify them according to their function. One useful exercise is to classify meetings according to their dominant feature, as we have done in Figure 14.2. Dominant features vary from acting out a ritual to disseminating facts and achieving commitment. Many of the problems that arise in meetings arise because managers behave in one context in

Figure 14.1   Some Kinds of Groups

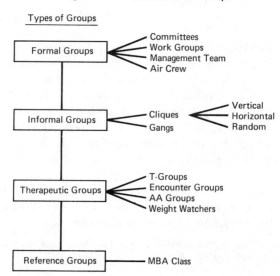

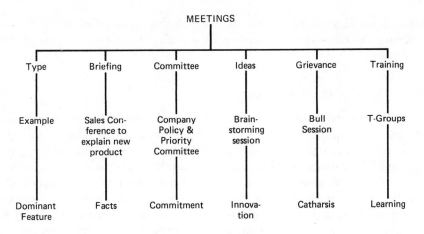

Figure 14.2   Types of Meetings

a manner appropriate to another; for example, they turn a load meeting to schedule the weekly production plan into a debating chamber for higher quality control standards.

The Committee

Functions

A committee's functions may include any—sometimes all—of the following:

1. communicating information,
2. generating alternatives,
3. recommending a solution,
4. "selling" a solution,
5. implementing solutions, and
6. reviewing performance and policy.

Forming a committee to perform these functions is not always appropriate. Committees are useful when subordinates have information or expertise unavailable to their superior, when power must be shared, when risk syndication is required, or when decisions must be delayed.

Structure

Contrary to current behavioral science wisdom, committees need not be small to discharge their functions. Regardless of a committee's

311

size, a small group of three to five people usually does most of the talking. A committee is made up of a chairperson and the rest of the members.

Duties of the chairperson

In general terms, the chairperson is meant to act as *primus inter pares,* first among equals. The chair's administrative chores include arranging the logistics, booking the room, arranging for coffee, preparing "the papers," sorting out the agenda, and preparing the minutes.

The chair should solicit members' opinions and views, especially when disagreements look likely. People often imagine that they disagree when in fact they are simply talking about different things. What is required here is to get behind the words to the actual meanings members are trying to convey.

The chairperson must maintain good eye contact with the group. When talking, he or she should talk to the group as a whole. At the same time, the chair should be searching for feedback, for reaction to what is being said. Eye contact is good for the morale of the group.

Finally, a general guide to the chairperson must be: Keep your ears to the ground. No rules or regulations can substitute for a sensitive approach to what is going on in the group. At all times the chair must maintain a balance between getting the job done and keeping the group's morale high.

Members of the group have a very important part to play in the discussion. Unless they are properly briefed about the subject in advance, their resources cannot be properly exploited. Seeing that members have been briefed is the chairperson's responsibility.

The meeting should not end with simply a general recommendation. If the members believe that further research is required, the chair should ask what kind of research and who is to carry it out. The end of a conference should be the beginning of its usefulness. After a week or so, the chairperson should send a one-page digest of decisions that were reached; this should be followed within a month by a report that fairly covers all opinions.

The committee cannot function in a structureless environment. It needs order and direction. Thus, the chairperson must spell out a tentative agenda and win approval for the adoption of either the original or an amended version. The chair should then attempt to guide the group systematically through its business. A good way to test your knowledge of the group dynamics of committee meetings is to examine the seating layout shown in Figure 14.3 and try to answer these two questions:

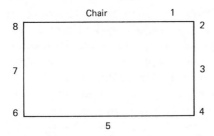

Figure 14.3   Committee Seating Layout

1. If you were the chairperson of the group and had prepared name cards that allowed you to position members, where would you put the troublemaker? (*Answer:* According to behavioral scientists, put the troublemaker in position 1, on the chair's left. The logic is that the chairperson, like most people, is probably right-eyed dominant. Thus he or she can ignore the troublemaker's attempts to get in.)

2. If you want to challenge the chairperson, which seat should you select? (*Answer:* Number 5. In the number 5 position, an opponent can achieve a confrontation eyeball-to-eyeball. This can be very disconcerting to the chairperson, especially if number 5 keeps his hand up, indicating that he is waiting to contribute.)

THE PROCESS OF DISCUSSION LEADING

The seminal research in the area of discussion leading was carried out by R. F. Bales when he was professor of social relations at Harvard. Based on his analysis of groups solving human relations problems, Bales concluded that the process could be broken down into three steps: clarification, evaluation, and decision.

The first and third phases are essentially logical in character and are concerned with the processing of information. The middle phase, evaluation, deals with the emotional issue of assessing choice, both task and human.

More modern research suggests that many diverse things happen at meetings. For example, one theory, known as the garbage bin theory of decision making, argues that three things travel in corporate space: problems, people who can solve them, and occasions that allow problems to be solved. Problems travel from meeting to meeting until the right collection of executives is at the right meeting with the right problem.

This seems an obvious restatement of the basic distinction between efficiency ("doing things right") and effectiveness ("doing the right things right") originally made by Peter Drucker. Thus, at a lot of meetings, nothing much happens because the wrong people may well be in the wrong room with the wrong problem.

This explains why executives at meetings frequently act in ways impossible to interpret by any logical approach. For example, executives may suddenly have important telephone calls to make when a meeting is about to begin, even though they had plenty of time beforehand.

How do meetings actually work? Frequently they work by doing something that creates a remainder, which has to be settled at another meeting elsewhere. One study of executive behavior was concerned with the work of production managers in a light engineering factory. A group of managers met every week with the departmental manager and his two staff officers, the production engineer and the production controller, to arrange the work for the following week. The company rules required that this meeting be run as a command session. Information was transmitted in a structured environment that did not allow much feedback or negotiation. Following the meeting, the production managers would meet in the cafeteria and sort the problems out in an informal session with the two staff managers. The departmental manager was absent at these informal meetings.

Process

Even when the structure is right and the spatial arrangements are appropriate, the committee must still have a process. Process in committees is sequencing informational, decisional, and emotional flows. R. F. Bales' analysis of the process divided it into three stages:

- □ Clarification—What are the facts? What assumptions are necessary?
- □ Evaluation—How do we feel about this issue?
- □ Decision—What are we going to do about it?

Values

Committee values represent a dilemma. Democratic members wish to conduct business one way, task-oriented members another. Figure 14.4 shows some of the areas of tension.

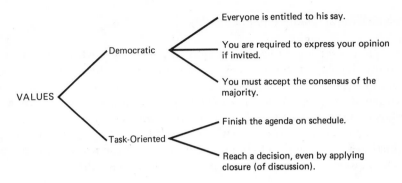

Figure 14.4   Two Contrasting Committee Values

GROUP DECISION MAKING

Typically, executives make decisions in groups. As we have already noted, groups tend to make riskier decisions than do individuals.

The T-Group

Kurt Lewin invented a three-step paradigm for describing change: unfreezing, change, refreezing. One can unfreeze an individual or any social system by recognizing that the interacting forces are becoming unstable and by helping to break them up by a little KITA (kick in the pants). KITA unbalances the system and gets it moving. Next, one points the system in the right direction, gets people to learn attitudes by emulating others with the correct attitudes (identification), and encourages people to practice these new values and attitudes as if they were their own (internalization). Finally, these values and attitudes are refrozen into the individual's personality.

This technique of change, which is used by T-group practitioners, presupposes a considerable degree of tension in the system. Such tension is generated by some technological, social, or economic failure. The generation of change is inevitably a high risk exercise requiring considerable skill. The large fees ($500 to $1,000 per diem) that are charged by consultants generate large expectations, create tensions, and mobilize energies, which are all to the good. Massive change involves executives in power equalization (or its illusion) and can be somewhat manipulative when used by neophyte consultants. Therefore, a change agent must be selected with care.

People's Intractability and Potentiality

The T-group practitioners and the executives who formed these groups developed a new view of human beings that took them well beyond Freud. Psychoanalysis was originally intended to help seriously disturbed people, but it has evolved into a treatment mainly for well-adjusted middle-class people with a few minor neurotic traits. The same law of compensating success with success applies to T-groups. T-groups, which were designed to help people understand themselves, turned out to be powerful behavioral engines of organizational change.

New Idea of the Executive

From the T-group a new idea of the executive began to emerge. People wanted to feel alive, to feel confirmed in the authenticity of their own nature, to reject traditional authority. Furthermore, they began to insist that their jobs be made more meaningful and relevant to their real needs.

Gradually, however, the T-group died as a training device, and OD (organizational development) emerged. Its philosophy was not to train the manager, not to train the group, but to train the system. The system became the learner, and the training regime was T-group technology. The central problem of OD is to change the culture, as well as the structure and process of the system.

ORGANIZATIONAL DEVELOPMENT

Organizational development (OD) aims to increase organizational effectiveness by integrating individual needs for growth, self-actualization, and authenticity with organizational goals. OD is a planned change effort. It aims to first change values, then process, and then structure, in accordance with the organization's mission.

OD is an attempt to change people's values towards their work, to make work more exciting, creative, challenging, and even fun. The basic presumption is that people have the capability and motivation to grow, and they can cope with the conflicts necessary to resolve differences. But to do so they need full information, not only about hard facts but also about values, attitudes, needs, and expectations.

OD requires a planned organizationwide effort, which begins at the top and utilizes planned intervention in the actual processes of the organization. OD begins by examining the organization's values, its shared assumptions about legitimate behavior and attitudes in that particular system. Because structure, process, and values in any organization are somewhat cohesive, any attempt to introduce changes is inherently intrusive, subversive, and, to some degree, nonrational.

In OD, the emphasis is not on the definition and solution of problems but on the process and the method of intervention. When one focuses on a "problem," one presupposes a simplistic single cause and a "best" solution. OD accepts the basic ideas of systems theory, especially the notions that there are a variety of acceptable end states and that a specific point of departure or beginning can lead to many different end states.

Thus, OD is not a program or a project but a process that is ongoing and involves the total system. The aim is to develop better rituals and routines (rules, roles, and relations) and a supporting culture for organizational growth and adaptation.

A Comparison of Management Development and OD

Management development emerged in the fifties as a major training technique for improving executive performance. In its instructional techniques, management development was a logical outcome of TWI (training within industry), which was developed during World War II to train foremen in instructional methods, grievance handling, and job methods. Management development's aim was to teach the manager new skills (instructing, interviewing, discussion leading), to enhance his conceptual framework of management (the techniques of delegation and staff work), and to give encapsulated versions of new management techniques (PERT, linear programming, value engineering). The basic reason for initiating such programs was that there was something wrong with the individual manager that could be set right by giving him or her new philosophies and policies. Many a pleasant Friday was spent by training officers picking out both the victims who "needed" the training and their destination.

Management development was also reinforced by job rotation, management traineeships, conferences, and planned reading programs. Of course, there was a fair amount of individual resistance to such training, which was seen in many cases as an infringement of individual freedom.

OD in Action: The Grid

Grid organization development is R. R. Blake's solution to the inadequacies of management development. This strategy was designed to handle the two most recurrent obstacles to corporate excellence: communication and planning. Both are symptoms of more significant and far deeper difficulties. Problems of communication actually reflect difficulties in the character of supervision. The way to overcome problems of communication is to use people properly; then they will automatically attain the required production and the desired excellence. Planning problems indicate either an absence of a valid business strategy or a strategy that relies on faulty business logic. According to Blake, planning obstacles can be overcome by designing an ideal strategic model.

Neither communication nor planning exists in isolation. Each either exaggerates or reduces difficulties in the other. Blake points out that finding the solution for one may make solutions for the other easier to come by. The effect is not additive but, to use Blake's terminology, it is synergistic: the effect is greater than the sum of the separate parts acting independently.

From the recognition of these two elements, Blake developed a Grid® (see Figure 14.5), which plots the task-oriented, or the "concern for production," as opposed to the human relations, or the "concern for people," approaches.

The degree of concern for production obviously varies from individual to individual. It is visualized on a nine-point scale on the horizontal axis of the grid: 1 represents a low concern, 9 a high concern. The vertical axis gives the scale for the concern for people, again from a low of 1 to a high of 9. The intersection points in the grid represent different ways of viewing how to achieve production through people.

The most clear-cut and straightforward theories are five in number. They are labeled the 1,1; the 1,9; the 5,5; the 9,1; and the 9,9. Each is a particular view of the optimum mix of the two concerns. We will discuss how each of these five theories would deal with avoiding conflict and, when that is not possible, how they would manage conflict.

The 1,1 corner exemplifies a low interest in production and a low interest in people. A person operating with the 1,1 approach will remain neutral in the face of any conflict. If his intervention is solicited in any conflict, he applies a basic rule to his conduct: "What a person does is not important as long as he keeps busy." Still another is to study problems and delay any answer. In a few words, stalling is his technique

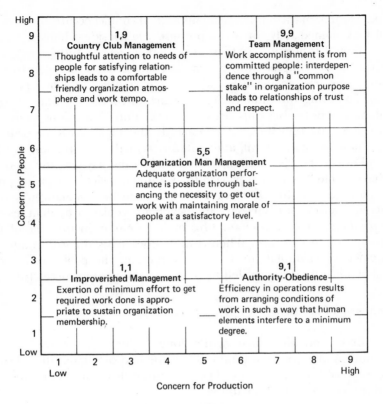

Figure 14.5   The Managerial Grid
The Managerial Grid ® figure from *The New Managerial Grid,* by Robert R. Blake and Jane Srygley Mouton. Houston: Gulf Publishing Company, Copyright © 1978, page 11. Reproduced by permission.

in face of conflict. He doesn't want to be involved, and therefore he doesn't involve himself to start with.

The 1,9 corner of the grid is already a step further along the continuum. Although there is a low concern for production, there is, on the other hand, a very high concern for people. Here the person will do anything, even let a subordinate become lax in his work, as long as the harmony between them is not disturbed. If conflict does arise, the boss will stress the "big happy family, every cloud has a silver lining" approach. As Blake aptly puts it, conflict is smothered along with the subordinate in a cozy, calm, peaceful atmosphere.

The 5,5 position illustrates the middle of the road. To avoid conflict, the manager will do nothing to stand out of the mainstream, either in production or in the human relations area. If conflict occurs, the manager will look immediately for a compromise. He considers himself flexible.

The 9,1 position is that of a person whose high interest for production is coupled with a very low concern for people. To avoid conflict, he tries to make his wishes, expectations, and orders crystal clear. Following the same logic, he manages conflict by reiterating his orders. Conflict arises only because people don't know how to listen to his orders. By repeating his commands and making his subordinates learn how to listen, he will automatically remedy the situation.

Finally, the 9,9 position is what Blake calls a synergistic theory of behavior. This theory's approach to avoiding conflict is to use empirical data as the basis for problem solving and decision making. As Blake puts it, "Faith is out; facts are in." Dogma is replaced by data, evasion by obedience. One can change his or her opinion in the face of facts without any loss of face. When conflict does arise, the group attempts an objective examination of the very roots of the problems. A great deal of sincerity is demanded to render this approach successful.

Six Stages of the Grid

Blake and Mouton have developed a highly structured strategy for putting the grid into action. Their method of organizational development requires six phases. The first three deal with communication and the last three with planning.

Phase one: seminar

Phase one typically involves participation in a week-long seminar in which a selected group learns theories of organization, including Likert's System Four and McGregor's Theory X and Theory Y. Usually this seminar is conducted on an in-company basis, and the members of the training group include staff and line managers drawn from several levels of the organization. The main objective of phase one is developing the 9,9 model as a prototype. The Blake grid uses T-group technology; it compels the attending executives to face up to the comparison between their actual and self-perceived grid scores. The whole exercise, according to participants, resembles a kind of pressure cooker. It usually works, but it can have explosive side effects.

Phase two: teamwork development

Phase two repeats the technology of phase one, but this time different work teams apply grid theories to improve their effectiveness.

The work group discusses with each member the specific steps that must be taken to increase individual effectiveness.

Phase three: intergroup development

Phase three concerns itself with building up intergroup cooperation. The departmental groups must cooperate to achieve results.

Phase four: developing an ideal strategic model

As William F. Dowling points out,

In Phase 4, by definition a top-management activity, key executives design an ideal strategic model by applying "pure reasoning" to six interdependent corporate elements: (1) key financial objectives; (2) the nature of the business; (3) the nature of the market; (4) the structure of the organization; (5) basic policies to guide decision making; and (6) development requirements for future growth.

Once again, as in Phases 1 and 2, "the ideal is a searchlight for seeing the real." As Blake and Mouton express it specifically in describing Phase 4, "When an ideal model of what is possible is contrasted with the existing situation, significant motivational energy is released." The initial formulation of the ideal model involves a week of concentrated team effort guided by a Grid organizational development specialist from Scientific Methods, Inc., and preceded by no less than 100 hours of individual prework in which the participants absorb the same fundamental concepts of business logic. Even the week of concentrated effort, Blake and Mouton admit, is only the beginning: Weeks or months may elapse before top management has agreed on its objectives in the six key areas.[1]

Phase five: planning and implementation

Phase five consists of a detailed revamping of the organizational structure to conform to configurations required by the ideal model. It requires a coordinator who reports directly to the chief executive officer and who heads a strategy implementation team.

[1] Reprinted by permission of the publisher, from "Using the Managerial Grid to Ensure MBO" by William F. Dowling, *Organizational Dynamics* (Spring 1974). Copyright © 1974 by AMACOM, a division of the American Management Associations. All rights reserved.

Phase six: systematic critique

Phase six is an all-inclusive critique. The group reviews the total effort to consolidate progress and to plan the next steps of development.

An Evaluation of the Managerial Grid

William F. Dowling has described how the grid was applied to Union Mutual, an insurance company with assets over $400,000 million and about 1,000 employees. It applied the grid as a means of making its MBO program more effective. The two years during which it was used were the most successful in Union Mutual's 126-year history. As Dowling points out, other factors may also have been involved, however:

> Take the situation at Union Mutual. We have two undeniable phenomena: Things have never been better—1972 witnessed a whole series of performance records in dollar gains from operations, dividends to policy owners and beneficiaries, investment income, and sales. At the same time, the top-management team had involved itself in several stages of the Grid. 1973 was another outstanding year and a year in which top management deepened its involvement in the Grid and the next level of management went through the beginning phase of the Grid. Cause and effect? Possibly. Hampton—and who is in a better position to judge?—is willing to give the Grid a large measure of the credit for increased profitability and effectiveness.
>
> To assert the likelihood of substantial cause and effect is easy; to prove it is impossible. Take, for example, the demonstration project of one group of second-level managers who developed criteria for identifying policies that might be subject to excessive claims in case of a recession. What if there hadn't been a Phase 2? Wouldn't Hampton or the man in charge of the group's division have appointed a team—possibly the same men—to work on the problem, which certainly demanded attention? And wouldn't they have emerged with the same results? Of course, the game of "what ifs" is a sterile one, in which we can never know any of the answers. But it illustrates one of the problems encountered in attributing direct benefits to the Grid or any other organization development effort.
>
> Another area of ambiguity: Was the unquestionable improvement in performance at Union Mutual due to the Grid mechanism, or was it due more to the continuing pressures for improvement generated by Hampton in his leadership role? In other words, was the Grid possibly more a symbol than a cause? Again, we have no way of *knowing* the answer. And, of course, we always have the force of economic, environmental, and political factors external to the organization that

have an undoubted, if elusive, impact on its performance and profitability.[2]

REVIEW AND RESEARCH

1. Define group dynamics.
2. List and cite examples of the various kinds of groups that the executive
    is likely to encounter.
3. List the various kinds of meetings that the executive is likely to take
    part in.
4. What are the functions of a committee?
5. Describe the process, structure, and values of a problem-solving
    group.
6. What is a T-group? Why have T-groups fallen into disrepute among
    executives?
7. Define organizational development. Compare and contrast manage-
    ment development and organizational development.
8. Explain the concept of the Grid. Briefly describe the five main
    management positions of the Grid.
9. Describe the six stages of the Grid.
10. Make a list of the basic tenets of group dynamics that every executive
    should be familiar with.

CALVIN C. KNOX

You are the project leader responsible for the implementation of a new
computerized accounting system for your company. The new system
must be operational in six months, and you are approximately two
weeks behind schedule. There are eight members in your project team,
all of whom report directly to you. The working atmosphere is open;
that is, the people feel free to ask questions of one another and offer
constructive criticism.

   Recently, however, upon return from a two-week business trip,

---

[2] *Ibid.*

you discover that a young man named Calvin C. Knox has been assigned to your project team without your knowledge, approval, or advice. Your first reaction is one of gratitude, since you do require additional manpower to complete the project on schedule. But soon you discover that Knox has a reputation among the other project leaders as disruptive and a troublemaker. In fact, he has been tossed from project to project like a hot potato.

Immediately you call in two responsible members of the project team and ask them for a report of the situation. Much to your surprise, they both state that work is moving along well; it has actually picked up since the addition of Knox. They tell you that it is true that at first Knox seems abrasive. But as you get to know him, you discover that this is a defense mechanism. The younger members of the team find him amusing and entertaining; and the work is not only finished faster but with fewer errors. Knox appears to be learning the job.

The problem you face is whether or not to keep him on your project team. What are you going to do?

15

Managing
the
Organization

List the stages a company goes through in moving from a one-man business to a large organization.

Describe the significance of a crisis in helping an organization to move from stage to stage.

Identify the significant steps in an organization as it goes into its decline and ultimate death.

Define the factors of organizational effectiveness.

Organizations are goal-seeking organisms that have to adapt and learn in order to survive and grow. Like organisms, organizations are conceived and born; they adapt, grow, learn, achieve adolescence, live through crises, somehow mature, achieve uniqueness, slowly decline, and finally die.

Birth of an Organization

Usually businesses begin as one-person firms, out of which managerial tissue is developed. For example, a person might start a short-order restaurant, which he runs by working a 16-hour day, doing all the chores, and perhaps even sleeping in the back room. The restaurant develops from stage 1, the boss and two employees all working together as cook, counterman, and dishwasher, to stage four, in which the cooks are connected to the waitresses by runners. As the restaurant evolves into a more complex organization, it develops functional specialization. The dining room is managed by a maître d', who supervises a number of waitresses, waiters, and busboys. Overseeing both of these entities is a captain who integrates both systems to the needs of the clientele.

The Organizational Crisis

As the organization grows and moves from stage to stage, it experiences a series of sharp crises. Lippitt and Schmidt have argued that at each stage of the organization's growth, it has to go through a crisis to enter into the next stage. Each stage involves key issues of decision making about the risks and the consequences it faces if it fails to meet the challenges. At each stage the organization needs to correlate its structure with the business strategy of the firm. In the first stage, a new firm's main problem is producing a product and finding a market for it. Leadership is basically entrepreneurial.

The Organization in Its Adolescence

As the organization passes from youth (50 to 100 or fewer employees) to adolescence (200 to 1,000 employees), it experiences all sorts of stresses and strains. Table 15.1 shows some of the differences between small and large companies. Differences in size alone call for different managerial strategies.

In the small company, the top management meet every morning

Table 15.1 Typical Organizational Characteristics: Small Versus Large Companies

Small Company	Large Company
1. Most important decisions are made at the top, either by one individual or by a small group. There is little delegation of authority to lower levels.	1. A distinction is made between routine and exceptional decisions. Routine decisions are delegated to lower levels.
2. Workers and top management are in frequent contact with each other. Middle management is rudimentary and constantly bypassed.	2. Middle management has been strengthened and is less frequently bypassed by either subordinates or superiors.
3. Lines of authority and responsibility are loosely defined. Titles mean relatively little. Almost every member of top management feels free to participate in decision making regarding every problem that comes up.	3. To a greater extent authority flows from title, not personality. Every job has definite duties and responsibilities.
4. Communications are largely face-to-face, oral, and unspecialized. There are no set procedures that distinguish among types of decisions and the way they are to be processed.	4. Communications are more often in writing; standard operating procedures have been established for routing information and decisions from department to department.
5. There are few explicit policies or rules.	5. Explicit rules have been laid down to define the freedom with which subordinates may act.
6. The staff function is weak and poorly defined.	6. The staff function has considerably expanded; it has well-defined areas of responsibility; its expertise is respected.
7. Members of top management personally check employee performance. There are few statistical controls, if any. Accounting performs primarily a historical function.	7. Formal, impersonal statistical control measures, such as accounting, quality control, and time study, are established. The concept of supervision by exception is accepted, as well as its corollary, the distinction between normal behavior and variance.

to open, read, and discuss the day's mail and to make decisions about designating responsibilities pertaining to that day's developments. As the organization grows, top management is less and less able to keep up with daily developments. Decision making breaks down, jobs outgrow people, and new levels are introduced into management; new technical experts bring in new values, and the old management becomes alienated. (See Box 15.1, which describes the growing pains of a company.)

A personnel director of a company going through the change of adolescence voiced his frustrations this way:

The Thatcher Company has 800 employees today, compared with 150 five years ago and a mere dozen back in 1958. In the community, it has the reputation of a fine place to work—the pay is excellent, there is a liberal profit sharing plan, almost no one ever gets laid off. And most of nontechnical management has risen from the ranks. Bill Thatcher, the founder, prides himself on the informality and lack of paperwork in the plant, as well as on the opportunities he tries to provide every employee—whether in management or among the hourly paid workforce—to show initiative and accept responsibility. Many of the company's best ideas have come from workers on the line and salesmen in the field.

Yet the Thatcher Company is in trouble. Costs are out of control. Coordination of sales, engineering, and production, once excellent, now seems to be breaking down. In spite of personal efforts by Thatcher himself to straighten things out, small orders are sometimes lost, and deliveries of large orders are often delayed. Thatcher is somewhat perplexed by the turn of events. As he sees it, relations are just not as smooth as they once were:

> Communications are still good at our [top-management] level, but we seem to have trouble reaching people further down. Oh, the oldtimers are fine, but you

Continued on next page

Frankly, I'm not getting anywhere. I get no backing, no support. Sometimes I find it hard even to get an answer. I tried to start a supervisory training program. They told me to work with the foremen (though it's higher management that needs it most), and after three weeks they dropped it because of the need to get out a rush order. The trouble is that I'm never consulted on policy or included in the policy-making group.[1]

To meet the problems of adolescence, Strauss argues that management should set a timetable that relates growth to structure. A periodic check should be made to find out how tensions are being handled.

The main problems of an organization in adolescence are how to gain stability, establish reputation, and develop pride. They are problems of organization, review, and evaluation. If the organization does

---

just can't seem to motivate the newer men. Lower management, and particularly the staff people, just won't take responsibility; they seem to lack team spirit; there's too much petty bickering and not much feeling for the company as a whole. I'm beginning to wonder whether they don't need a good training program in the nature of management principles.

The Thatcher Company's problems seem to be typical of those of many rapidly growing companies that are reaching a critical period in their development, during which they must shift from informal, face-to-face, rule-of-thumb means of control to those involving greater formality. The problem is that they have become too big for their present mode of operation. When these companies were smaller, communications flowed freely upward and downward and across departmental lines; the boss knew what everyone was doing; and decisions could easily be made at the top. These easygoing days are now gone, and the informality that helped spark their early growth has now become a stumbling block to efficiency. What was once everybody's business has become nobody's business, and the result is inefficiency, buckpassing, and delay. Greater formality is now required—paperwork (bureaucracy, if you wish), the assignment of definite responsibilities, and impersonal methods of feedback and control.

---

not cope effectively with this crisis, it will fail to attract good personnel and clients. Adolescent organizations' problems have to do with direction; they need to set up standards and cost centers. Centralized, autocratic management does not know how to integrate these concepts into the decision-making process. Management also experiences problems in delegation.

The Crisis of Growing Complexity

Donald K. Clifford, Jr., has argued that an organization faces a major problem as it moves from the entrepreneurial stage to a larger corporation. The company has to go through a critical trouble zone. These threshold companies, which experience an explosive rate of increase in product complexity, present the chief executive officer (CEO) with a tremendous problem. Figure 15.1 explains some of the complexities companies meet.

This growing complexity radically changes the management requirements, both at the very top and in beginning functional positions. The

	Low	Moderate	Substantial	High
A. Product Complexity				
1. Number of products	Single line	Several related	Several related some not	Diverse complex
2. Complexity of individual products	Simple design	Multiple components	Intricate, sensitive	Complex, technical systems
3. Degree of forward/ backward integration	None	Partial, one step	Extensive	Highly integrated
4. Rate of product innovation	Slow	Slow/ moderate	Moderate/ rapid	Rapid
B. Market Complexity				
5. Geographic scope	Regional	National	National significant export	International
6. Distribution channels	Single	2–3	Several	Multiple/ complex
7. End-user groups	Single, well-defined	2–3	Several, distinct	Multiple/ diverse
C. Environmental Complexity				
8. Competitive intensity (price, product, marketing)	Low	Low/ moderate	Moderate/ intense	Very intense
9. External pressures (economic, govern- mental, social, labor)	Stable	Stable/ moderate	Moderate/ heavy	Volatile

▇ Small company example   ▇ Larger threshold company example

Figure 15.1   Dimensions of Product/Market Complexity
Reprinted by permission of the publisher, from "The Case of the Floundering Flounder"
by Donald K. Clifford, Jr., *Organizational Dynamics* (Autumn 1974). Copyright © 1975
by AMACOM, a division of the American Management Associations. All rights reserved.

CEO, according to Clifford, has to revamp his management role and
style. He has to spend more time selecting, training, and motivating
others to carry out the main functions of the business. The CEO's job
is compounded by stress and uncertainty. What the CEO has to do,
according to Clifford is

1. Give the old guard a chance to develop new capabilities, but be
willing to face up quickly to proven inadequacy.
2. Bring in new talent and give it growing room.

3. Create a challenging yet supportive organizational climate.[2]

To be effective, one has got to create a new climate. The CEO who cannot cope frequently fails because he juggles priorities, acts on gut feelings rather than rational analysis, engages in too much one-way communication, and in general talks too much.

But Clifford believes these problems can be overcome by developing structural changes to harness new skills and control growing complexity. For example,

> The CEO can exploit this need for structural change to reinforce his efforts to modify his own role. For example, one CEO of a complex $100 million company appointed his top division manager as chief operating officer with direct-line responsibility for all domestic profit centers plus most staff functions. The CEO retained the international division plus the financial control function and strategic planning. These moves (not atypical of many growing threshold companies in the $100 to $200 million sales range) shifted the balance of his time allocation in the right direction and provided the younger man with an exceptional opportunity to grow.
>
> It is vital for the CEO to lay out a specific program for himself, linked where appropriate to planned changes in the corporate organization. This program should include written descriptions of the successive roles he foresees for himself at specific times, and it should also lay out the resources and mechanisms he plans to use to achieve it.[3]

Figure 15.2 shows how the CEO's time allocations change with a company's complexity.

Fighting for Maturity

The final stage of organizational development requires the firm to achieve uniqueness and adaptability and to determine its contribution to society. The main issues here are whether and how to change and whether and how to share. This can be a very difficult stage for a firm. The main problem the firm faces at this time is the need to engage in collaboration. Realizing and accepting this need requires social control and self-discipline. For example, to survive or perhaps only to postpone its demise, a firm may be forced to merge with other firms or acquire

[2] Reprinted by permission of the publisher, from "The Case of the Floundering Flounder," by Donald K. Clifford, Jr., *Organizational Dynamics* (Autumn 1975). Copyright © 1975 by AMACOM, a division of The American Management Associations. All rights reserved.

[3] *Ibid.*

Degree of Complexity

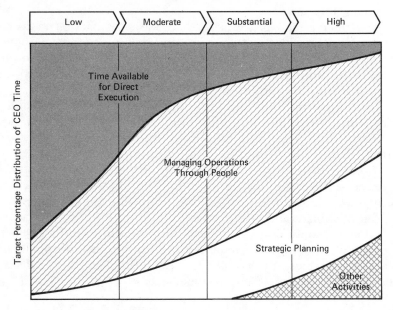

Figure 15.2   The Changing Role of the Chief Executive

other companies. Pepsico, for example, has merged with or acquired Frito-Lay, Wilson Sporting Goods, and North American Van Lines since 1965.

How can the change from one stage to another be facilitated? Usually, the chief executive comes under pressure to improve performance; a new executive or consultant is introduced into the organization; a new policy emerges that polarizes the management; a conflict breaks out, and a war of attrition ensues; and a firm either survives and prospers, or it fails to recognize the realities of the situation and fails.

TECHNOLOGY AND ORGANIZATIONAL STRUCTURE

One of the most important factors affecting organizational growth is technology. When we speak of technology, we mean not only tools and machines but also know-how and applied science. Management theorists were first made aware of the importance of integrating technology by some work carried out by the Tavistock Institute of Human Relations in London, England.

In Britain after World War II, there was a change over in the coal mines from a primitive method of cutting coal to complex machinery, which cut away a whole wall of coal. The old way allowed men to work in pairs; the modern method required miners to work in fairly large teams, which made them feel isolated and alone. The Tavistock people reorganized the teams so that the miners could create some kind of social fabric that would give their lives meaning in these new, large teams. Out of such simple beginnings came the idea of sociotechnical systems.

From these beginnings, we have learned that modern industry not only needs a liaison between sales and customers but frequently between research and development, between development and pilot plant, and between pilot plant and manufacturer.

Modern, sophisticated, innovative organizations need a vast army of technical messengers; companies are now more horizontal than vertical hierarchies. By its very nature, technology is the decisive determinant of organizational arrangements.

Three Types of Technology

Technology and structure are intimately interlocked: one depends upon the other.

Long-linked

Long-linked technology is mostly to be found in mass-production industry, such as car assembly plants and appliance manufacturing. In the automobile assembly line, for example, technology is based upon "serial interdependence" of tasks necessary to the completion of production. Wheels can be put in position only after the work has been completed on the front and rear axles of the car.

Mediating technology

Mediating technologies are found in firms that provide linking services between customers or clients. A bank, which provides a link between the depositors and the borrowers, uses mediating technology.

Intensive technology

Mobilizing and forming a wide diversity of skills, concepts, and ideas for a single client is characteristic of intensive technology. A good example of this type of organization is a hospital. The aerospace industry also provides many examples of this type of technology.

THE ORGANIZATION AND ITS ENVIRONMENT

A new view of organizations is emerging that stresses the importance of the environment. Research in human relations has established that executives need to manage the coalitions within the firm. To keep things in balance, managers operate by satisficing; that is, rather than requiring the maximum, they take just a little more than they need, making sure that such other interest groups as stockholders, organized labor, the government, and consumers also get enough to discourage them from interfering with the manager's business.

Managing the environment means treating organizations as open systems whose prime problem is the transformation of inputs into outputs. Therefore, managers must be highly involved collecting intelligence about the environment to transform it and make it more munificent.

Definition of the Environment

The environment consists of all the external sources and factors to which an organization is potentially responsive. These include physical, social, and cultural elements.

The Nature of the Environment

Emery and Trist have developed a typology for classifying environments.[4] They distinguish four kinds:

1. *The placid, randomized environment,* which is relatively unchanging and

[4] F.E. Emery and E.L. Trist, "The Causal Texture of Organizational Environments," *Human Relations,* 18, 1 (1965), 21–32.

homogeneous. Demands are randomly distributed and change slowly over time.

2. *The placid, clustered environment,* which is also slow to change but in which threats and rewards are clustered, rather than randomly distributed. Such an environment might be a monopolistic market, for example, the Bell Telephone system.

3. *The disturbed, reactive environment,* in which there is competition among similar organizations; each organization seeks to block the development of its rival. An example would be the auto industry in the United States.

4. *The turbulent field environment,* which is dynamic and rapidly changing and in which organizations continually review their standing in regard to external forces. A good example of such an environment is the aerospace industry in the United States.

Different kinds of organizations emerge in different environments. For example, in the race to the moon, NASA had to employ a complex sociotechnical form of organization. Normal work roles and loyalties were broken down and replaced by a very different set of relations. In the NASA project, organizations did not passively accept the conditions that surrounded them; they actively shaped the environment to meet their needs. Technical experts of aerospace firms were absorbed into the structure of NASA to eliminate potential sources of opposition. Convoluted, informal organizations circumvented traditional organizational relations. But these adjustments were achieved at a high price for the individuals involved. In a good number of cases, marriages and careers were torn apart.

As the NASA example illustrates, organizations co-opt other organizations and individuals to enhance their own chances of success. Co-optation is widely employed in business as a means of controlling the uncertainties of the environment. If firms are subject to government regulation and have high needs for capital, for example, boards of directors tend to co-opt lawyers and bankers. A more subtle form of co-optation is trading executives. Another means of dealing with the environment is to engage in merger and acquisition. In most cases, the objective of merger and acquisition is to reduce the organization's dependence on its environment. Another method employed to control uncertainty is to insist on long-term contracts.

Invisible Organizations

By discovering the pervasiveness of informal organizations, human relations pointed out the existence of "invisible organizations" within or along with formal organizations. We know that the power often lies with these informally organized interest groups, invisible as they may be. But they are not confined to the shop floor. Ethnic groups (in spite of the melting pot hypothesis), elite groups (Ivy League MBA's, for example), ritual groups (the Masons and the Knights of Columbus) and cousinhoods (the intermarrying families that "control" the London financial system) run the business of life. Research reveals that informal groups at all levels are bound together in webs of values-norms-reinforcements-sanctions. These informal groups achieve what the open, formal system cannot. Occasionally, of course, the price becomes inordinate and indeed unpayable.

ORGANIZATION THEORY

Organization theory seeks to explain that curious social phenomenon the "organization." It has been described as a quasi-independent science, which draws primarily on the disciplines of psychology and sociology. But the organization has also been affected by developments in industrial engineering, politics, and economics and more recently by findings from such diverse fields as social anthropology, social psychiatry, operations research, and computer science. In more technical terms, organization theory can be defined as the study of the structure, processes, and values of organizations; the behavior of groups and individuals within them; and the interaction of the organization with other behavioral systems in its environment.

MANAGING ORGANIZATIONAL CHANGE
FOR PERFORMANCE

In this chapter we are concerned with the subject of change. What particular structure, process, and values are appropriate to different change situations?

As we move into the last quarter of the twentieth century the only constant seems to be change. The executive who is in his late forties has witnessed dramatic changes. He or she has lived through the depression, World War II, and several recessions. He has lived through the period when the main way of crossing the Atlantic has changed from trans-Atlantic liners (even the fastest of which took just over three days) to supersonic jets, which take a few hours.

Now, with these changes have come unanticipated problems. With the supersonics, for example, came the dangers of sonic booms. When there are massive and constant changes, people need a theory of change to help them understand both the present and the future. To be effective, managers have got to be able to develop strategy and tactics for change. Only then can they develop structures, processes, and values in a changing environment.

Structural Changes

By structure we mean the rules, roles, and relations of the managerial process, which determines a system of communication and a system of authority. Structural changes are usually concerned with such issues as centralization versus decentralization.

Structural change has been the major thrust of the classical organization theroists. Typically, consultants are brought in. They are usually qualified either in engineering or accountancy, and they can rapidly develop new organization charts, policies, and role descriptions. These structural changes are still widely employed, and they draw their authority from the use of unilateral power. In the decree approach to change, a "one-way announcement" is made by the chief executive and passed down the line to the actual troops. Under the replacement approach, key people are replaced. The changing relationship approach requires new relationships of subordinates.

The Technological Fact

Closely related to structural considerations is the technological fact. Since the turn of the century, American management has been dominated by the ideas of assembly line production, maximal task breakdown, time study, and method study. All these ideas have come to us from engineers who are preoccupied with making production scientific. Latest in this line is the computer. Out of computer technology have come operation research and sophisticated management information systems.

Unfortunately, when new management science concepts have been put into action, they have frequently had to overcome considerable resistance to change. This is because changes in organizational structure may dramatically change the life styles of the people who have to live within these structures. Employees carry around in their heads a kind of psychological contract, which spells out a fair day's work, a fair day's pay, and generally determines their perception of the rules and relations governing their role. Employees resist changes because a new behavior violates this psychological contract. Therefore, for change to be effective, a process has to be developed that can negotiate employees out of their psychological contracts.

Process of Change

Significant changes cannot take place unless historical forces facilitate those changes. Most managers who have lived through substantial organizational change would agree with Kurt Lewin's three phases of change: unfreezing, changing, and refreezing.

The unfreezing stage cannot take place without a sense of crisis. For example, the American automobile manufacturers would never have changed from large to smaller cars without the crisis engendered by the OPEC cartel.

But a crisis by itself is not sufficient; it has to be exploited. This means bringing in a change agent, usually a new top executive and/or a prestigious consultant. Consultants follow a planned change process, which has the following steps:

1. Recognizing a crisis
2. Exploiting the crisis by creating an awareness of the need for change.
3. Making a diagnosis of the problem, which specifies the need for change and develops a change vector.
4. Communicating the change to those that are going to be changed.
5. Monitoring the change and fine-tuning it.

Diagnosis of the Problem

Diagnosis of the problem is essentially an exercise in drawing the right conclusions. Sometimes one must employ a variety of diagnostic techniques: T-groups, conferences, task forces, brainstorming sessions, questionnaires and surveys, informal conversations, and so on.

Only when the diagnosis has been properly completed is it possible to develop a plan for change.

Values

If technology or structure or process is changed, values are automatically changed as well. For example, a man who has been trained as a professional engineer brings his values of precision and accuracy to the job of time and motion engineer. But in the process of becoming a time-study man, he may carry over the idea of treating people as things, which may have the effect of generating some shop floor opposition. When the same engineer later in his career becomes an expert on computer-based management science projects, his own values will undergo an even sharper change. He may become more numerate, more information-oriented, more analytical, yet more open and nonlinear.

Classical structural changes, based on rationality and economic common sense, nearly always mobilize opposition. Human relations, on the other hand, has been preoccupied with overcoming resistance to change. In the human relations approach, the object is to use not only reason and logic but persuasion, warmth, and spontaneity. Descended from this approach is change strategy, which is presumed to work better with total participation.

Behavioral System

To help managers achieve changes, behavioral scientists have developed a whole raft of techniques. These range from T-groups to encounter groups to organizational development. The central idea of these new techniques is to create more power sharing, more openness, more trust, and more energy. The idea is to change the psychological contract and help people accept the fact that change is legitimate.

REVIEW AND RESEARCH

1. Describe the different stages a growing organization goes through. Why does an organization have to go through a crisis to get from stage to stage?

2. What are the four problems an organization faces as it grows away from its clients?

3. Discuss the relationship between technology and organizational structure. Illustrate your answer by looking either at computers and banking or computers and the airline business.

4. How do companies manage the environment? Select a particular company and show how it has adapted to its environment.

5. In what ways could the informal organization be described as a sacred secret society?

6. What does decline and fall of *The Saturday Evening Post* tell you about organizational pathology?
7. What is the Peter Principle?
8. How can organizational change be managed to get performance?
9. What makes working in one organization different from working in another? Discuss what is meant by the statement, different organizations have different climates. Explain why the climate means the perception of the internal organizational environment.

SELLING MANAGEMENT

Many American corporations are in the field of selling management expertise as well as a product. A good example of a company in this category is the Marriott Corporation, a $1 billion food and lodging company which began as a nickel root beer stand just over 50 years ago and is still booming. In 1978 no other corporation was as aggressively building new hotels as Marriott. The Marriott success has been achieved by strategies that reflect a distinct change in management concepts. The Marriott Corporation, a most diversified business of hotels, fast-food restaurants, theme parks, cruise ships, and contract food service to airlines, has begun to place a heavy emphasis on profit margin as opposed to volume. The company has decided to concentrate on a smaller number of high margin areas. The company is increasing its efforts in hotel and food service businesses, for these are the most profitable areas. Where the company is losing money—cruise ships, for example—they are standing fast.

One of the most creative aspects in the business, however, has been the recent $92 million sale of five profitable hotels to the Equitable Life Assurance Society of the United States. Marriott will continue to operate these hotels for a management fee and a percentage across operating profits. The company's objective is to get into a position for constructing "pipelines" within which they can build new hotels, operate them for a time to develop a track record, then sell them and operate them for a management fee and a share of the profits. Thus Marriott is increasingly in the management business. They make money both by buying and developing properties and by selling their skills to manage these properties.

What are the advantages for a company in pursuing this policy of "selling management"?

16

Diagnosing
and
Managing
Conflict

Identify four different kinds of conflict situations.

Describe the causes and cures of classical conflict.

List the advantages of and limitations to three human relations approaches to conflict.

Give an example of how systems conflict can develop in the modern airliner between the front crew and the back crew.

List the several methods of diagnosing and alleviating conflict.

The classical view of conflict is concerned with the problems that arise in organizations because they are hierarchically structured. The causes of conflict are essentially structural and arise either from poorly defined rules, roles, and relations or because the environment has changed and the structure is no longer appropriate. In our discussion of the classical approach to conflict, we will consider the relationships among authority, aggression, space, and stress. This will take us into consideration of the territorial imperative, the geography of conflict, and the dysfunction of too much aggression.

The second, the human relations view of conflict, deals mainly with the problems that arise from faulty communication and inappropriate stereotypes. Coping with conflict then becomes a question of introducing one stereotype to another, reestablishing communications, and using third parties as intermediaries.

The third approach, derived from systems theory, deals with inter- and intraorganizational conflicts. The critical question for the modern corporate society is the control of large, multinational corporations, many of which are more potent than the governments of small countries.

The last approach to conflict is existential in character. The aim in this section is to show how conflicts affect individual managers and force them into an agonizing reappraisal of their identities and career trajectories.

WHAT IS CONFLICT?

One expert has defined conflict as:

> ... a struggle over values and claims to scarce status, power and resources in which the aims of the opponents are to neutralize, injure or eliminate their rivals.[1]

The social science view stresses the idea that conflict is one of the central forms of interaction. In this view, conflict is seen as a method of achieving some kind of unity. In this chapter, we will examine the kinds of conflicts managers must often deal with. How can managers use conflicts to strengthen their organizations?

---

[1] L.A. Coser, *The Functions of Social Conflict* (Glencoe, Ill.: The Free Press, 1956), p. 8. Copyright © 1956 by The Free Press, A Corporation.

THE CLASSICAL VIEW OF CONFLICT

In classical theory, most conflict is presumed to be jurisdictional in character.

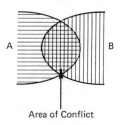

Area of Conflict

Figure 16.1   Overlapping Areas of Conflict

Typically, two job roles expand until there is an overlap, which causes a demarcation dispute (see Figure 16.1). Britain is beset with such conflicts. One classic example took place in British shipyards. The fitting of portholes traditionally required three specialists, a carpenter to mark the holes, a torchman to cut the holes, and another tradesman to fit the porthole cover. All were organized in different unions. When modern technology allowed one semiskilled man to do the whole job, an intense conflict arose. Who should do it, and what happens to the others? Many similar problems exist in North America. In the U.S., the classic illustration of a demarcation dispute was the problem of negotiating the firemen (who used to shovel coal in the steam engine) out of the cabin of the diesel railroad engine.

Structural Conflict

The formal leader of an organization, the chief executive officer, often develops conflict among middle executives. The chief executive is often so overwhelming that his behavior inhibits the very change he desires for his organization. Chris Argyris describes the following behavioral characteristics that are typical of most CEOs:

1. They are articulate, competitive, and persuasive.
2. They stimulate "win-lose" competition among subordinates, which leads to conformity and avoidance of risk taking.
3. Despite a professed desire for subordinates who are like themselves,

the CEOs' behavior leads subordinates to mute their own competitiveness and to avoid frank expression of their feelings.[2]

Given these traits it should not be surprising to learn that CEOs see themselves as dynamic leaders who are concerned with achievements that bear their unique imprint, who set difficult goals and then pursue them with single-minded devotion to duty, and who look all the while for continuous feedback on their accomplishments. Such dynamic people are generally not overly concerned with executive subordinates' feelings. They tend to view unfavorable feedback as unsolicited and gratuitous advice or irrelevant carping. Given this double bind situation, it is not surprising that middle-level executives seek to avoid their bosses rather than speak frankly. They do so to protect not only themselves but also the organization, which may need a driving leader (the personality of the leader may be deeply hurt by rejection of his thoroughly sincere efforts to do a good job). Some of the comments quoted by Argyris illustrate the attitudes of the CEO toward subordinates:

"I want a situation where it is not hard to show clearly what I did . . . and few of us want to be stopped by others. Right! Give us our turf and look out!"

"I believe that a real business leader is incapable of generating a climate where people can grow."

"Hell, none of us would work for people like ourselves."[3]

Despite the self-awareness shown by some of these comments, Argyris found that CEOs rarely discussed these ideas with their subordinates. Sometimes they had become aware of the problem too recently; some felt such a discussion would be threatening to their subordinates; and all felt that such discussions were "not the thing to do." Box 16.1 explains why business executives, like everyone else, often find themselves doing things they'd much rather not do.

The powerful impact of the CEO's personality and the general reluctance to examine its effects pose serious problems for the development of healthy mid-level executives. What it amounts to is that the CEO has a tremendous need for power and knows how to exercise it.

---

[2] "The CEO's Behavior: Key to Organizational Development" by Chris Argyris, *Harvard Business Review* (March-April 1973). Copyright © 1973 by the President and Fellows of Harvard College; all rights reserved.

[3] *Ibid.*, p. 57.

The Abilene paradox was invented by Jerry Harvey, an associate professor of management at George Washington University. Harvey got his inspiration some time ago when he, his wife, and his parents-in-law were at a house in Coleman, Texas. The temperature was 104 degrees, and a dust storm was blowing. Sheltered from the dust, the four sat under a fan, sipping iced lemonade, whiling away the afternoon playing dominoes.

Suddenly, the father-in-law came up with the idea of getting into the car, which had no air conditioning, and driving 53 miles to Abilene to eat in a cafeteria. Everyone readily agreed. They got into the car and sweltered in the dust all the way there, ate a terrible meal, and sweltered all the way back again.

Once back in the house everyone was silent and tense; soon they all fell to bickering. First the mother-in-law, then Harvey, then his wife made it plain they would have rather stayed at home sipping lemonade, gazing at the fan, and playing dominoes. They had agreed to make the trip simply because the others wanted to. The surprise came when the father-in-law declared that he had come up with the idea only because he thought the others might be bored.

The Classical Organizational Imperative: Maintain the Pecking Hierarchy

Executives who have fought their way to the top will welcome the news that behavioral scientists have established a curious connection between authority and power on the one hand and aggression, space, and stress on the other. Apparently, both senior executives and top apes maintain the authority and power of the pecking hierarchy in their respective turfs by swashbuckling aggressive posturing. This relationship connecting the factors of good order and hierarchical discipline, turf or territory and aggression is part of the field of ethology, which is the study of animal behavior and its relationship to man. Most people now accept the once unthinkable idea that men and beasts are species in the same animal kingdom and have comparable patterns of behavior in regard to aggression and territoriality.

Classical Control of Conflict

A major feature of the classical control of conflict is dominance. When two hostile parties meet, both have to consider the options of fight or flight. The more dominant party may well try to eliminate the weaker. In organizations, the domineering manager may dominate

Here were four sensible people who as individuals knew what was best for them (to stay as they were), yet as a group they readily agreed to do the exact opposite. Thus "Going to Abilene" is the title of the process by which four "no's" can be put together to come up with a collective "yes," or vice versa.

Of course, Jerry Harvey had no problem in finding corporate illustrations of the Abilene paradox. One American company nearly bankrupted itself by continuing an expensive research project even though the top brass knew the project was hopeless. People, executives included, are frightened to stand up in committees and act on their own beliefs. What terrifies executives is the threat of being ostracized. So dire is this threat that it appears in some manuals as "social amputation." This fear of social amputation distracts us from looking rationally at real risks. Group members are so busy suppressing conflict that only when they get to Abilene do they realize what they got themselves into.

because of his formal authority or power. The weaker party may be forced to defer to his more dominant opponent.

A major way of resolving conflict in organizations is to force the weaker party to resign. But conflicts in organizations rarely proceed at this individual level. Typically, cliques and cabals are formed. Modern organization theory accepts the necessity of coalitions to control the infighting and overt rivalry within the executive group.

Formal appeal mechanisms

A major virtue of the classical structuring of organizations into hierarchies is that a conflict that cannot be resolved at one level can always be referred to a superior for resolution. Thus, if managers follow the principles of the chain of command, any two parties in conflict can refer the problem to a common superior. In spite of the attacks on bureaucratic forms of management, the existence of the hierarchy provides a useful method of review. This judicial aspect of the executive system requires managers to live with the consequences of due process.

The personal factor

The classical management of conflict presupposes that individual managers will absorb some of the stress in the system without necessarily passing it on to superiors or subordinates. Sometimes it's very hard for young managers to accept their roles as buffers in the system. But the reality of corporate life is such that managers have to be prepared to spend at least part of their time listening to their subordinates' and occasionally their superiors' complaining.

THE HUMAN RELATIONS VIEW OF CONFLICT

Human relations argues that conflict is caused by faulty stereotypes, which will disappear as a result of good communication. For the human relations aficionado all problems are ultimately problems of communication. The question then becomes, how do you solve problems in communication?

Human relations experts have devised a whole range of techniques to improve and facilitate communication, including T-groups, encounter groups, group feedback sessions, VTR (videotape recording) assisted interviews, and so on.

These techniques bring the adversaries of a conflict together, usually in a neutral setting where they can deal with some pseudo-task such as solving a case study problem.

In this learning context, the adversaries can learn not only about group dynamics but a good deal about each other.

Stereotypes Stultify

There is some evidence that executives form stereotypes about other executives and about other people with whom they interact. This perceptual distortion exaggerates the differences between groups. For example, many American executives have somewhat negative attitudes towards the managerial capacities of members of minority groups and women.

But among executives there is a great variety of stereotypes. Managers whose only qualification is an undergraduate degree in engineering often have a strong negative picture of newly qualified MBAs, whom they perceive as uppity, pushy, overzealous know-nothings who want to move into the top levels of business without serving their apprenticeship in the technical bowels of the organization. Production people have stereotypes about personnel managers, whom they see as soft and pseudo-democratic. Moreover, American executives have stereotypes about their British counterparts and vice versa.

Coping with Conflict the Human Relations Way

Arguing from the viewpoint that conflict is "bad" and should be eliminated; that conflict results from breakdown in communication and the holding of false stereotypes; and, above all, that people are essentially good, human relations researchers have developed a whole range of techniques to deal with conflict.

Introducing one stereotype to another

One technique has had remarkable success in generating a cooperative problem-solving relationship between hostile groups. Such warring groups could include unions and management, production and sales, or research and pilot plant development.

The method is deceptively simple.

1. The two groups must express a basic interest in ameliorating the relationship.
2. Each group is placed in a separate room and commits to paper its perception of "self" and the "other."
3. The two groups are brought together, and a presentation is made of these four different perceptions. The object of this stage is to allow the process of assimilation, questioning, rebuttal and reexamination.
4. The groups then return to their separate rooms to analyze the discrepancies in their perceptions.
5. The groups then meet again and try to develop reasons for the different perceptions.

Using this diagnostic technique, researchers have been able to reduce misperceptions, to improve the fidelity of communication, and to establish trust in conflicts between opposing groups.

Superordinate goals

Another technique proposes that group hostility can be resolved through a search for superordinate goals. A superordinate goal is one that is absolutely essential to both groups and can be ignored only at the peril of their survival; further, the goal can be achieved only by mobilizing the resources and energies of both groups. For example, during the Second World War a coalition government emerged in Great Britain because both political parties recognized the importance of the superordinate goal, defeating Germany and Japan. In an organizational context, management and labor are often willing to cooperate, but only if such cooperation is a sine qua non of the company's survival. Perhaps it is worth noting that a critical disadvantage of this coping technique is that conflict may well break out again after the accomplishment of the superordinate goal.

Third party conflict resolution

Some experts recommend interpersonal peacemaking through confrontation and third party consultation. If two departmental groups are in conflict with one another, a third party skilled in interpersonal peacemaking may intervene to bring the two sides together. The third party stimulates an agonizing reappraisal of viewpoints through open dialogue and confrontation.

Human relations game playing

To stimulate communication, some human relations experts recommend "playing games;" that is, talking to people in conflict in a way that will cool their emotions and make them feel important. The rules of game playing are:

1. Always look the other person straight in the eye.
2. Wear a smile and nod a lot. Above all, appear to listen intently.
3. Always address the other person by his first name. It helps you to remember his name.
4. Keep summarizing his or her position.
5. Never use a word when a sentence will do.
6. Remember that all problems are ultimately problems of communication.
7. Treat the other person as a patient, a client, someone who needs help. You are the helper; he is the helpee.
8. Remember: "When the attitudes are right, production will start flowing out the gate."
9. Remember to treat people as you would like to be treated yourself. At least they will know what you like.
10. Remember that although attitudinal changes are important, structural changes are more important.

THE SYSTEMS VIEW OF CONFLICT

It is possible to have conflict within individuals, between individuals; within groups, between groups; and within organizations, between organizations. Where systems theory can help is with the last category,

intra- and interorganizational conflict. Intraorganizational conflict occurs among subunits of the organization (between production and
marketing, for example). Interorganizational conflict occurs among
different organizations (among Ford, General Motors, and American
Motors, for example).

The characteristics of conflict, according to the systems approach,
are:

1. Conflict is a struggle for scarce resources.
2. The aim is to neutralize, injure, or eliminate opponents.
3. Conflict is a central form of interaction designed to resolve divergent
   dualism.
4. Conflict requires cooperation for the game to be played out.
5. Conflict is linked to cooperation.
6. Conflict takes place at every level in every society.
7. Conflict can be good for you.
8. Conflict is a function of regulating the interaction of systems and
   subsystems; and conflict can be optimized by getting the system
   properly designed and regulated.

Coping with Intraorganizational Conflict the Systems Way

The systems approach to conflict is based on the notion that most
conflict arises from faulty or inadequate communication processes and
infrastructures. Thus, the solution to most problems of conflict involves
the installation or fine-tuning of a spindle.

The systems approach to interdepartmental conflict argues that
people who work in different organizational departments develop
different cognitive perceptual orientations. Thus, a marketing expert
thinks in quite a different way from an R & D expert. Getting these
different "thinking" groups to cooperate takes a high level of integration. Managers in different departments have different goals, different
time orientations, and different interpersonal orientations. Therefore,
it may be extremely difficult for a research scientist (who is working on
a project to harness solar energy for heating buildings with a time
perspective of five to ten years) to communicate with a production
manager (who wants him to redesign the windows that are to be
installed in a high-rise apartment in six months). To meet these
problems of differentiation and integration, an integrator acts as a
liaison between departments. These integrators openly confront the
conflicting parties and rather than smooth out the differences, they
unilaterally force a decision.

Decoupling and Buffering

A major way of reducing conflict is to disconnect the conflicting parties. You may recall, for example, that the spindle was invented as a means of partially decoupling the waitress from the cooks in short order restaurants.

EXISTENTIAL CONFLICT MANAGEMENT: RECONCILING CONFLICTING CONCEPTIONS OF A JOB ROLE

System theory can provide insight into how different subsystems' interaction can affect the way roles are executed within the total system. Consider how the role of the director of in-flight service in a modern airline has changed. The director of in-flight service on an aircraft like the 747 can have as many as thirteen staff attendants under command. The director is responsible for getting the passengers on board, having them properly seated, explaining the safety instructions to them (usually in several languages), and making sure that they are supplied with meals and drinks. In an emergency directors play a major part in putting the escape and survival procedures into action.

Many directors of in-service flights have conflicts with pilots over their respective roles. A good way to get at this problem is to gather a group of pilots and a group of flight directors to establish and contrast their perceptions of each other's role. This existential exercise can be carried out with some gusto using VTR (videotape recording). Both groups meet in separate rooms and develop a perception of the flight director's role. The group is given an account of some incident involving interaction among the pilots, the flight attendants, and the directors.

Using this incident as a trigger, the groups come up with some ideas on the role of the directors of inside services. The two perceptions are quite different.

How the Directors of In-flight Service Perceive Themselves

1. They believe they come under the command of the captain of the airliner only in emergencies.

2. They feel isolated from the front end and believe that they do not have sufficient information to respond to the passengers' inquiries.

3. They are upset when the captain decides to land the aircraft twenty minutes ahead of schedule without consulting them or giving them sufficient time to get everything stowed away.

4. They feel the captain of the aircraft makes too many personal demands; for example, he may want his meal served at a particular time, which may throw their work schedule off.

5. They find that the pilots frequently ignore them and make it impossible for the director of in-flight service to initiate contact.

6. They resent the fact that the captain requires them to report all incidents that arise with awkward passengers, even when the aircraft is on the ground taking on passengers. They feel they should be in command of the back-end area when the aircraft is loading or unloading.

7. They feel that pilots are unable to comprehend the tremendous volume of transactions that are involved in serving passengers when the flying time is short.

8. They feel that the captain should interact with flight attendants only through the flight director.

How the Pilots Perceive the Director of In-flight Service

1. In general the pilots feel that there is no problem. In their view, the schedules of the front-end crew and the back-end flight attendants crew should be synchronized so that both work together for a period of time, say a month.

2. Given this arrangement, the captain could get the hang of handling the directors. "Some will need to be smoothed down"; "others will need to be psyched up"; "others will need to be given time to sound off to the captain." "What they really need to remember is that the captain is flying *his* plane and what happens in the plane is *his* business." "The captain is completely in command, no *ifs* or *buts*."

3. Some pilots feel that there should be only a limited, functional interaction between the back end and the front end. Pilots think they should have their meals when they want them because they know about upcoming turbulence.

Confronting Perceptions

With VTR it was possible to get both groups together and to show each group's perceptions.

The pilots were surprised that the directors were willing to be responsible to the captain only in emergencies. This led to a lot of discussion.

General Recommendations

1. Both crews should be joined more effectively. Both could be briefed together before the flight by the captain of the airplane.

2. Some effort should be made to familiarize both the front-end and the back-end people about the others' job.

3. The captain should ensure that the directors of in-flight service have the proper information about flight plans and any changes.

4. Both groups felt that something should be done about the fact that larger aircrafts and shorter flight times have changed how these two groups work. Basically what has changed is the balance of power.

Box 16.2 gives overall recommendations for resolving conflicts.

REVIEW AND RESEARCH

1. Define conflict. List and explain four different kinds of conflict.

2. What are the basic causes of structural conflict? How can they be overcome?

3. Why does the chief executive officer make life so difficult for his immediate subordinates?

4. What does the Abilene Paradox tell us about consensus formation in management committees?

5. Why does top management place so much value on maintaining the pecking hierarchy? How does the classical manager control conflict?

6. In the human relations view of conflict the presumption is that all difficulties are ultimately problems of communication. Explain.

7. The human relations way of coping with conflict usually involves "introducing one stereotype to another." Explain what this statement means.

8. What are the basic rules of human relations game playing?

9. Describe the systems approach conflict. The systems method of resolving conflict usually involves "de-coupling and buffering." Explain what this statement means.

10. Conflict has developed in modern airlines between the captain on the

The following . . . are characteristics of confrontation or problem solving as a method of managing superior-subordinate conflict:

1. Both people have a vested interest in the outcome.
2. A belief on the part of the people involved that they have the potential to resolve the conflict and achieve a better solution through collaboration.
3. A recognition that the conflict or the problem is in the *relationship between the individuals* and not in each person separately. Thus, if the conflict is in the relationship, it must be defined by those who have the relationship. In addition, if solutions are to be developed, the solutions have to be generated by those who share the responsibility for seeing the solution work and making the relationship last.
4. A concern with solving the problem not accommodating different points of view. This process identifies the causes of reservation, doubt, and misunderstanding between the people confronted with conflict and disagreement. Alternative ways of approaching conflict resolution are explored and tested.
5. Problem-minded instead of solution-minded; "fluid" instead of "fixed" positions. Both people together search out the issues that separate them. Through joint effort the problems that demand solution are identified, and later solved.
6. A realization that both aspects of a controversy have potential strengths and potential weaknesses. Rarely is one position completely right and the other completely wrong.
7. Trying to understand the conflict or problem from the other person's point of view, and from the standpoint of the "real" or legitimate needs that must be

Continued on next page

From Ronald J. Burke, "Methods of Managing Superior-Subordinate Conflict: Their Effectiveness and Consequences," *Faculty of Administrative Studies* (York University, Reprint 17).

flight deck and the director of inflight services in the cabin. What are the causes of this conflict and how can it be dealt with?

11. Make a list of the basic rules for conflict resolution.

EXECUTIVE CONFLICT: SHOOTOUT AT THE JOHNS-MANVILLE CORRAL

The chief executive of Johns-Manville Corp. felt confident and secure last month as he journeyed from the company's spectacular new headquarters—a 10,000-acre cattle ranch near Denver to New York City for a regular board of directors' meeting. During five and three-quarter years as J-M president, W. Richard Goodwin had reorganized and rejuvenated the once sleepy building-materials company. Sales

recognized and met before problem solving can occur. Full acceptance of the other.

8. Importance of looking at the conflict objectively rather than in a personalized sort of way.

9. An examination of your own attitudes (hostilities, antagonisms) before interpersonal contact on a less effective basis has a chance to occur.

10. An understanding of the less effective methods of conflict resolution (e.g., win-lose, bargaining, etc.).

11. Present "face-saving" situations. Allow people to "give" so that a change in one's viewpoint does not suggest weakness or capitulation.

12. Try to minimize effects of status differences, own defensiveness, and other barriers to working together.

13. An awareness of the limitations of arguing or presenting evidence in favor of own position while degrading opponent's position. This behavior often stimulates the opponent to find even greater support for his position (increased polarization). In addition, it leads to selective listening for weakness in opponent's position rather than listening to understand his position.

Organizations can increase the amount of confrontation and problem-solving in the area of interpersonal conflict by providing organizational rewards for superior-subordinate co-operation, and altering the relationship between superior-subordinate to reduce the attitudinal barriers to collaborative effort. Training in leadership and followership is one fruitful possibility. Although conflict can and does erupt between individuals, there is a sound basis for achieving acceptable and high quality resolutions.

were up 91 percent, and earnings during the first half of 1976 had set a company record. Goodwin planned to tell his fellow directors that the company was in great shape.

He never got the chance. Three directors, representing a majority of the board, came to Goodwin's hotel room the night before the meeting, and demanded and got his resignation. Ironically, Goodwin was undone by some of the very qualities that had brought him success. His flair for corporate showmanship sparked the company, but his style irked the rather staid directors. And when he proposed to enlarge the board, the directors, as one of them puts it, became "disturbed."*

The puzzle of this story is that Goodwin had achieved everything that the directors had hired him to do. His was a dazzling success story. He had reorganized and rejuvenated a slow-moving building materials

* Herbert E. Meyer, "Shootout at the Johns-Manville Corral," *Fortune*, October 1976.

company. Goodwin was a unique president; he had, for example, a Ph.D. in experimental psychology.

When Goodwin had arrived in his hotel suite on that evening, he had found a message from William F. May, chairman of American Can Company and the director of Johns-Manville, saying that he had called and would call back in a few minutes. When May called back, the unsuspecting Goodwin suggested that they meet later. "We'll be there in ten minutes," replied May. Soon May arrived with two other outside directors of Johns-Manville. Goodwin was informed that the three represented the nine outside directors of Johns-Manville, and that they all wanted him to resign.

> "Why?" stammered Goodwin, who was caught totally by surprise.
>
> "Under the bylaws of this corporation," replied Schroeder evenly, "we don't have to give you a reason."†

Caught off balance, Goodwin agreed to resign, and a separation agreement was negotiated on the spot.

At the board meeting the following morning, John P. Schroeder, vice-chairman of Morgan Guarantee Trust Company, called the meeting to order and stated the first item on the agenda was the election of a successor. John A. McKinney, a company executive, a senior vice president, and the company's top legal officer, was appointed president. "It all happened so fast," McKinney said, "I almost missed it."

The rise and fall of Dick Goodwin provides an interesting executive saga full of insights about both the executive process and the management of conflict. Goodwin transformed Johns-Manville Company from a stodgy, starchy, and sleepy organization, which was largely production-oriented, to a dynamic company, which was very strong in planning and marketing. Goodwin had been brought in as a private consultant. At the same time he was consulting he was giving a course entitled "Systems Approach to Business" to night students at New York University's Graduate School of Business Administration. He developed a planning system for one of the company's divisions and was so successful at doing so that he was invited to come aboard as the company's vice president for corporate planning. Goodwin was named president and chief executive in December 1970. He reorganized the company and pursued a policy of acquisition and divestiture. He also moved the company's headquarters from New York to Denver, Colorado. To the company Goodwin brought a dynamic new management style, which was truly democratic but casual.

† *Ibid.*

Two crises preceded Goodwin's resignation. To handle an upcoming large offering of common stock, Goodwin suggested that the company would benefit from the advice from more than one investment banker. Traditionally, the company had always worked with J.P. Morgan (the holding company that owns Morgan Guarantee Trust Company). Schroeder, the director who was vice chairman of Morgan Guarantee Trust, was upset and voiced doubts about this proposal. The second crisis arose from the fact that Goodwin proposed that the number of directors be increased from twelve to fifteen and eventually to twenty.

By this time in the company's development, after so much change, there was a general feeling that the company ought to take more conservative action and turn these changes into profits—in McKinney's phrase, "to get the most squeal from the pig." What the firing of W. Richard Goodwin tells us about the management of conflict is that executive life is full of hazard; moving too swiftly and visibly can be dangerous. Goodwin forgot who was boss and failed to take into consideration that the ultimate power of the board is to hire and fire the chief operating executive. Apparently, the major consideration in the rejection of Goodwin was his idiosyncratic life style, which was so democratic and casual that it mobilized the opposition of his executives. Finally, Goodwin brought two controversial issues to the surface at the same time. These issues challenged his opponents and threatened their voting power. In the shootout at the Johns-Manville Corral, Goodwin was shot down by some of the very qualities that brought him success. His flair for showmanship made him an obvious target.

Do you agree with this assessment of Goodwin's failure?

What could he have done to avoid being fired?

17

Executive
Behavior,
Personality,
and
Communications

OBJECTIVES YOU SHOULD MEET

List three questions to ask executives about their jobs.

Describe a typical day in the life of a manager.

Describe the executive's need for achievement, power, and affiliation.

Specify the principles of effective communication.

Argue the problems that women face in becoming executives.

Develop a success strategy for the new manager.

Our chapter begins with an attempt to develop a full behavioral picture of the executive. Then we look at executive personality as assessed by personality questionnaires and projection tests. Using projection tests, we review three basic executive needs: the need for achievement, the need for affiliation, and the need for power. Having caught a quick glimpse of the executive career, we turn to more rigorous observational studies of executive communications which, we hope, will give us a scientific snapshot of the manager and all his fleeting contacts.

EXECUTIVE BEHAVIOR

Asking the right questions is the key to successful enquiry. But what are the right questions? Let's assume you were given the assignment of studying a particular executive. What questions would you formulate in advance, before approaching your executive?

Who Are You?

Besides the person's name, this question also touches on deeper issues of identity and as such is frequently used for selection purposes. The sequence in which a person lists his roles can help reveal how such a person might be employed. For example, the WAY (Who Are You?) test was used in the selection of astronauts. A candidate who described himself as a jet fighter pilot, a scientist, an American, a father, and a husband would be a somewhat different kettle of fish from a man who put these roles in the reverse order. Ultimately, the "who are you" question takes in the whole issue of identity and purpose and can become somewhat abstruse.

A less abstruse question is, "What are you?" Here your subject will presumably (but not always) answer by describing his occupation and usually with a word ending in er, such as manager, fitter, turner, and so on. As the "what" indicates, this question points to a person as a thing or an instrument.

To get further into your subject, you might ask the executive questions like, "What do you think about . . . ?" One example might be, "What do you think of executive unions for managers?" This sort of enquiry means an exploration of attitudes, which usually means questionnaires, sampling, computer programs, and frequently complex statistical analysis.

Statistically, this is the preferred method of behavioral science research.

What Do You Do?

Since our field is behavioral science, it should focus on behavior. Our question should be, "What do you do?" If we could take a leaf out of the lawyer's book, we would not accept an answer as the truth until we had applied some rules about admissible evidence.

In studies of executive behavior, the eyewitness or trained observer is preferred. Curiously, however, observational studies frequently turn things upside down. For example, observational studies have shown that many managers spend nearly half of their time communicating laterally, even though most management texts treat leadership as an hierarchical affair. Observational studies are less likely to make a priori decisions about causality. In general terms, observational research comes out with a description of a sequence of events and thus is process-oriented.

What Do Managers Do?

The major issue of this chapter concerns the question, "What do managers do?" Researchers have tried to answer this question by asking managers questions and by observing their behavior. They must also ask questions of themselves:

1. What should I look for? What kinds of activities? Talking, walking, sitting, using hands but not deciding, organizing, planning.
2. What should I look at? The executive, colleagues, secretaries, written documents (diaries, letters, list of telephone calls, etc.)
3. How long do I have to look?
   Three to four weeks preceded by pilot studies and interviews. The actual period selected will influence the results.
4. Does looking at somebody change his behavior?
   Yes. Therefore, a variety of methods should be employed, including direct observation, self-recording, activity sampling, and critical incident analysis.
5. How accurate are my observations?
   All observational research should include significant exercises on cross-checking to ensure data are reliable.

There are very few executive behavior studies. Why? First, it is hard work collecting the data—if you can find a manager willing to be studied. Most managers are so totally involved in their work that they find it impossible to let some researcher record what they do. Observation does distort behavior, and it does take time to explain to observers what the executive was actually doing, for example, on the phone. Further, many things managers do are delicate and confidential. In spite of these difficulties, however, it is usually possible to study the manager's subordinates. They are fair game, and the executive would like to find out what they do anyway.

The senior manager can usually overcome all the difficulties that his subordinate managers come up with. You may well ask, "Are they willing subjects?" Curiously enough, a surprising number of executives enjoy being the subjects of observational studies.

What Does It All Add Up To?

Once you have got your subject, negotiated access, figured out what the job is, looked at role descriptions and organization charts, interviewed everybody connected with the subject, read the technical literature, and finally collected your data, what does it all add up to? Usually the researcher has mountains of forms, loaded with descriptive statements and marked tables. But what does it all mean?

Now is when the real work begins. Data have to be grouped under activities (programming, technical, personnel), interactions (with whom: superior, peer, subordinates), and method of communication (phone, letter, face to face, etc.). Finally, some dramatic new research conclusion must be reached; and it helps to get the article published. Perhaps it is clearer now why so few observational studies of executive behavior have been published. So few have been carried out; and those that have, have never been replicated.

Though there have been many anecdotal accounts of executive behavior, there are few studies of managerial behavior using scientific techniques of recording. Scientifically, the data may be collected by observation or by the subject keeping records, or by activity sampling procedures as opposed to the method of continuous observation.[1]

---

[1] Based on Joe Kelly, "The Study of Executive Behaviour by Activity Sampling," *Human Relations*, Vol. 17, no. 3, 1964.

Top Managers

The most frequently quoted investigation in this field is the work of Sune Carlson, who studied ten directors from various businesses. Most of the material was collected by the self-recording technique, though some of it was recorded by other people. The study was based on a five-point plan: contact with persons and institutions; place of work; technique of communication; nature of the question handled; kind of action taken. Carlson also studied the informal organization of the directors' firms. It was found that the executives studied worked excessive hours, that they spent a third of their working time outside the firm, that they were subjected to constant interruptions so that they had little time for reading or thinking, and that they considered this problem of pressure a temporary abnormality.

Middle Managers

Tom Burns studied a group of four departmental executives in a British light engineering firm. The self-recording technique was used to study communications (intra-department, inter-department, and extra-department), work content, and the interaction process. It was shown that in 80 percent of the total time spent by these executives at work, they were talking. The study revealed a tendency for some executives to overestimate the time spent on production work and to underestimate that spent on personnel work.

First-Line Managers

A. D. Ponder compared the behavior of twelve "high effective" foremen with that of twelve "low effective" foremen in the General Electric Company: in the area of operating responsibility, he showed that the effective foremen spent twice as much time on personnel administration and only half as much time on production as the less effective foremen. Four different studies confirm that most of the foremen's work with other people is devoted to close details of work. Three areas, technical, programming, and personnel, account for between 63 and 89 percent of all activities. Could it be that the task approach to management . . . has enabled this increased emphasis on the details of work as reported here?

The Section Manager

The section manager spends two-thirds of his time with other persons and a fifth of his time with his unit manager. It may be observed that approximately one-third is with his colleagues and half with his subordinates. The unit manager meets him mostly at the morning meeting. A great deal of informal rearranging takes place, especially at a rather extended break in the morning. He spends half of his time on the shop floor, a quarter in the Production & Engineering Department, and the balance in other sections or outside the unit. His work is mainly programming (a half), followed by technical (a quarter), and only a little personnel work (a tenth). Compared with other first line managers, he spends more time on the close details of work. In a phrase, he is a "task specialist." It may be observed that approximately one-third of the total interaction time is devoted to peers. Indeed, it is probable among organizational equals that much of the real coordination of work flow and operations takes place in the nonformal behavior system.

Executive Personality

Is there a particular type of personality that is suitable for the executive role? From behavioral research on executive personality we know that executives have a high need for achievement, that they are dominant, that they score high on political-economic scales of value tests, that they enjoy taking risks, and that they are opposed to regimentation. From observational studies of executive behavior we know that they work excessive hours at an unrelenting pace, that they spend most of their time communicating, mainly by the spoken word, and that they like dealing with immediate, solvable problems.

We also know that managers employ a variety of executive styles. Popular books on management have introduced us to a variety of different executive types. For example, there is the organization man, who is seen as a conformist who arrives early at work and leaves late. Another common stereotype is the human relations manager, who seems to be preoccupied with participation, getting people involved, and improving the climate of the work place.

Studs Terkel has collected a whole set of oral histories from real people, who tell what it feels like to be working.

The executives interviewed by Studs Terkel liked their work for three main reasons: prestige, power, and money. Although dislikes were seldom mentioned, one top executive declared that considerable pressure is exerted on a president by the board of directors, and the result is great insecurity. (The same executive commented that he saw the business world as a vicious competition in which everyone was after the boss's job.) In spite of the fact that most executives made no adverse comments about their jobs, virtually all of them showed signs of stress and alienation from society. They had been driven to physical deterioration (usually an ulcer), and almost all of them held people in very low esteem. Loyalty and friendship were nonexistent in the business world. It was always simply a matter of making the largest profit.

THREE BASIC EXECUTIVE NEEDS

A useful projection test is the Thematic Apperception Test (TAT), which consists of twenty pictures. The person being tested is asked to tell a story that can explain the events in each picture. Using the TAT, David McClelland has built up a picture of executive motivation.[2]

The achievement motive, or "n-Ach," is the need to master or overcome difficulties. Since n-Ach is learned, it should be possible to teach it. If an executive is obsessed with his job and corporate excellence, he has a bad attack of n-Ach. Such an n-Ach executive actively seeks to take responsibility for getting things done. The achieving executive enjoys managing the means. The higher achiever is not interested in gambling if the outcome is mainly determined by chance, but he or she likes risks if efforts are a significant factor in determining the consequences. Therefore, he or she sets moderate goals and takes calculated risks. To reach their goals executives are good at devising a set of alternatives, which they can evaluate against a set of criteria and make an intelligent selection. High achievers can spot blockages impeding their intentions and figure out how to get around them. They have strong needs for feedback to keep them on track. Middle-level managers are high on n-Ach.

The executive who is obsessed with how to manipulate others as an end in itself has a strong need for power. The "n-Pow" executive desires to possess people, to punish them, to bend them to his will, and to browbeat others in argument. Bedeviled by a compulsive need to influence others, the n-Pow has an argumentative, polemical, verbally

---

[2] "Power Is the Great Motivator" by David C. McClelland and David H. Burnham, *Harvard Business Review* (March-April 1976). Copyright © 1976 by the President and Fellows of Harvard College; all rights reserved.

fluent life style. He or she is forceful and outspoken but also hardheaded and demanding. Not too surprisingly, others feel they have to respond to n-Pows. They enjoy persuading, cajoling, and "seducing" as a means of influencing, directing, and controlling others. They enjoy teaching and public speaking. People who make it to the top in business are usually n-Pow people.

People who are obsessed with getting others to love them have a strong need for affiliation. Such n-Affil people seek opportunities for friendly interactions and are most attracted to personnel positions.

THE EXECUTIVE CAREER PLAN

The executive career can be broken into three large stages: the beginning, the middle, and the end game. The first describes the period when the trainee is put through initiation and basic training, when he or she is "properly" inducted into the organization. When he has completed his basic training, which always involves denial of previous statuses and roles, he is given some kind of status and his first regular assignment, which to his mind is meant to make or break him. If he makes it, he is given a series of assignments, usually as a section manager in charge of operators or salesmen (if he is in sales), but not of other managers.

The middle game takes him or her from being a young departmental manager through to senior management status. The manager now has corporate tenure; at least he is guaranteed "a job." He is, however, expected to perform and produce. At one time most managers believed in tough standards and were given to making statements such as, "If I'm not performing, I should be told to get the hell out." With changing technologies, turbulent environments, and better trained young managers competing for their jobs, many of these same managers are finding it hard to cope effectively. Given such dramatic rule changing, middle game ends in frustration and failure for an increasing number of managers today.

The end game covers the period from being a director of a major function through the rank of vice president up to possession of the much-sought title of president. Corporate tenure is not so common during this period, but contracts are. Incidentally, contracts (which are a commonplace for professors, lawyers, and doctors) for junior and middle-level executives are practically unknown.

MANAGERIAL COMMUNICATION

We know from observational studies of executive behavior that executives can spend up to 80 percent of their time communicating. Contrary to what one might expect from the conventional theory of hierarchy, a great deal of this communication takes place in the horizontal dimension; that is, executives spend a great deal of time communicating with peers.

Therefore, it is very important to get an insight into how this communication process operates. Essentially, communication consists of the transmission and reception of information between at least two people. In this context, information includes not only facts but also values, attitudes, needs, and expectations. Managers transmit information not only by the spoken and written word but also in nonverbal ways. Indeed, a whole psychology of body languages has emerged, a knowledge of which can help a manager to understand his own behavior and that of his colleagues.

A manager should keep in mind that there are a great number of obstacles to effective communication. Since failure in communication can cause serious errors, delays, bottlenecks, and misunderstandings, the manager should ensure that:

1. the message is received by the other party;
2. the message is interpreted in the same way by the recipient as by the sender;
3. the message is remembered; and
4. it is applied.

Research based on studies of executive behavior suggests that managers spend most of their time not writing letters or memos but in face-to-face contact with their colleagues.

Executive behavior studies suggest that managers are interested in live action and in getting into human contact with the informal network of information. Minzberg suggests that a great deal of managerial activity is carried out in a somewhat superficial manner.

> Half of the observed activities were completed in less than nine minutes and only one-tenth took more than an hour. In effect, the managers were seldom able or willing to spend much time on any one issue in any one session. . . . [3]

[3] Henry Mintzberg, *The Nature of Managerial Work* (New York: Harper and Row, 1974), p. 33.

Effective Communication

To communicate effectively, one should take these steps:

1. First the manager should analyze the problem into its component parts and determine exactly what his objectives are.
2. He or she should check with his superior and his colleagues before communicating.
3. He or she should try to ascertain in advance what the probable impact of his message will be on his audience. To do this, he should try to see the message from the other person's point of view.
4. He or she should decide which media to employ. Should the message be communicated by memo or by word of mouth? If it is done face to face, is it better in a group or in a one-to-one situation?
5. He or she should assess the effectiveness of the communication. This is normally done by encouraging feedback.
6. The manager should be careful to ensure that he is hooked into the informal system.

THE WOMAN EXECUTIVE

In spite of the fact that women are entering the job market at an extraordinary rate, making up fully 40 percent of the labor force, the number holding managerial positions is still meager. Most of these female executives occupy positions in the middle and lower parts of the managerial hierarchy. In the executive suite they remain largely invisible. Many companies claim that they want but cannot locate talented women managers. A major problem here is the companies' compensation policies, which are designed for men.

After years of outright discrimination and corporate resistance, women have finally arrived in the management ranks. Their right to a place in the corporate world is no longer disputed. Traditionally women have made their way in business in functional positions: in personnel, public relations, market research, and jobs specifically earmarked for women in the areas of fashion. Now an increasing number of women are asking to make the transition to line jobs. Here they are breaking new ground with both super- and subordinates.

These new female executives have arrived like a new immigrant wave in male America. Women's lives are profoundly changing, and with them the traditional hierarchical relations are also changing.

Encouraged by the formal feminist movement, women are in the process of trying to take up their proper positions in executive organizations. But very few of them occupy managerial positions. In fact, of the nearly half-million managers in the United States whose annual salaries are $25,000 or higher, only 11,000 (or 2.3 percent) are women. Why do so few women make it through to top managerial positions?

Probably the main reason is that men grow up knowing they will have to work to support not only themselves but probably others as well. This compels them to develop autonomy and independence and to make their career choices early in life. Women typically make career decisions in their late twenties or early thirties. Basically young women have been brought up to think that they can become nurses but not doctors, secretaries not bosses. How do we know all this? Some very useful and important evidence has come to us from *The Managerial Woman* by Margaret Hennig and Anne Jardim.[4] This book describes research based on interviews with twenty-five women who did make it to the top as vice presidents and presidents of major companies.

Women aspiring to be executives have to overcome certain critical differences between themselves and their male competitors. First of all there is the matter of late career decisions, which we have already mentioned. Secondly, most women experience a sense of passivity. There is an overwhelming sense of waiting to be chosen. What it amounts to is that men relate their jobs to some concept of career advancement; women see a job as something that has to be done in the "here and now." Another difference has to do with personal strategy. For a man strategy is defined in terms of winning or scoring a goal. Women don't tend to think in terms of game strategies. These differences create different mind sets for men and women.

A woman's mind set emerges from the way she is brought up. Girls are brought up to conform more readily to both parents and teachers. In their study of the twenty-five women who made it, Hennig and Jardim describe the career paths of successful managerial women. One critical characteristic was that a great majority of the successful managerial women were either elder or only children. These highly successful women remember their childhoods as having been happy. They had a special relationship with their fathers. Their elementary school years were times of high achievement; they became members of many youth organizations, and they rose to positions of leadership. They were usually good at games. They had a high drive to achieve, an orientation to task, a desire to be respected for their abilities, and the desire to compete. Yet strangely enough these little girls developed these masculine qualities without giving up their notion of being females. In high school they all did well academically. They all attended coeducational universities. When they left college, they consciously chose to put more of an effort into their careers than did most of their friends.

With their male peers at work the managerial women had few contacts, and most relationships tended to be work-centered. Their male colleagues considered them to be serious, highly skilled, work oriented, and certainly ambitious.

By their mid to late thirties, these women had moved to upper managerial positions. Now the matter of marriage and motherhood had to be considered. As one subject of the study pointed out:

> I finally had to face the fact that I wasn't married, I didn't have any children, and I damn well better decide now whether I wanted either. Time was finally calling me to task and I had to come to some decisions on issues which I had put off for years. Way back when I first started, I had convinced myself to put off marriage for a time so I could give all of myself to my career. But I was still young then and questions of biological age were not important. Then, suddenly, the few years was twelve years, and I was thirty-six. I had already achieved what had been faced with the same kind of decisions as I had to face at twenty-four. Only now it was a crisis situation. I was smart enough to know that going on to try to achieve top management would be as different as night and day from my previous jobs and might well be just as time- and life-consuming as my previous career. I seemed to be much less sure of the relationship between marriage and career for me than I was ten years ago.

> I saw three possibilities: marry and quit; marry and stay at my same position; or not marry and go forth on my next career stage. I knew there was a fourth alternative—find a very unique type of man to marry who would be willing to go along with the time and personal investment of having a career-striving wife—but I figured I would never be unique enough to make a go of such a marriage if I could find such a rare fellow. No matter how I looked at it, I still had to decide on marry or not marry first. Somehow that seemed to come before the career.

> I decided I needed time—something I had not had in years. So I decided to let the career ride for a year or so to see what I could do about my personal and social life. Somehow I felt just like an adolescent again, starting out to achieve my first dates. I figured the question of having kids had better follow finding the husband, and I was not at all adverse to adoption or taking on a widower's family. I

did know that I'd never be happy just staying home all day so I figured that at least I'd hang on to my present position.[5]

Half of the women studied married. Those who did, married widowers or divorced men, all of whom had children. In the next few years all of them rose to become presidents or vice presidents of their firms.

THE NEW MANAGER

The first principle for the new manager is "to thine own self be true." This underlying principle of "what I can be, I must be" guides his or her every choice. The new manager seeks out assignments with visibility and creativity. He or she wants jobs that provide new encounters and enhance his or her independence financially and socially.

This means choice, change, and chance. Choice is required to ensure the right assignments—to make sure he or she is in on such projects as "acquisitions and mergers," or "selection of new models," or blue ribbon task forces created for the elimination of a specific competitor. It means change, in terms of function, industry, and location. It means chance because there is always an element of gambling, of beating the statistics.

The new manager places great value on being mobile on the principle that it is easier to change systems than change the system. He or she also operates on the assumption that he or she will not be doing the same thing forever. He or she places a major value on the consulting—coaching—teaching—public speaking skills. Inevitably part of his or her career is going to be spent in consultancy, both at the beginning to increase salary and at the end to get in touch with new opportunities. Again, his or her career is likely to involve a spell in a university business school, most likely part-time but possibly full-time for the "in-betweens." Public speaking, which is apparently an activity for those high in n-Pow, affords the liberated manager visibility outside his or her own organization.

The new executive knows that the best work group is made up of a mix of types. Typically in a top management group there will be a classical manager, perhaps in charge of production (where structuring, task-oriented skills, capacity to break down jobs and functions, and

[5] *Ibid.*, pp. 140–142.

ability to work to tight deadlines are immensely helpful); with a bit of luck there will be a human relations manager (ideally in charge of personnel or advertising, where human interest obsession will work for him); an information mechanic/systems person (to manage the information function either through MIS or the controller); and many others.

The new manager is more concerned with the scenario, the script, the exits and entries than with the nuts and bolts of corporate life. In brief, the liberated manager is an actor in the drama of management, not an innocent bystander.

Executives, like everyone else, want to live joyously. Most are desperately engaged in a search for sanity in the face of insanity. They are searching for commitment in a world that makes faith impossible and even absurd. Existentialism says that people must create the meaning they once desired from faith. Previously, many executives gave meaning to their lives by working hard for some organization that supplied a supportive setting. This comfortable if somewhat stunting relationship has gone. Organizations are transient; relations are temporary; and new values that recognize such human needs as authenticity, inter-dependence, openness, and trust are needed.

These are just the needs that existentialism fosters. The central issues of existentialism are the needs to exercise choice, to act in good faith, and to make life meaningful—all in the here and now. A central theme of existentialism is that people owe it to themselves to reject despair. Difficult this may be, but one must be ready to begin again each day and impose meaning on, perhaps, what has none. Existentialism represents an attempt to humanize fate, an attempt to convince everyone that when he or she throws in two bits' worth, he or she should make it count. Every decision must be made as if it were both the last and the first.

REVIEW AND RESEARCH

1. Design an interview schedule listing the questions that would enable you to carry out an interview in depth with an executive. Select an executive that you know and carry through the interview.

2. Develop a set of characteristics for the executive who is high on n-Ach, n-Affil, and n-Pow. Evaluate your own standing on these three needs.

3. Prepare a research plan to carry out an observational study of a group of executives in any organization you are familiar with.

4. Why are there so few observational studies of executive life?

5. Write a book review of Henry Minzberg's *The Nature of Managerial Work.*

6. Why does executive life involve so many fleeting interactions?

7. Construct an optimistic career trajectory for yourself, listing the appointments, the probable salaries, the locations, and the difficulties. Develop a corresponding curve for your family life, listing dates of marriage, divorce, disease, and other dysfunctions. Make a list of the major crises you expect to encounter. How can you best prepare yourself for such crises?

JOHN CARR, W. C. PENJACK COMPANY, LTD.

John Carr had been in the employment of W. C. Penjack Company for two and a half years. He had joined the company as a management trainee and after a period of eighteen months had been promoted to the position of technical field service representative. John derived immense satisfaction from the position and was seriously considering making the technical service end of the business his career (not necessarily, of course, with the Penjack Company).

Generally speaking, John's dress and personal appearance were of a "conservative" nature. Since joining the company, he had gradually allowed his hair to exceed its normal length by several inches. Until a week ago his hair had been the longest of any staff member. However, no one had ever approached him on the subject, and he had assumed that his hair length was acceptable to everyone, including senior management.

John's wife, Veronica, had encouraged him to allow his hair to grow. Lately she had been after John to have his hair properly styled. John's conservative side had resisted such a suggestion, but on the spur of the moment one lunch hour he dropped into a local hairstylist's shop.

John requested the hairstylist to style his hair, hoping that his ignorance of what exactly that meant would pass unchallenged. The hairstylist suggested that John's hair could not be properly styled without the application of a "treatment," which would give it body. John was hesitant but decided that after all this was what he had come in for.

The treatment turned out to be a permanent set. At the end of the visit, John's long, straight hair had been transformed into waves that ran from the front to the back of his head. He was too shy to state his disapproval to the hairstylist, thinking that when he returned to his office he would only have to wet his hair and comb out the waves.

On arriving back at his office, he discovered to his horror that in wetting his hair, in an attempt to straighten it, he had succeeded only in transforming the waves into tight Afro-style curls. After some twenty minutes of combing he managed to return his hair to a wavy condition. At this point he had the first intimation that the so called "treatment" was permanent (he was later to learn that such was indeed the case and that short of shaving his head he would just have to wait until his hair grew to a length at which the curls could be clipped). Being somewhat stoic by nature, John decided that he would just have to live with it. Putting on his sternest "don't dare say a word" look, he walked out to his desk. The look seemed to work, for apart from a few raised eyebrows no one said a word.

By the end of the first week John had become somewhat adjusted to his new appearance and had even come to like it (especially in the absence of any comments from his fellow workers; his wife liked the "new" John and praised his courage and taste). All was not well, however. This morning John had been requested to come into his boss's office. Mr. Clarkson, after an initial perfunctory greeting, engaged John in the following dialogue:

Clarkson: John, I don't think, ah . . . no, let me rephrase that. I know that a man's hair has no bearing on his ability to do a job, but ah . . . I think it would be more in keeping with the general company image if you were to revert to a more normal hair style.

John: (Noticeably taken aback) Has someone complained about my appearance?

Clarkson: Well, no, not exactly. Nevertheless you must give me some credit for knowing the standards of the Penjack Company. After all, I will have completed my twenty-seventh year of service at the end of this month. Let me tell you that the absence of comments is just as dangerous as out and out condemnation.

John: I was very embarrassed by my own appearance to begin with, but to tell you the truth, I now like it very much and really don't want to change it.

Clarkson: Please don't misunderstand me, Mr. Carr. I personally have nothing against the style you've chosen. I'm only thinking of your own best interests. You young people don't seem to understand how to get ahead in this world. All in all, it would be better for your career

with this company if you were to change your haircut back to a more
normal style.

John: But my wife and I like my hair the way it is.

Clarkson: You're a bright young man, Mr. Carr, and to date we have
found your work to be more than satisfactory. I hate to see you
damage your chances of promotion by flaunting your hair in such a
strange fashion. In a few weeks you are slated to start visiting
customers. To be quite frank, your queer hairdo is not in keeping
with our company's image. I'm almost sure that our vice-president
will be upset by this whole affair. As a matter of fact, and I had hoped
you would be more understanding about this whole unfortunate
incident, I strongly recommend that you take immediate action to
redo your hair before he decides to take a hand in the matter. You
understand, of course, that I personally have nothing against such a
queer hairstyle. Well, John, I'm sure you have lots of work to finish
up before lunch hour. Would you be kind enough to ask my secretary
to come in as you pass her desk? Thank you.

What should John Carr do?

V

MANAGING
THE
FUTURE

18

The
Liberated
Manager

Develop a profile of the new mobile manager.

List some ways that work may be made more joyful.

Develop a new leadership style.

Define the characteristics of the gamesman.

Work out a game plan of how to become a more effective manager.

THE PICTURE OF THE MODERN "MOBILE" MANAGER

In the mid-fifties, W. H. Whyte painted a brilliant portrait of the organization man or classical manager just as he was going into a decline as a model for practicing managers. The man in the grey flannel suit, essentially a conformist, keen to win over colleagues and influence superiors, was a product of Weber-style bureaucracy, which came of age in 1914 and was dying by the mid-fifties. Organization man started to make his exit from the executive scene, not because the rest of society didn't like his looks or his dedication to achievement, affluence and aggression, but because a new style of organization . . . was emerging. And a new type of executive, the liberated manager, was making his debut.[1] (Box 18.1 describes him.)

What Is He?

A liberated manager likes to select problems that interest him, utilize his trained capabilities, and give him high visibility. The sort of assignment he likes is serving on an acquisition and merger project management group with computer, logistics, and secretarial support and which can give him the kind of interactions he so earnestly craves. He is motivated by "get a new job, master it and move on" and believes that "strengths travel better than weaknesses." He puts loyalty to his career first, likes corporate slots with academy companies such as Procter and Gamble or a spell teaching in a crack university business school. He argues the view that managerial style is related to speed of movement.

The new mobiles have a different response to conflict: they welcome it as a means of clarifying issues, resolving conflicts of interest and achieving personal growth and development (PGD). Indeed, a job offer is judged by the criteria of how it will effect one's PGD, which is the ultimate existential issue.

The existential executive has a love-hate relation with corporate organizations. Both are born of the fact that organizations employ other existential executives as corporate headhunters to spot, ring, and earmark the young neophyte, who then has to learn the ropes, to loop

---

[1] This section is based on Joe Kelly, "The Very Picture of the Modern 'Mobile' Manager," *The Production Engineering Magazine*, Vol. 23, No. 5 (May 1976). Reprinted with permission of the publisher.

Box 18.1: By These Yardsticks, You May Be "Mobicentric"

The Mobicentric Man, or the mobility-centered manager, is presently replacing the insider and the Organization Man. He is typified by the following characteristics:

- ◻ He holds the psychological view that movement is not so much a way to get someplace or a means to an end, as it is an end in itself.
- ◻ He values action and motion not because they lead to change, but because they are change, and change is considered to be his ultimate value and most important goal.

In particular the mobicentric executive exhibits the following traits and characteristics:

- ◻ He is always in motion.

---

the loop, and to work his passage to earn his place in the sun. Choosing their victims from preselected and pedigreed batches (e.g., by insisting all managers interviewed have MBAs from top ten schools), organizations do not select—they socialize.

He's a Job-Hopper

Many young managers and professionals no longer swear allegiance to the company with which they work. They expect independence and detachment, prefer maximum choice and mobility, and welcome conflict on strategic issues. Hence the dramatic increase in labor turnover among executives. Michigan State's Eugene E. Jennings has argued that turnover among executives is increasing rapidly. And nowhere is this labor turnover more marked than among MBAs who speak in terms of "I interviewed IBM yesterday, I'm only interested in overseas assignments. . . ." Jennings calls the liberated, existential executive the *Mobicentric Man* because he is mobility-centered. Jennings studied 1,500 managers and executives, and 230 presidents from 500 large industrial firms, over a period of 16 years. He concluded there is an increasingly close relationship between mobility and success. Two out of five executives who become presidents do so after entering the corporation at a high level, rather than working their way up the ladder at one company.

The average mobicentric executive moves laterally once for every two moves up. He moves outside his own technical area once for every two moves in it. He changes location geographically once for every three moves with the corporation. His mobility gives him a broad knowledge of corporate structures, and provides him with a realistic understanding of the executive scene within which he must operate.

384

- He travels a lot.
- He and his family move around a lot, both because his job requires it, and also for recreation.
- He often changes positions, sometimes within the same company and sometimes between companies.
- He views freedom as a form of movement.
- He places faith in himself and not in any institution.
- He accepts a new job in order to move on, and not simply to get a better job.
- He feels that success is represented by moving and movement, rather than by position, title, salary or performance.

Social adjustment is approached with the same philosophy as work. He enjoys meeting people, especially those who are different from himself. His approach to love and sex is exemplified by change. When a relationship stops growing it ends, and he moves on. For the mobicentric, change is the secure element in his life. He becomes anxious when he stands still, but not when he is on the move. However, individuals who are highly mobicentric in one of the three major areas of life (i.e., career, social adjustment, and love and marriage), are not so in the other areas.

What He Really Wants

Nobody ever said it was easy to be an existentialist. . . . Today's executives are continually assailed by a sense of personal doom which leaves them with a feeling of impotence and fear. On a global scale we are threatened by the doomsday syndrome which predicts catastrophe at every cut and turn of the computer.

What the liberated manager wants is more joy in his work, to live and work more fully, to have authentic and aware relations with those who work with him.

Executive life, being what it is, demands considerable strength of ego. In business, problems do not present themselves in such a fashion that an executive can make a decision which is certainly correct. Usually many options will be open to him; none will be absolutely free of risk or disadvantage. He must make a decision which inevitably will only reduce the degree of uncertainty, not eliminate it. In many, if not most cases, it will be impossible to say whether he was right. Given this problem of objective verification, most managers opt for the "best decision" and hope for consensus from superiors and colleagues. The need to rationalize decisions is only too painfully obvious. The executive act is iterative; you can't solve the "equations" involved exactly but can only get approximate solutions which you then resubstitute in your original "equations" to improve the accuracy of the decision-making process.

The existential style is essentially a search for an alternative and a supplement to the analytic style which is good for problem solving but has nothing to say about either problem finding or solution implementation. Getting beyond the analytic style (which is highly numerate, preoccupied with decomposing problems into components and convergence) requires an effort in lateral or divergent thinking. Instead of moving vertically in a linear train of A, B, C's, the existential executive tries to move laterally in a mental context where intelligence and feel (a compound of hunch, hypothesis, hype, vibes, and experience which cannot yet be treated by Bayesian statistics) count—to try and find the real problem. To try and find out if "there is a crisis;" to find out "what we really want."

In cognitive terms, the existential executive is trying to turn on his metamorphic, intuitive and analogic processes (e.g., Why does the giraffe wear red sneakers?—So it can hide in cherry trees.), which means switching on his right cerebral hemisphere, which Western education has left in cold storage. What our educational system is good at (and our business schools best of all) is tuning up the left cerebral hemisphere, which is good at linear, rational, and digital thought—the kind of intellectual activity that takes place when someone says, "Let's be logical about this."

What the existential executive is trying to do is to supplement and find an alternative to his analytic skills, to get beyond what Wertheimer, the father of Gestalt Psychology, characterized as an emphasis on generalization.

His Most Important Goal

The most important thing for the existential executive is to realize his personal destiny. But how do you find your destiny? The essence of the existential approach was first stated by Henrik Ibsen, who argued that a man ought to decide what destiny decided him to be and be it. O.K. for Ibsen, you might think. Ibsen found all sorts of ways of indulging his neurosis, including dining at home in uniform bedecked with his medals. The corollary of the Ibsen thesis of being yourself is to find an organizational role that will allow *you* to find *your* destiny. Ideally, the organization should be designed for Ibsen, not Ibsen redesigned for the organization.

In the last three decades the heady belief has grown that man can become a more active force in shaping his destiny. No one has done more to advance this notion than Rollo May. While May feels that existential psychology owes a debt to Freud for his emphasis on man's intractability, he believes that Freud gave insufficient weight to man's potentiality. May is arguing for a view of man which emphasizes the capacity and need for love, grace, creativity, music, literature, and art instead of focusing on the irrational and repressed elements of man's psychopathie which is frequently both hostile and unacceptable. A new ethos, pathos, and logos must be introduced into the study of man. The ethos, which refers to the moral frame of reference, must concern itself with the ethic of intention based on the tenet that each man is responsible for his own actions and their effects. When the ethos has been properly established among men in a community, a framework of legitimacy will have been created, which will allow people to act in good conscience. One test that such an ethic exists will be a decrease in violence. Violence will languish as people begin to feel they are being treated as ends in themselves and not as means.

And for the existentialist there is no ethos without pathos. Pathos is the ability to move people emotionally. For it is recognized that the heart has reasons which the head can never understand. Man is not a machine, not a piece of apparatus, not a cog in the bureaucratic machine, not even a computer. Man has both great potentiality (if he can recognize his destiny) and tremendous intractability. And out of his intractability comes his capacity to rebel.

Existentialism has its own particular logos, its own specific intellectual infrastructure. But it is not an intellectual structure which gives primacy to logic, but rather attempts a somewhat unsuccessful fusion of ethos, pathos, and logos. Existentialists seek a society which has a basis of legitimacy, which recognizes men have feelings, but which also has a vision of freedom. Somehow these three factors have to be put together to make man's life meaningful.

The poetry of life, existentialism, is an imaginative expression of the drama of life and involves the spontaneous overflow of powerful feelings. The proper and immediate object is the business of living, in all its gory detail. It tries to give meaning to both the happiest and the best as well as the saddest and the worst moments of life. It turns about such fundamental questions as, "Who am I?" and "Where am I going?" Thus, the existential executive is engaged in a lifelong identity crisis, trying to figure out how far he has come and how far he has still to go. (See Box 18.2 for a way to find out if you are an existentialist.)

THE GAMESMAN

A different new kind of executive is also making his way to the top of America's high technology companies. This new executive, who has been labeled the gamesman, is highly motivated, not to build or preside over empires but to lead winning teams who beat out the competition. The new gamesman is an existential figure who is excited by problems in business that involve both counting probabilities and taking considerable risks. The gamesman is not as hardhearted as the autocratic entrepreneurs who built the American industries, nor is he as loyal or dependent as the organization man. The man who discovered the gamesman is Michael Maccoby. Maccoby conducted interviews with 250 managers from high technology companies, most of whose sales exceeded $1 billion a year. The subjects of Maccoby's study had invented managerial techniques and strategies; they were the envy of their peers. Maccoby used not only interviews but tests to try and plumb the depths of the managers' psyches.

Maccoby described four ideal types of managers. The first, the craftsman, holds essentially traditional values and thinks of himself as somebody who makes something. The second type, the jungle fighter, lusts for power. For him, the corporate world is a sea of internecine strife. (There are two types of jungle fighters, lions and foxes. The lions go forward by force, and the foxes advance by cunning.) The third type is the company man, who sees his destiny in a protective organization. The fourth type is the gamesman.

388

The gamesman seems to have stepped out of the pages of a modern textbook on management. Corporate life seems to come to him as a set of options, each with an attached probability and utility. He has a compulsive need to take calculated risks and is fascinated with new management techniques. Says Maccoby,

> The modern gamesman is cooperative but competitive; detached and playful but compulsively driven to succeed; a team player but a would-be superstar; a team leader but often a rebel against bureaucratic hierarchy. . . . His main goal is to be known as a winner, and his deepest fear is to be labeled a loser.[2]

Modern organic technostructures are densely peopled with gamesmen, who rise through the hierarchy and develop their intellects but not their emotions. Because the gamesman is emotionally detached, he becomes overly concerned with protecting his career and amputates idealistic, compassionate, and courageous impulses that might interfere with it. Maccoby, who is a psychoanalyst, believes that the individual's sense of identity and integrity is injured as he ascends the bureaucratic hierarchy. Echoing Eric Fromm, Maccoby believes that these high-flying executives suffer from a nagging sense of self-betrayal because they have given so much to their careers and so little to the needs of self, family, and society.

[2] Michael Maccoby, *The Gamesman* (New York: Simon & Schuster, 1976), p. 100. Copyright © 1976 by Michael Maccoby. Reprinted with permission of the publisher.

Maccoby has found that many managers seem to be wondering whether they amount to much of anything. He points out,

> A highly successful executive, in charge of product development in a large company at the age of forty, already feels himself a failure. "I am considering whether all this is worth it," he said. "I started thinking about this four or five years ago. I feel a lack of joy. I don't see where all this is leading to."
>
> I asked him whether he felt his life lacked meaning. "Yes," he replied, "it is running full tilt without direction. This environment is continually in a crisis mode. It's all high speed. You can't talk about trivia. It turns me off when my wife wants to chatter. It's stupid when you think about it; what else can you do but listen?"[3]

Maccoby is arguing that the executive has got to get his head and heart together. Executives must use their intellects to analyze problems, design products, provide alternatives, and make choices. But at the same time the executive must develop his moral sensitivity so that he can find values that go beyond winning the game. For Maccoby, careerism, as practiced by the gamesman, can produce executives who lead empty lives and who are dangerous not only to themselves but to society. They may fail to develop a strong independent sense of self and lose touch with their deeper strivings.

TOWARDS AN EXISTENTIAL MODEL OF MANAGEMENT

Management is a very exciting thing as an activity, but as a scientific discipline it is often associated with such long lists as POLE— planning, organizing, leading, evaluating. In spite of hefty investments in the behavioral sciences, management theorists have failed to come up with an explanation of management that feels right to practicing managers. To try and develop a new perspective, a new process for looking at management, we have set out to examine management, as a combination of theater, information, and existentialism.

An increasing number of people are discovering that management is drama. The model we have adopted in this book assumes an imaginative integration of structure (the cast), process (the sequencing

[3] Michael Maccoby, "The Corporate Climber Has to Find His Heart," *Fortune,* December 1976.

of events), and values (myths, magic, and mystery) to achieve corporate excellence. The organization becomes the theater of action.

The modern environment requires an essentially bilingual (information and existentialism) and bicultural (linear and nonlinear) perspective. People in our society want both affluence and achievement on the one hand and awareness and authenticity on the other.

Combining existentialism, drama, and information is a new type of executive, the liberated manager. In his or her life style, intention and decision making are central. For liberated managers, a new point of departure is needed, and this is where existential management begins: by uniting the structure, the process, and the values.

The Drama of Managing

Management does not emerge from the simple arithmetic addition of structure, process, and values (S + P + V) but arises from their dramatic integration in some multiplicative way (S × P × V). Once one has fixed the structure, arranged the process, given the values full sway, the situation assumes full command, and the dramatic character of management becomes clear.

The existential executive's job is to put the structure, process, and values together in an imaginative way that will get things done. "Getting things done" can be producing the right quantity and quality of goods on time at a reasonable cost. But it can also include achieving the feeling of élan that comes from a job well done.

Efficacy

Good management, like good drama, helps to create an image of something important having been lived through. The actors in a corporate drama can come away from action feeling exhilarated and released. This corporate catharsis can in itself be a measure of executive efficacy.

Efficacy is to be preferred to either efficiency or effectiveness. Efficiency reflects the performance of functions in the best possible and least wasteful manner; the best measure of efficiency is the ratio of work done to work put in. Effectiveness is the achievement of a desired purpose. Efficacy, on the other hand, is the capacity for producing a desired result and effect. We use efficacy in this context to highlight not only economic effectiveness and human satisfaction but also the idea of joy and delight at something accomplished. Efficacy also implies "not a closed system"; thus a priori definition of purpose or aims does not lock the manager to a static outcome. Efficacy is an amalgam of economic achievement, exhilaration, and joy of a kind that cannot be fully predicted from or predicated on a definition of a priori aims. The drama of management both deals with uncertainties and generates new uncertainties.

REVIEW AND RESEARCH

1. Why are managers so interested in forecasts of the future? What role do "think tanks" play in this process?
2. Why are books like George Orwell's *Nineteen-Eighty Four,* Aldous Huxley's *Brave New World,* and Anthony Burgess's *A Clockwork Orange* so influential in determining people's attitudes about the future?
3. List the main methods of forecasting the future. How reliable are these methods? Can they be used to improve the quality of planning in a business firm?
4. What is future shock? What event in your life has given you the most future shock? How can future shock be minimized?
5. Who is the liberated manager? Why is he so mobile?
6. What is the divergent cognitive style? How does it help executives solve problems?
7. Describe two leadership styles according to Argyris's Model I and Model II. How would you find out more about these two leadership styles?
8. Are you an existentialist? What characteristics, styles, and behaviors mark the existentialist?
9. Compare and contrast the gamesman and the organization man.
10. How can executive effectiveness be improved?
11. Find out what impact computer chips will have in the development of the microprocessor. Look particularly at calculators, watches, telephones, cash registers, and automobiles.
12. Is management an inviting prospect for the young university student? Why or why not?

EXECUTIVE OBSOLESCENCE

Being effective as a manager is a highly rewarded activity. But executives have to pay a personal price for taking their place at the top of the corporate tree, as the case of William Agee, chairman of the Bendix Corporation, shows:

> Since joining Bendix, Agee has forsworn most community activities in favor of family recreation. He gave up downhill schussing, lest an accident keep him away from the board room, but enjoys cross-country skiing with his wife Diane and their three children near their home in McCall, Idaho. Agee admits to fighting the temptation to take a "systems approach" to his kids—"sitting them down and saying, 'All right, in the next half-hour we're going to take care of all the things that are on your mind'"—but he has already given some hard analytic thought to top-level personnel issues at Bendix. He wants to expand the uppermost management team, and has also, within a month of becoming chairman, started thinking about his own successor. Agee feels that chief executives outlive their usefulness after "ten to 15 years—perhaps that's the outer limit." But in 15 years, Bill Agee will be only 54. He is not likely to take up knitting.*

Do you agree with Bill Agee's view on executive obsolescence?

* From "Room at the Top," 21 February, 1977. Reprinted by permission from *Time*, The Weekly Newsmagazine; Copyright Time, Inc. 1977.

NAME INDEX

Ackoff, R.L., 124, 218, 219, 221, 222
Adler, R.D., 44, 45
Argyris, C., 36, 61, 162–65, 346, 347

Bales R., 313, 314
Barnard, C.I., 52, 54
Bennis, W.G., 41, 273
Blake, R.R., 318–23
Boehm, G.A.W., 132, 160
Brenner, S.W., 277
Brown, R.L., 231, 232
Brown, W.B., 220
Burke, R.J., 357, 358
Burnham, D.H., 74–79, 368
Burns, T., 9, 66, 67

Campbell, J.P., 172, 173
Carey, A., 34
Carlson, S., 7, 8, 366
Cartwright, D., 309
Chamot, D., 68–70
Chandler, A.D., 108
Clarke, D.G., 127–30
Clifford, D.K., Jr., 330–33
Coons, A.E., 203
Coser, L.A., 345
Cuddihy, B.P., 185, 186

Dale, E., 7
Dalton, M., 79, 80
Davis, S.M., 161–63
DeBono, E., 251, 252
Dickson, W.J., 33, 78
Dowling, W.F., 321–23
Drucker, P., 111, 112
Dunnette, M.P., 172, 173

Emery, F.E., 335, 336
Etzioni, A., 83
Ewing, D.W., 156–59

Fayol, Henry, 11, 12
Fiedler, F.E., 205–209
Foulkes, F.K., 103
Ford, R.N., 297–99
Fuller, R.B., 289

Galbraith, J.K., 272
Galbraith, J.R., 165, 166
Gibson, J.L., 245
Goldberg, B.E., 99, 100, 109
Gordon, G.C., 99, 100, 109
Gyllenhammar, P., 62

Hall, J.J., 303
Harvey, J., 348, 349
Heany, D.F., 136, 137
Henning, M., 372–74
Herzberg, F., 36, 295–99
Heskett, J.L., 138
Hobbs, J.M., 136, 137
Homans, G.C., 77
House, R.J., 209

Jardim, A., 372–74
Jennings, Eugene, 384, 385
Johnson, J.H., 74

Kahn, H., 127
Kahn, R.L., 36
Katz, D., 36
Kelly, J., 17, 18, 365–67, 383–89
Kolodony, H., 161–63

395

Korda, M., 86
Kotter, J.P., 212, 213

Lasagna, J.B., 111, 112
Lawler, E.E., 172, 173, 301, 302
Lawrence, Paul R., 42, 161–63
Leidelker, J.K., 303
Lewin, K., 315
Likert, R., 153–55
Lippitt, R., 309, 327
Lorsch, J.W., 42
Luthans, F., 300, 301

McCaskey, M., 67, 68
McClelland, D.C., 74–79, 368
Maccoby, M., 388–90
McCreary, E., 247–50
McGregor, D.M., 36
Maier, N.R.F., 245, 246
March, J.G., 243
Martin, N.H., 81–83
Marx, Karl, 239
Maslow, A., 293–95
Mayo, E., 27, 33, 34
Meadows, D.H., 128
Meyer, H.E., 357–60
Mintzberg, H., 8, 149, 150, 370
Molander, E.A., 277
Morgan, H.M., 103
Mouton, J.S., 318–23
Myer, M.S., 303, 304

Norcross, D., 62

Oberg, W., 188–92
Odiorne, G.S., 114

Patton, A., 175, 176
Patz, A.L., 188–93
Pavlov, I.P., 289
Piotrowski, Z., 8, 9
Porter, E.H., 64, 65

Robbins, S.P., 90
Rock, M.R., 8, 9
Roethlisberger, F.J., 33, 78
Ruch, W.A., 262–64

Sashkin, M., 245, 246
Sasser, W.E., 211
Simon, H.A., 156, 238, 243
Simons, H., 257–59
Sims, J.H., 81–83
Skinner, B.F., 290
Skinner, W., 211
Slater, P.E., 41
Smith, Adam, 29
Stalker, G.M., 66, 67
Steers, R.M., 107–109
Stodgill, R.M., 203
Strauss, G., 328–30
Sturdivant, F.D., 44, 45

Tarnowieski, D., 16
Tarrant, J.J., 111, 112
Taylor, F.W., 27–29, 34
Thant, U, 237
Tinnin, D.B., 102
Toffler, Alvin, 273
Trist, E.L., 335, 336

Urwick, Lyndall, 7, 29–31, 34

Vancil, R.F., 122, 123
Vroom, V.H., 300

Walters, K.D., 56, 57, 58
Webber, R., 55
Weber, Max, 27, 31, 32, 272
Weik, K.E., 172, 173
Wheelwright, S.C., 127–30
Whyte, W.F., 64
Whyte, W.H., Jr., 7
Wiener, N., 38

SUBJECT INDEX

Adhocracy, 160–65
Administrative management, 29–31
Alienation, 390
Ameng Inc., 22, 23
Assessment centers, 180, 181
Attitudes, 16, 17
Authority:
    challenging of, 56, 57, 58, 68–70
    charismatic, 54
    definition, 54
    delegation, 55–57
    legal, 54
    legitimacy, 348
    modern dilemma, 159
    obedience to, 346–47
    power and, 347, 348
    process, 53–57

    relations, 347
    structure, 51–53
    traditional, 54

Basic needs, 293–95
Behavioral science, 48
Behavioral technology, 290, 291
Blowing the whistle, 56–58
Budgeting:
    control and, 225–28
    financial, 229
    planning, 225–27
    purchasing, 229
    sales, 228
    zero-based, 231, 232
Bureaucracy, 31, 32

Cabals, 34, 76–80
Change, 337–40
Chain of command, 59
Chevette, 139–41
Chrysler Corporation, 114–17
Classical theory, 28–32
Cliques, 34, 76–80
Codetermination, 167, 168
Committees, 309–15
Communications, 370, 371
Computer analogy, 222–25
Conditioned responses, 289
Conflict:
  causes, 345
  classical, 346–50
  coping with, 348–50, 351, 353–57
  definition, 345
  existential, 354–56
  human relations view of, 350
  kinds, 345
  models, 345
  organizational, 357–60
  resolution, 357, 358
  structured, 346–50
  systems, 352–54
Consensus formation, 53
Conspiracy theory, 88, 89
Corporate culpability, 279, 280
Contingency approach, 41, 42
Control:
  computer analogy and, 222–25
  cybernetics and, 207
  information, 219–22
  steps, 218, 219
Creativity, 247–49
Cybernetics, 38, 39

Decision making:
  creative, 247–49
  dynamics of, 239
  quantitative, 250–64
  rational, 237, 238
  steps, 240
Decision selling, 245, 246
Decision trees, 247–50
Delegations, 55–57
Delphi method, 126, 127
Dysfunctions of control, 232, 233

End products, 20, 21
Environments of organization, 335, 336
Executive:
  behavior, 7–11, 363–67
  ethics, 277–80
  future of the, 44, 45
  obsolescence, 393
  personality and motivation, 367–69
  roles, 149, 150
  selection, 180, 181
  talent, 175, 176
  top, 44, 45
  woman, 371–74
Executive honesty, 280
Executive personality, 367–69

Existentialism, 280, 281
Existential personality, 304, 385–87, 388, 389

Firing:
  firee and, 186, 187
  steps in, 185–86
  systematic, 183–86
Forecasting:
  computer-assisted, 131, 132
  computer simulation and, 128, 129
  delphi technique, 126, 127
  methods of, 127–30
  problems of, 132–35
  scenario writing, 127, 128
  technological, 129
Future:
  executive, 44, 45
  limits to growth, 128

Gamesman, 388–90
Goals, 105–107, 135
Grid, 318–23
Group:
  conformity in,
  definition of, 309
  discussion, 311–15
  process, 313
  selection procedure, 180, 181
  structure, 312
  spatial factor, 312, 313
  think, 138
  values, 314, 315
Group Dynamics:
  definition of, 309
  limitations, 309

Hawthorne studies:
  bank wiring, 34, 35
  illumination experiment, 33
  relay assembly test room, 33, 34
  review, 34
Hiring, 171–81
Human relations, 32–37
  evaluation, 37
  human resources, 35–37
Human resource planning, 36, 37

Information:
  environment and, 220
  processing, 238
  system, 222–24
International Supplies Inc., 224–26
Interviewing:
  interviewee strategy, 178, 179
  interviewer strategy, 177, 178

Job design, 301
Job enrichment, 297–99
Jobs, 148–50

Leadership:
  assessment, 180, 181
  classical, 201, 202
  cognitive complexity and, 207, 208

Leadership: (*cont.*)
  contingency model, 205–11
  cult of great man, 200, 201
  definitions, 199
  existential, 211, 212
  functions, 202, 203
  group approach, 201–205
  human relations, 201–205
  path-goal theory, 209
  situational, 206, 207
  structure and consideration, 202, 203
  systems, 205
  trait approach, 200
Lordstown syndrome, 60, 61
LPC scale, 206

Machiavellian, 81–83
Management:
  definition, 3, 4
  design, 144–68
  existential, 390–92
  levels, 6, 7
  process, 11–14
  schools, 25–45
  structure, 4–6
  supervisory, 366, 367
  top, 346, 347, 366
  values, 15–17
Management by objectives, 110–14
Management information system, 224–26
Manager:
  classical, 201, 202
  effective, 391, 392
  mobile, 383–85
  new, 374
Managerial grid, 318–23
Matrix Management, 160–65
Mechanistic organizations, 66, 67
Meetings, 310, 311
Mobicentric Manager, 383–85
Models, 17–21, 38, 39
Motivation, 289, 302, 303
Motivation-hygiene theory, 295–99

Needs:
  to achieve, 368
  for affiliation, 369
  for power, 368

Objectives:
  composite, 104, 105
  increase earnings, 104
  market share, 103
  operationalizing, 108–10
  social responsibility, 104
  suboptimization of, 105
Objective setting:
  importance of, 99, 100
  types of, 101
Operational budgeting, 225–32
Organization:
  birth, 127
  conflict, 328, 329
  crisis, 327

  dilemmas, 330, 331
  effectiveness, 108
  environments of, 335, 336
  future, 162–65
  goals, 105–107
  information processing system, 238
  maturity, 332, 333
  mechanistic, 66, 67
  organic, 66, 67
  process, 339
  structure, 338
  technology and, 333–35
  values, 339
Organizational change:
  process, 339
  structure, 338
Organizational development, 316–23
Organizational politics:
  cabals and, 76–80
  cliques and, 76–80
  contingency approach, 90
  dysfunctions of, 90, 91
  effective, 91
  group level, 76–80
  individual level, 73–76
  Machiavellian, 81–83
  politicking, 88
Organizing:
  classical, 145–53
  contingency, 165–67
  human relations, 153–55
  informational technologies and, 157
  participative, 156–59
  systems, 155–59

Parable of the spindle, 64, 65
Participation, 156–59
Perception:
  communication and, 370
  definition of, 292
  selection and organizing, 292
  as a transaction, 292
Personality:
  definitions of, 289
  existential concept, 304
Performance appraisal:
  hindrances, 190–92
  making it work, 192, 193
  techniques, 188–92
P-G man, 300–303
Pin factory, 29
Planning:
  definition of, 121
  forecasting and, 126–34
  logistics and, 138, 139
  operational goals, 135, 136
  policy and, 139
  strategic, 121–26
Power:
  definitions of, 83
  exercising, 85
  how to get it, 86
  organizational factors, 84
  personal expertise, 84

reaction to, 87
    structural bases of, 83–85
    systems of, 88, 89
Problem solving:
    diagnosis, 240–42
    evaluation, 242–44
    implementation, 244–47
Profits, 101, 102
Project management, 166
Psychological distance, 205
Psychological tests, 179, 180

Quantitative techniques:
    correlation, 255, 256
    inventory models, 253, 254
    linear programming, 262–64
    networks, 256, 257
    PERT, 257–59
    queuing theory, 254, 255
    sampling, 252, 253
    simulation, 257, 258
    situations of total ignorance, 260, 261
    tips, 261, 262

Responsibility, 55, 56
Risk syndication, 53
Role:
    concept of, 145–48
    conflict, 346
    definition of, 145
    managerial, 149, 150
    playing, 148
    set, 148

Scenario, 127, 128, 131
Scientific management, 28, 29
Self-actualization, 294, 295
Self-concept, 294
Semantic differential, 206
Socio-technical systems, 336
S-O-R man, 291–93

Span of control, 57–59
S-R man, 289–91
Staffing, 170–95
Status symbols, 146, 147
Stereotypes, 350, 351
Strategy, 121–26
Structure:
    classical, 51–53, 59–61
    contingency, 66, 67
    human relations, 61–63
    linking pin, 153–55
    relations, 19, 52
    roles, 19, 52
    rules, 19, 52
    systems, 64, 65
Success ethic, 16, 17
Systems management, 38–40
Systems theory:
    characteristics, 41
    evaluation, 224
    handling complexity, 64, 65

Tavistock Institute, 335, 336
Technological forecasting, 129
Technology, 333–35
T-group, 315, 316
Theory X, 36, 37
Theory Y, 36, 37

Values:
    classical, 271–73
    definition, 271
    existential, 276, 277
    human relations, 274, 275
    organizational, 339
    systems, 275, 276
    WASP, 272
Volvo, 61–63

Zig Zag Thinking, 251, 252
Zone of indifference, 53, 54